Enactments

EDITED BY RICHARD SCHECHNER

To perform is to imagine, represent, live and enact present circumstances, past events and future possibilities. Performance takes place across a very broad range of venues from city streets to the countryside, in theatres and in offices, on battlefields and in hospital operating rooms. The genres of performance are many, from the arts to the myriad performances of everyday life, from courtrooms to legislative chambers, from theatres to wars to circuses.

ENACTMENTS will encompass performance in as many of its aspects and realities as there are authors able to write about them.

ENACTMENTS will include active scholarship, readable thought and engaged analysis across the broad spectrum of performance studies.

RECENT **ENACTMENT** TITLES
AVAILABLE FROM SEAGULL BOOKS

Festive Devils of the Americas
EDITED BY MILLA COZART RIGGIO, ANGELA MARINO AND PAOLO VIGNOLO

Grotowski's Bridge Made of Memory
Embodied Memory, Witnessing and Transmission in the Grotowski Work
DOMINIKA LASTER

Death Tourism
Disaster Sites as Recreational Landscape
EDITED BY BRIGITTE SION

Performing the Nation
Genocide, Justice, Reconciliation
ANANDA BREED

Celebration, Entertainment and Theatre in the Ottoman World
EDITED BY SURAIYA FAROQHI AND ARZU OZTÜRKMEN

Humanitarian Performance
From Disaster Tragedies to Spectacles of War
JAMES THOMPSON

Beijing Xingwei
Contemporary Chinese Time-Based Art
MEILING CHENG

Pop Goes the Avant-Garde
Experimental Theater in Contemporary China
ROSSELLA FERRARI

PERFORMING UTOPIA

EDITED BY

RACHEL BOWDITCH AND PEGGE VISSICARO

LONDON NEW YORK CALCUTTA

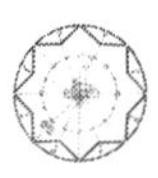

Seagull Books, 2017

ISBN 978 0 8574 2 386 3

British Library Cataloguing-in-Publication Data
A catalogue record for this book is available from the British Library

Typeset by Seagull Books, Calcutta, India
Printed and bound by Maple Press, York, PA, USA

Dedicated to
Sophie, John, Caio, Ari, Vito, Bruce, Mark, Kirsten
and our parents.

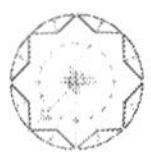

CONTENTS

ACKNOWLEDGEMENTS

The seed for this book was planted with a fellowship awarded by the Institute for Humanities Research (IHR) at Arizona State University (ASU) to develop an anthology focusing on 'Utopias, Dystopias, and Social Transformation'. Principal investigators Rachel Bowditch, Tracey Fessenden and Pegge Vissicaro held weekly seminars with the other IHR fellows Ann Kaplan, Luis Alvarez, Anne Feldhaus and Megha Budruk from August 2009 to May 2010. The book was further developed in tandem with an international working group, 'Play, Fiesta, and Power', founded in Argentina in 2007 at the Hemispheric Institute Encuentro. The nucleus of scholars from throughout the Americas include Paolo Vignolo (Universidad Nacional de Colombia, Bogotå), Angela Marino (University of California, Berkeley), Milla Riggio (Trinity College), Rachel Bowditch (Arizona State University) and Zeca Ligiéro (UNI-RIO, Brazil) among many others. The small, ongoing research group on fiestas and carnivals convened again at the Hemispheric Encuentro in Bogotá, Colombia, in August 2009 as well as at the American Society for Theatre Research Conferences (ASTR) in Puerto Rico in November 2009, Seattle in 2010, the Performance Studies International conference at Stanford in 2013 and the Hemispheric Encuentro in Montreal in 2014. This book would not be possible without the support of Richard Schechner, Diana Taylor, Tamara Underiner, Naveen Kishore, Bishan Samaddar, Sally Kitch, Daniel Gilfillan, Mariellen Sandford and our IHR research assistant Erica Ocegueda.

Rachel Bowditch
Pegge Vissicaro

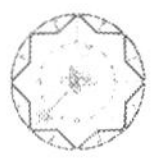

INTRODUCTION

Rachel Bowditch and Pegge Vissicaro

> Live performance provides a place where people come together, embodied and passionate, to share experiences of meaning making and imagination that can describe or capture fleeting intimations of a better world (Dolan 2005: 2).

In *Utopia in Performance*, Jill Dolan departs from historical writings on utopia that suggest social reorganization and the redistribution of wealth as utopian, arguing instead that utopia occurs in fragmentary 'utopian moments' often embedded within performance. Dolan's project does not propose a self-contained utopic community but, rather, how utopia might be 'imagined or experienced affectively, through feelings, in small incremental moments that performance can provide' (2001: 459–60). Drawing on Richard Dyer's notion that 'utopianism is contained in the feelings it embodies,' Dolan interrogates what utopia would feel like rather than how it would be organized (2005: 33). This somatic approach gives rise to what she calls the 'utopian performative' (2001: 460). She states, 'Performance can be employed and experienced as politically activist as well as aesthetically new and invigorating, as perhaps, utopian' (ibid.: 461). The ephemeral coalescing of community, what Victor Turner referred to as communitas (1967), Dolan offers as a springboard towards a momentary utopia (ibid.: 473). During moments of communitas, a community moves towards possibility, hope and political agency (ibid.: 477). She posits that performance

> can move us towards understanding the possibility of something better, can train our imaginations, inspire our dreams and fuel our desires in ways that might lead to incremental cultural change [. . .]. This, for me, is the beginning (and perhaps the substance) of the utopic performative: in the performer's grace, in the audience's generosity, in the lucid power of intersubjective understanding, however fleeting. These are the moments when we can believe in utopia. These are the moments theatre and performance make possible (ibid.: 460, 479).

As fleeting utopic landscapes, performances and the moving bodies within them can be studied to reveal 'signs' or 'signals' of evolutionary developments in society, providing a potent space where new forms of economic and political possibilities are rehearsed and enacted (see Morris 1946[1893]: 27, 91). While Dolan focuses on the utopian performative within a theatrical context, we expand her theories to encompass performance in public life—from diasporic hip hop battles, Chilean military parades, commemorative processions, Blackfoot pow-wows and Mardi Gras post-Katrina to the Philadelphia Mummers Parade, Quadrilhas Caipiras in Brazil, the Renaissance fairs in Arizona and neo-burlesque competitions. Her theory offers a way for us to see these dances, celebrations, contests, tributes and protests as potential sites to glimpse utopian moments when a community performs its notion of an ideal world.

Theories surrounding utopia have evolved from abstract literary, fictional utopias[1]—blueprints for a new ideal model for living in the world—to concrete utopias to heterotopias,[2] dystopias and momentary utopias.[3] The utopian impulse can be seen since the beginning of the written word—the desire to dream of a better world representing the noblest aspirations of humanity. In *The Utopian Impulse in Latin America*, Kim Beauchesne and Alessandra Santos explain: 'Will and agency are certainly part of the vocabulary surrounding utopia: the will to imagine a better life, an ideal community, and the agency to concretize such possibilities' (2011: 4). The term 'utopia', coined in 1516 by Sir Thomas More in *Utopia*,[4] blends two Greek words: *topos* or place, and *u* that means 'no' or 'not'. Thus, *utopia* can be translated as 'noplace' or 'nowhere' (Claeys and Sargent 1999: 1).[5] In *Rabelais and His World*, Mikhail Bakhtin states that in the earliest stages of cultural development, in particular during carnival, participants entered a 'utopian realm of community, freedom, equality, and abundance' (1984: 9). As a time of utopic freedom and anarchy, carnival allows for a temporary suspension of rules and regulations. This utopian spirit, according to Bakhtin, is one of inventive liberation from established truths, clichés and norms that engender the imaginings of new social realities (see ibid.). Expanding beyond carnival, collective bodies gathered in public life become a productive site to understand how utopia operates in rhizomatic nodes across a variety of contexts.[6]

Contemporary Utopian Discourse

Modern utopian literature—including H. G. Wells' *A Modern Utopia* (1905) and feminist utopias such as *Herland* (1915) by Charlotte Perkins Gilman—depart significantly from historical utopian theories. In the 1970s, feminists embraced utopianism as a vision for an alternative future. Several feminist utopias—including Topolobampo, Mexico, and Llano del Rio, California (1874–1917), designed by Marie Stevens Howland and Alice Constance Austin—were cooperative colonies that advocated for kitchenless homes to free women from the confines of domestic life. However, Sally L. Kitch warns of the dangers of utopia in feminist thought, arguing that utopianism can easily slip towards totalitarianism (2000: 55).

According to Kitch, utopias establish a false dichotomy between 'us' and 'them' that is destructive (ibid.: 56). These segregated societies enact 'fanatical closure' that seals the group's demise, as was demonstrated in 1978 in Guyana by Jim Jones and the Peoples Temple, originally founded as a utopian community.

The other side of utopia, it could be argued, is dystopia. Barbara Goodwin and Keith Taylor argue that the quest for utopia is highly subjective and culturally specific: 'One man's Paradise is another's Inferno' (2009: 17). For them, utopia is 'an instant or imminent transition from the present system, a break with history. [. . .] The creation of a utopia has the double effect of throwing into sharp relief the imperfections of the present and providing a standpoint for criticism [. . .] offering an accessible replacement, the ideal future' (ibid.: 26–7). One person's ideal society is usually at the expense and exclusion of others; Adolf Hitler imagined he, too, was creating an ideal society. Vernon Louis Parrington states, 'from the very beginning, Americans have dreamt of a different, and usually of a better world. America is a Utopia' (1964: *vii*). Archibald MacLeish similarly notes, 'America was built on promises [. . .]. From the first voyage and the first ship there were promises' (1939: *vvi*). The earliest writings of the conquest envisioned the Americas as a 'terrestrial paradise', a 'utopic' land of abundance and natural resources.[7] Ambivalence regarding the conquest's history is reflected, on one side, as the 'utopian discovery' of the New World—a land of abundance, promise and fecundity—and, on the other, as a dystopian narrative of death, destruction, disease and colonial invasion of indigenous societies. The 'discovery of the Americas' is at once utopian and dystopian depending on one's vantage point.

The twentieth century saw the emergence of dystopian fiction, and satire such as Aldous Huxley's *Brave New World* (1932), George Orwell's *1984* (1949) and Ray Bradbury's *Fahrenheit 451* (1953).

These novels imagined a world where the state controls individual agency—from thoughts to reproduction. Big Brother, a mechanical hound and other methods of surveillance became the status quo. We note a resurgence of interest since 9/11 in utopia as well as dystopia as a site of theoretical and artistic inquiry, evidenced by the number of publications and films dedicated to the subject. Recent utopian and dystopian scholarly contributions include *Utopia in Performance: Finding Hope at the Theatre* (2005) by Jill Dolan, *Cruising Utopia: The Then and There of Queer Futurity* (2009) by José Esteban Muñoz, *On the Edge of Utopia: Performance and Ritual at Burning Man* (2010) by Rachel Bowditch and *The Utopian Impulse in Latin America* (2011), edited by Kim Beauchesne and Alessandra Santos, as well as a plethora of dystopian blockbuster films: *Day After Tomorrow* (2004), *Children of Men* (2006), *I am Legend* (2007), *Blindness* (2008) and *The Road* (2009).

As film scholar E. Ann Kaplan has noted, since 9/11 there has been a surge of what she calls 'Future-Tense Trauma Cinema' and the 'Post-Traumatic Futurist Disaster Film'. In the former, 'viewers witness probable futurist dystopian worlds, as they are imagined on film *before* they happen' (Kaplan 2013: 53). Kaplan also states:

> The paradox is that humans face a real challenge of catastrophe from climate change while at the same time governmental forces exploit fears generated by this and other dangers—terrorism, immigration, global financial markets, the economy. Interest in catastrophic imaginaries reaches into unconscious denial of what humans have produced, relieving mental tension and allowing us to confront in fantasy (and survive) what we cannot face in reality (2016).

As Kaplan points out, at the end of these dystopian imaginaries is embedded a utopic note of hope—the dawning of a new day, the rebirth of a civilization or the opening of a gate into a new future.

> Sigmund Freud all but offers a theory of the ways in which utopian and dystopian thought are but two sides of the same psychological coin. He suggests that his despair about what humans are doing to humans may be due to his having held too high an expectation of humanity, suggesting that utopian thinking necessarily dissolves into dystopia. But instead of asking if utopian thinking leads to dystopian nightmares, one might ask if dystopian vision may inevitably produce utopian thought. If utopian thought, in its impossibility of success, leads via disappointment to dystopian imagery or models, conversely, dystopian discourses inevitably spiral upwards in search of hope, a beneficent future arising out of the ruins of what had seemed to be the end of the world (2014: 366).

Visions of utopia through this renewed attention in literature as well as other media provides a coping mechanism to counteract the fear, trauma and destruction caused by acts of terror, real and imagined. Just as the utopian impulse to imagine a better world pervades the history of thought, so too does the dystopian impulse to envision our own destruction and demise as perhaps a rehearsal for what is to come. Therefore, any investigation of utopianism reveals its dystopian counterpart.

The Utopian Body

Through movement and everyday performative gestures, performances in public life embody utopian possibilities. The body becomes a locus for enacting the production of cultural memory, empowering marginalized and subjugated communities. Joseph Roach's analysis of the New Orleans Mardi Gras Indians offers theoretical insight by calling attention to what he names a 'performance genealogy' that draws on the idea of 'expressive movements as mnemonic reserves, patterned movements made and remembered by bodies'

(1996: 26). The moving bodies and gestures are a microcosm of culture. Often overlooked, these micro-expressions of performative behaviour can be seen as cultural palimpsests with complex layers of meaning and history. Performative behaviour makes visible the ways in which people interact to socially construct and embody knowledge, catalysing and strengthening communal organization. These processes deepen our insight about the symbiotic relationship between performative behaviour and community development.

Bodies act as sites of resistance against ideological hegemony and for the transmission and dissemination of alternative cultural memories and histories (ibid.: 24). The bodily archive of cultural memory is what Pierre Nora and Diana Taylor refer to as the 'repertoire'. According to Nora, the repertoire is '*true memory* that exists in gestures and habits, in skills passed down by unspoken traditions, in the body's inherent self-knowledge, in unstudied reflexes and ingrained memories' (1994: 284). Nora distinguishes between 'places of memory', artificial sites for the production of national and cultural memory such as museums, and 'environments of memory' which are oral, corporeal and performative (ibid.: 289).

Taylor notes that the understanding of cultural memory and identity is impossible to imagine as disembodied (2003: 86). The body carries cultural memory and is 'Specific, pivotal and subject to change. [. . .] The bodies participating in the transmission of knowledge and memory are themselves a product of taxonomic, disciplinary, and mnemonic systems [. . .]. The body becomes a receptor, storehouse, and transmitter of knowledge that comes from the archive' (ibid.: 86, 82). Taylor argues that the ways in which people transmit cultural memory through performance varies from group to group and is culturally specific. She gives an example of a mestiza woman whose body 'functions as the site of convergence binding the individual with the collective, the private with the social, the diachronic and the synchronic, memory with knowledge' (ibid.: 82). She goes on to say that memory that is 'embodied and sensual, conjured through the senses, links the deeply private with the social, even official practices. Memory, like the heart, beats beyond our capacity to control it, a lifeline between the past and future' (ibid.: 82).

As Taylor, Nora and Roach argue, the 'repertoire' of bodily memory works in tandem with the 'archive' of official memory stored in 'written records, spoken narratives, architectural monuments, and built environments' (Roach 1996: 27). These performing bodies become 'environments of memory' for witnessing, transmitting and understanding the 'true memory' of a given community. Randy Martin proposes that it is the collective of bodies and the power of presence en masse that make transformation possible (1998: 50–1).

Study of embodied performances in public life facilitates understanding of what Ernst Bloch called the 'not-yet-conscious' (2000: 191) of a given community, which is 'knowable, to some extent, as a utopian feeling' (Muñoz 2009: 3). Muñoz articulates how Bloch's *The Principle of Hope* (1954–59) makes a 'critical distinction between abstract utopias and concrete utopias, valuing abstract utopias only insofar as they pose a critique function that fuels a potentially transformative political imagination. Abstract utopias falter for Bloch because they are untethered from any historical consciousness. Concrete utopias are relational to historically situated struggles, a collectivity that is actualized or potential' (ibid.: :3). Utopias embedded within performance hover in that liminal space between an abstract and a concrete utopia; they are abstract utopias in that they activate a potentially transformative political imagination yet they are tethered to the historical consciousness of a given community. Muñoz further explains that

'Bloch would posit that such utopian feelings can and regularly will be disappointed. They are nonetheless indispensable to the act of imagining transformation' (ibid.: 9). In public life, these bodies are fertile ground for 'utopian potentiality' (ibid.: 6), a way for communities to imagine transformation—political, communal, personal, local and global. The utopian impulse to visualize a better world stimulates change; performing bodies manifest this vision to transform society.

Overview of the Volume

Our book offers a diverse collection of case studies focusing on utopias, dystopias and heterotopias enacted through the performing body. How do these performances rehearse and enact visions of a utopic, ideal world? What can the lens of utopia and dystopia illuminate about how performing bodies negotiate and reshape communities, identities, values and beliefs across time and space? What conditions motivate these processes and why? Structurally, the book is divided into three sections with each chapter uniquely addressing ways in which a particular community imagines itself into being through performative utopian moments.

Part One, 'Embodied Utopia', explores performing bodies as sites of resistance, critiquing social relations of class, gender, ethnicity and race. Corporeal protest and persistence against hegemonic and often disembodied ideologies of colonialism, capitalism, globalization and modernization destabilize power and authority. Three diverse contexts—hip hop / rap artists in the global diaspora, First Nations in Western Canada and citizens in São Paulo, Brazil—reveal how participants confront and subvert change through a 'dance' of cultural politics. Authors Luis Alvarez, Lisa Doolittle and Anne Flynn, and Pegge Vissicaro explore the capacity of performing bodies to reveal 'alternative archives of history, the shared memories, experiences, and aspirations of ordinary people'

(Lipsitz 2007: *xi*). Tensions created by 'hidden' possibilities unite people's disparate struggles to inspire and effect real social transformation.

Alvarez's work examines the politics of travel, ethnography and culture in the production and content of Maori hip hop artist and activist Dean Hapeta's documentary, *Ngātahi: Know the Links*, which connects local hip hop, spoken word, poetry and activist scenes around the world. Alvarez argues that Hapeta, the folks in his films and the many they identify with are part of a diaspora, 'one based on interlinked struggles for dignity and against global capital rather than any place or ethnicity-based affiliation'. This work illustrates ways in which hip hop culture circulates political struggle; global justice functions as social and cultural labour; and efforts for utopia are grounded in everyday, often spontaneous activities.

Doolittle and Flynn focus their essay on how First Nations people of Western Canada established agency and political leverage through performance and cultural patrimony. In the late nineteenth and early twentieth centuries, overlapping containment strategies and legislation banned dancing and traditional celebrations, confining Indigenous populations to reservations and their children to residential schools.[8] Through an examination of archival photographs of dance and dancing bodies, tensions between processes of containment, protest and accommodation are analysed and critiqued.

In the third essay, a comparative process provides a framework for Vissicaro's ethnographic study of Festas Juninas, midwinter rituals characterized by Quadrilhas Caipiras. Her research looks at these dances as a space to rehearse encounters with difference by embodying the *caipira*—a pejorative term given to people from Brazil's countryside who were drawn to major urban centres for economic opportunities during the early twentieth century. This essay examines how the contemporary context of urban São Paulo, with its increasing cultural heterogeneity, provides ideal conditions for creativity and community to flourish, exemplified through Quadrilhas Caipiras performance.

Part Two, 'Utopian Laughter from Minstrelsy to Burlesque', focuses on three case studies: the Arizona Renaissance Festival, the Burlesque Hall of Fame Weekend and neo-burlesque in Las Vegas, and the New Year's Day Mummers Parade in Philadelphia. As Bakhtin asserts, carnival laughter, like carnival itself, is ambivalent. He posits that laughter reveals a 'second truth', and that through laughter and humour, a deeper reality and truth are revealed (1984: 84).[9] Laughter unleashes the 'indestructible joie de vivre' (ibid.: 142) of the carnival spirit, allowing participants to experience a social pressure valve outside the realm of authority that is both therapeutic and cathartic (ibid.: 67). In all three case studies, the body becomes a landscape of pleasure and excess, whether it be through the practised moves of a neo-burlesque dancer or the high kicks of a mummer performing the cakewalk. As each case study also illuminates, beneath the eruption of laughter and the grotesque body exists a more serious engagement with history, race relations, sexual construction and the performance of self.

Kevin McHugh and Ann Fletchall trace the emergence and increased production of Renaissance fairs (faires) in the US. They offer a glimpse of the local rebirth of the carnivalesque and grotesque—in their words, 'a pastiche that jumbles, romanticizes and commodifies history'. This nostalgia for the second-world carnival condition can be found in particular in the eruption of festive laughter—*Le Rire,* as theorized by Henri Bergson. This indulgence in festive laughter triggers feelings of possibility that are inherently utopian.

In the Philadelphia Mummers Parade, complex social constructions are at play. Author Christian DuComb focuses on the pivotal year of 1963, when the Mummers Parade was pressured to ban blackface make-up, causing a series of changes within the procession. DuComb examines song lyrics and dances like the cakewalk, piecing together a picture of the complicated history the procession has with both race and gender. He tracks how the procession has had to evolve over time to become more inclusive despite opposition from the predominantly white male mummers.

As a contemporary example of the carnivalesque body, Laura Dougherty closely examines the Burlesque Hall of Fame (BHoF) Weekend that occurs annually in Las Vegas, Nevada. Since its founding in 1990, the BHoF brings together classic burlesque and neo-burlesque—a repertoire of burlesque history transmitted from body to body. This living archive becomes a rich site for understanding how specific gestures, movement vocabularies, routines and everyday performative behaviours of this specific community are transmitted. Framed as a competition, multiple generations of performers converge to display their moves and bodies to one another at this vital venue, ensuring the survival of the form by staging its evolution and transformation.

As a counterpoint to carnival laughter, Part Three, 'Heterotopias and Dystopias as Contemporary Spaces of Healing', explores the other side of the theatrical dichotomy. From the rescue of 33 miners in Chile in relation to the Chilean Military Parade and post-Katrina Mardi Gras in New Orleans to the All Souls' Procession in Tucson, Arizona, these case studies shine a spotlight on how public processions and parades serve as locations for the negotiation and processing of trauma as well as hope, helping each community cope and collectively heal.

Building on Michel Foucault's notion of heterotopias, Néstor Bravo Goldsmith juxtaposes three distinct but related events that created a new vision of Chile during its bicentennial year of 2010: the Chilean Military Parade celebrating Chilean independence; the hunger strike of 32 Indigenous Mapuche people; and the rescue of the 33 miners trapped in a San José mine. Placing these events in conversation with one another reveals the coercive role the Chilean government played in staging a national agenda for a global audience. The media representation of 'reality' constructed by the Chilean government presented an idealistic, utopic version of Chile on the international stage while masking the underlying realities of the broken socioeconomic systems of inequality at play.

Rachel Bowditch's chapter focuses on the Tucson All Souls' Procession, a grassroots effort that serves as a transformative agent for processing grief within the Tucson community. The All Souls' Procession, which occurs each November is a collective, community-invented ritual loosely drawn from practices surrounding All Souls' Day and Día de Los Muertos, both celebrated widely across the Americas, creating a festive palimpsest of meaning and symbolism. Several aspects of the event—the history and evolution of the procession, the complex relationship with the city of Tucson, the personal and community altars, the ritual of burning of the urn and the finale—serve as powerful modes of community healing. They act as a vehicle for what procession organizers Nadia Hagen and Paul Weir call 'festal culture', creating a necessary, hopeful utopian space to process trauma and create a sense of community identity.

Katherine Nigh's chapter interrogates the tension between media portrayal and the reality surrounding the first Mardi Gras after Hurricane Katrina in 2006 that became a site for both utopic and dystopic visions of a post-Katrina New Orleans. A number of krewes used the mediated platform of Mardi Gras to present counter-narratives to the dominant media headlines, expressing frustration and outrage towards the local and federal government about what had taken place in their city before, during and after Katrina. The differences in performances along racial and class lines only highlighted the social divisions. The role of Mardi Gras after the devastation of New Orleans became pivotal in the recovery process, offering an avenue of hope and restoration.

Our diverse selection of geographical sites from celebrations and contests to tributes, processions and protests represents a fraction of the myriad examples of utopian performatives within public life. We envision this book not as an endpoint but a springboard, a place of departure for future inquiry. It is through an in-depth analysis of performing utopia in public contexts that we will better understand the world, one another and ourselves.

Notes

1 Literary utopias can be seen in several ways; '1) a fantastic escape from an unpleasant reality; 2) a blueprint for a better society; 3) a better society which might exist in some far off time; 4) a better society which is desired but not achievable; and 5) an early plan for British Imperialism' (Claeys and Tower Sargent 1999: 119).

2 Heterotopias are defined by Michel Foucault as 'real places—places that do exist and that are formed in the very founding of society—which are something like counter-sites, a kind of effectively enacted utopia in which the real sites, all the other real sites that can be found within the culture, are simultaneously represented, contested, and inverted. Places of this kind are outside of all places, even though it may be possible to indicate their location in reality' (1986: 24). Heterotopias juxtapose in a 'single real place several spaces, several sites that are in themselves incompatible.' Festivals, according to Foucault, are temporal heterotopias in that they are a break from traditional time and place, simultaneously representing, contesting and inverting the everyday (ibid.).

3 Gregory Claeys and Lyman Tower Sargent track 'utopia', following Thomas More, through four main historical stages: 'First, religious radicalism in the sixteenth and seventeenth centuries; second, voyages of 'discovery' from the sixteenth century onwards; third, scientific discovery and technological innovation from the seventeenth century on began to hold out the promise of indefinite progress; finally, aspirations for great social equality emerged in the revolutionary movements of the late eighteenth-century North America and France, in which the utopian promise

of a new society of greater virtue, equality, and social justice was now projected onto a national scale' (1999: 3).

4 In More's *Utopia*, a fictional character by the name of Raphael Hythloday returns to the Commonwealth having lived among the Utopians for five years. He contrasts the social ills of sixteenth-century England thriving with idle noblemen, crime, starvation and social inequality with the ideal society of Utopia. Hythloday arrives in the capital Amaurot on the island of Utopia, earlier known as Abraxa, where the Utopians only work six hours a day followed by leisure activities, such as exercise, reading and gardening. Money is no longer used as every family is provided for within a shared labour economy. Core Utopian values are equality, justice, education, shared governance, happiness, honesty, reason, self-reliance, pleasure, wisdom, community service and family. Vices include idleness, sloth, material desire and gambling.

5 The concept of utopia has existed long before Thomas More. The Garden of Eden can be understood as one of the earliest utopias, an earthly paradise of abundance. From Hesiod (eighth Century BCE) to Ovid (born 43 BCE) to Virgil (70–19 BCE), the theme of a fecund earth of 'rivers of milk and nectar' (Claeys and Sargent 1999: 8), trees bearing low-hanging fruit and an abundance of water pervades these early utopias. In Lycurgus (46–120 CE), a highly structured social organization begins to emerge with the equal distribution of land and personal property and the removal of gold as currency to eradicate greed and corruption from society (ibid.: 16). The concept of the fountain of youth also appears: 'If anyone tastes of that spring he will suffer no weakness from that day on, and will always be as a man thirty two years old, however long he may live' (ibid.: 14).

6 The earliest utopian literary fictions introduced the concept of the 'ideal city' producing blueprints of urban architectural designs and the careful construction of public and social space from St Augustine's *City of God* (426), More's *Utopia* (1516), Johann Valentin Andreae's *Christianopolis* (1619), Tommaso Campanella's *City of the Sun* (1623) and Francis Bacon's *New Atlantis* (1624). Few of these designs were ever realized. As literary historian Vernon Louis Parrington argues, utopian visionaries could more accurately be called social planners, community architects with a vision of a new model for society and community living (1964: 4–5). Circular and semicircular designs are common among utopian architectural blueprints as seen in *Hygeia* (Tod and Wheeler 1978: 124), Ebenezer Howard's *Garden City* (1902) and Alice Constance

Austin's plan for the city of *Llano* (Hayden 1979: 283). In Tommaso Campanella's *City of the Sun*, the city was 'divided into seven huge rings or circles named for the seven planets, and each is connected with the next by four streets passing through four gates facing the four points of the compass' (Negley and Patrick 1971: 318). Each of the seven concentric circles contained murals designed to educate citizens of City of the Sun, worlds of knowledge from mathematical figures and astrological diagrams to biological natural worlds of biology, chemistry, mechanical arts, inventors and other realms of knowledge placed in an encyclopedic immersive experience of knowing (Claeys and Sargent 1991: 109). In the twentieth century, we see utopian architects and visionaries such as Charles Edouard Jeanneret-Gris (Le Corbusier), Frank Lloyd Wright, Buckminister Fuller and Paolo Soleri.

7 Since the 1680s, the United States has been the site for the founding of hundreds of utopian communities, both religious and secular. Popular US utopian experiments include Brook Farm (1841–47), Joyful (1880–90), Winters Island (1890–1900), Fountain Grove (1875–1900), Little Landers (1900–15), Fellowship Farm (1915–25), Llano (1910–20), Holy City (1920–50) and Tuolumne Farms (1945–50) (Hine 1966: 132–57). Nineteenth-century socialist utopians such as the Oneidas in New York and the Shakers in Massachusetts imagined and implemented societies founded on their individual utopian principles. Robert V. Hine defines such communities: 'A utopian colony, thus, consists of a group of people who are attempting to establish a new social pattern based upon a vision of the ideal society and who have withdrawn themselves from the community at large to embody that vision in experimental form' (1966: 5).

8 Enacted through the Indian Act, 1876 (see Titley 1986).

9 A complete and complex system, Bakhtin's 'second world' is characterized by carnival laughter, the carnivalesque body, grotesque exaggeration and clowning, and the spirit of creative destruction. As Bakhtin posits, the carnivalesque body is a liminal body of becoming that is never completed, straddling the crib and the grave embodying a cosmic topography of heaven (upper body) and earth (lower body), this unfinished body is a fecund site for abundance, excess, renewal and transformation. Often evident in the costuming of the body, travesty and exaggeration have assisted in the reversal of social hierarchies—the jester can become the king for a day and vice versa (1984: 317).

Works Cited

Bakhtin, Mikhail M. 1984. *Rabelais and His World.* Bloomington: Indiana University Press.

Beauchesne, Kim, and Alessandra Santos. 2011. *The Utopian Impulse in Latin America.* London: Palgrave Macmillan.

Bloch, Ernst. 2000. *The Spirit of Utopia* (Anthony A. Nassar trans.). Stanford, CA: Stanford University Press.

Claeys, Gregory, and Lyman Tower Sargent. 1999. *The Utopia Reader.* New York: New York University Press.

Dolan, Jill. 2001. 'Performance, Utopia, and the "Utopian Performative."' *Theatre Journal* 53(3): 455–79.

——. 2005. *Utopia in Performance: Finding Hope at the Theatre.* Ann Arbor: University of Michigan Press.

Foucault, Michel. 1986. 'Of Other Spaces' (Jay Miskowiec trans.). *Diacritics* 16(1) (Spring): 22–7.

Goodwin, Barbara, and Keith Taylor. 2009. *The Politics of Utopia: A Study in Theory and Practice.* New York: Peter Lang.

Hayden, Dolores. 1979. *Seven American Utopias: The Architecture of Communitarian Socialism, 1790–1975.* Cambridge, MA: MIT Press.

Hine, Robert V. 1966. *California's Utopian Colonies.* New Haven, CT: Yale University Press.

Kaplan, E. Ann. 2013. 'Trauma Studies Moving Forward: Interdisciplinary Perspectives'. *Journal of Dramatic Theory and Criticism* 27(2): 53–66.

——. 2014. 'Trauma Future-Tense (With Reference to Alfonso Cuarón's *Children of Men,* 2006)' in Julia Koehne (ed.), *Trauma and Film.* Berlin: Kulturverlag Kadmos, pp. 364–81.

——. 2016. Profile page of E. Ann Kaplan. College of Arts and Sciences, Stony Brook University, New York. Available at: http://goo.gl/HvUj7S (last accessed on 12 April 2016).

Kitch, Sally L. 2000. *Higher Ground: From Utopianism to Realism in American Feminist Thought and Theory.* Chicago: University of Chicago Press.

Lipsitz, George. 2007. *Footsteps in the Dark: The Hidden Histories of Popular Music.* Minneapolis: University of Minnesota Press.

MacLeish, Archibald. 1939. *America Was Promises.* New York: Duell, Sloan & Pearce.

MARTIN, Randy. 1998. *Critical Moves: Dance Studies in Theory and Politics.* Durham, NC: Duke University Press.

MORRIS, William. 1946[1893]. *News from Nowhere: Or, an Epoch of Rest, Being Some Chapters from a Utopian Romance.* Hammersmith: Kelmscott Press.

MUÑOZ, José Esteban. 2009. *Cruising Utopia: The Then and There of Queer Futurity.* New York: New York University Press.

NEGLEY, Glenn, and J. Max Patrick (eds). 1971. *The Quest for Utopia.* College Park, MD: McGrath.

NORA, Pierre. 1994. 'Between Memory and History: *Les Lieux de Mémoire*' in Geneviève Fabre and Robert O'Meally (eds), *History and Memory in African-American Culture.* New York: Oxford University Press, pp. 284–300.

PARRINGTON, Vernon Louis. 1964. *American Dreams: A Study of American Utopias.* New York: Russell & Russell.

ROACH, Joseph. 1996. *Cities of the Dead: Circum-Atlantic Performance.* New York: Columbia University Press.

TAYLOR, Diana. 2003. *The Archive and the Repertoire: Performing Cultural Memory in the Americas.* Durham: Duke University Press.

TITLEY, E. Brian. 1986. *A Narrow Vision: Duncan Campbell Scott and the Administration of Indian Affairs in Canada.* Vancouver: University of British Columbia Press.

TOD, Ian, and Martin Wheeler. 1978. *Utopia.* New York: Harmony Books.

TURNER, Victor. 1967. 'Carnival, Ritual, and Play in Rio de Janeiro' in Alessandro Falassi (ed.), *Time Out of Time: Essays on the Festival.* Albuquerque: University of New Mexico Press, pp. 74–90.

Part One

EMBODIED UTOPIAS

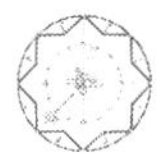

Chapter 1

LEARNING FROM NGĀTAHI

Rapumentary Film, the Utopian Imagination and Politics of the Possible

Luis Alvarez

In a segment of the docu/rapumentary film *Ngātahi: Know the Links* by Maori filmmaker, rapper, musician and activist Dean Hapeta, the scenes flip from Dedan Kimathi—Pan-African activist, former Black Panther, president of the Black Surfer's Association and host of the Los Angeles–based KPFK's 'Freedom Now' radio programme—to Pinay spoken word artist, writer and hip hop, Filipino and international women's rights activist Faith Santilla. Sitting in a living room in South Central Los Angeles with books scattered at his feet and Bob Marley, Free Palestine, African Liberation, George Jackson and Smash the FBI–CIA posters on the walls, Kimathi waxes poetically about racism as a global phenomenon. He underscores the need for 'the fight back' to cultivate links between Pan-African and Maori, Aborigine, Khoikhoi, Korean and Irish struggles against colonialism. As a helicopter hovers in the sky above her in the middle of an unnamed Los Angeles city street at dusk, Santilla delivers her own rhymes and verses condemning the neoliberal, for-profit exploitation of prison labour in the United States and the hyperfunding of prisons compared to the underfunding of state-sponsored education. She concludes her poem 'No More Prisons' with shout-outs to the Filipinos on death row. The scene shifts back and forth between the two camera shots: different political discussions and performances by different people now interconnected and in conversation with one another. They are united by the political content of their words, the power of their presentation, and their desire to imagine a future where seemingly disparate struggles bring people together rather than keep them apart, while the sounds of Hapeta's own Maori rap outfit Upper Hutt Posse (UHP) provide a soundtrack (see Hapeta 2007a).[1]

Armed with a handheld video camera, a few contacts in his destination cities, and hopes to capture on film the political and cultural struggles of aggrieved communities across the globe, Hapeta set out in 2000 from Aotearoa (the Maori name for New Zealand) to connect with local hip hop, spoken word and activist scenes around the world. His journey took him to more than fifteen cities in nine countries, resulting in dozens of encounters like the one in Los Angeles described above. The result was the docu/rapumentary film *Ngātahi: Know the Links*, Parts 1–2. Since flowering into a six-part film series on 'arts and activism amongst native and marginalized people in 20 countries', *Ngātahi* has been Hapeta's labour of love, as he is cameraman, director and editor all in one (Hapeta 2007a). He spent the better part of a decade accumulating hundreds of hours of spectacular footage from around the world. From New York to London to Wounded Knee, the West Bank to Bogotá to Manila and points in-between, Hapeta stayed afloat with personal funds and support from the Screen Innovation Production Fund (a partnership between Creative New Zealand and New Zealand Film Commission) and several Maori tribal councils, sleeping on couches and calling in favours to cut costs.[2] Back home in Aotearoa between trips, Hapeta put the Macintosh computer in his backyard film studio to use, producing concise, powerful and visually stunning films that, in his words, invite the viewer to 'step into a zone where hip hop and activism are one' and experience 'an elated dose of urban vitality immersed in conscious awareness' (Hapeta 2003). The stories, interviews, performances and organizing Hapeta shares with us chronicle how seemingly disconnected people around the world struggle against neoliberalism and legacies of colonialism in their own locales while finding common ground with those from faraway places.[3]

What does a lone Maori travelling the globe, seeking out underground hip hop gigs, house parties, poetry slams and political demonstrations have to teach us about popular culture, social movements and the utopian imagination? Quite a bit, if we listen to what Hapeta and the people he meets in his travels have to say about how and why they see themselves in one another. Underscoring that global capitalism is rooted in local conditions, the films offer snapshots of grassroots efforts by artists and activists to combat the poor living conditions and violence spawned by neoliberalism while they sketch the ways diverse people share similar experiences. Facing what George Lipsitz describes as 'a brand of economic fundamentalism favouring free markets', many in *Ngātahi* point out that the intensification of deregulation and global flows of capital, ideas and labour, along with the growth of mass technology and communications, has resulted in 'low wages, high unemployment, slow growth, high interest rates, and devastating declines in social spending on health, housing, and education' (Lipsitz 2007: 70). From Chicano muralists and Filipina poets in Los Angeles to native rappers in Whitehorse, Arusha and Mexico City, Hapeta encounters a cast of characters who passionately perform and speak their minds. They draw connections between their own land claims, battles against racism and police brutality and long histories of resistance to colonization with the experiences of Hapeta's Maori and other Indigenous and marginalized people. Among the films' primary messages is that while Indigenous communities have long shouldered the destructive consequences of privatization, development and colonial expansion, they have also sustained and regenerated cultural practices to survive, navigate, challenge and even thrive amid such seemingly dystopic conditions. Through Hapeta's extensive globetrotting and creative ethnographic style, we see people learning, identifying and exploring the links between themselves and others. *Ngātahi*, after all, means 'togetherness' in Maori.

In the six *Ngātahi* films, Hapeta skilfully weaves the stories of the people he meets in his travels. Hapeta himself is rarely seen, save for a few occasions when he shares a *hongi*, the traditional Maori forehead-to-forehead greeting, with his new friends. In Parts 1 and 2, released in 2003 as a double DVD set by Hapeta's own company Kia Kaha Productions, Hapeta visits Detroit, Ottawa, Toronto, London, New York, Paris, San Francisco, Washington DC, Medellín, Bogotá, Kingston, Havana, Honolulu, Sydney and his home turf of Aotearoa. Released in 2007, Part 3 includes stops in Los Angeles, Mexico City, Chiapas, Whitehorse, Wounded Knee and Rapid City. Part 4 charts Hapeta's visits to Capetown, Arusha and Tahiti. Part 5, released in 2008, sees Hapeta in the West Bank, Palestine, Belfast and Derry in Northern Ireland, and Manila and Baguio in the Philippines. In the sixth and final part that premiered in 2012, Hapeta visits Budapest, Belgrade, Beijing, Rio de Janeiro and Sao Paulo. The *Ngātahi* films move up and down the Americas, from Europe to Asia and from Africa to the Pacific Islands, exploring the connections between grassroots cultural and social movements on a global scale.

In addition to their sweeping geographical reach, the *Ngātahi* films encompass broadly defined cultural experience. While Hapeta's free-flowing camera work creates a unique aesthetic for each place he visits by capturing local geography and people, his footage generally falls into three different formats: informal interviews with local political activists; spontaneous performances of poetry, rap or dance; and recording of festivals, political rallies and protests. Although some scenes are clearly more planned or choreographed than others, the result is a montage of ordinary people saying and doing amazing things on city streets, in public spaces or in their own homes. The *Ngātahi* films present a picture of artists, singers, musicians, poets and activists whose everyday activity at once tells the story of how they seek to make their own locales better places to live and how the whole of such struggles might become more powerful than the sum of their parts.

Through an abbreviated exploration of *Ngātahi*, I propose that Hapeta, the folks in his films and the many they identify with are part of a diaspora, one based on interlinked struggles for dignity rather than any particular place or ethnic affiliation. The film uncovers and encourages a diaspora made up of the many local spaces and small politics that seek to make dominant neoliberal, race or power relations unworkable on the ground, even if only for a moment at a festival, spontaneous musical or poetic performance or house party. The project both documents and cultivates dignity's diaspora, showing how people make sense of and strike back against the forces of globalization. They reveal connections between a range of movements for autonomy and freedom. In the larger-than-life murals of pre-Columbian history in Los Angeles and revolutionary struggles in Belfast, the poetic verses thrown on streets in Rapid City and Cape Town or the public marches for the return of Indigenous land and against police brutality in San Francisco and the Philippines, *Ngātahi* illumines dignity's diaspora. Hapeta and the many new friends he makes along the *Ngātahi* trail show us that the small politics of cultural work and performance may not be so small after all.[4] More than just imaginary solutions to real problems, the cultural practices evident in *Ngātahi* enable people to speak back against their own erasure by making a record of events, injustices and calls for change that might be otherwise ignored or forgotten. Hapeta's films suggest that 'revolution' in the neoliberal, postmodern, postcolonial era may be more plausible with a small *r* and an *s* at the end. The artists and activists in *Ngātahi* ultimately practise a politics of the possible, demonstrating that utopian hopes for a better future can emerge from the dystopian and almost apocalyptic misery left in the wake of global capitalism and imperialism.

Ngātahi functions as a kind of cultural history of what some have labelled the Fourth World War, marked by contemporary struggles around the world against the effects of neoliberalism and following the First World War, the Second World War and the Cold War (Marcos 2001 [1999]; *The Fourth World War* 2004). The rest of this chapter samples from the films to consider how their production and content might help us think about the political and pedagogical possibilities of popular culture, social movements and the utopian imagination. The making of *Ngātahi* sheds light on (1) a theory of dignity and diaspora; (2) how pop culture circulates political struggle; and (3) how the utopian imagination rests on cultural labor, small politics and alternative interpretations of history.

Making *Ngātahi*

In the commentary track to Part 5 of *Ngātahi*, Hapeta and his radio and music producer friend Brent Clough sip beers and converse informally as they watch the film. An example of the exchange so evident in the movies themselves, their discussion provides clues to the range of methods Hapeta used to make the films, including his willingness to adapt on the fly, explore the unknown and embrace the possibility that something good might come from an apparent dead end. More than mere flexibility, Hapeta's open-ended approach to the making of *Ngātahi* reveals a politics that is decentered, rhizomatic and open to constant change. Describing to Clough how he made one set of contacts, for example, Hapeta explains that while still in Aotearoa,

> I was in the pub [. . .] and I met a guy. I was telling him I'm going to Ireland, man. I got some money and I want to go to Palestine at the same time. And he goes, 'You know what? I know someone over there you should meet up. She's from here, but she lives there now. Her name is Rita Simmons.' I says, 'Yeah right. When I've got my ticket I'm gonna be on your case to get her number.' I don't know, I say this to people and I wonder what they think. Anyway, I guess a year or so later I get back in touch with him, 'OK, can you get me Rita's number?' I got in touch with Rita. Said who I am, she could remember Upper Hutt Posse from when she was living here. She hooked me up with this other guy, put me in touch with the brother here (Hapeta 2008).

Through much more than just dumb luck, Hapeta crafted a network of global contacts, support and interlinked political struggles by following the organic, spur-of-the-moment and seemingly accidental opportunities that came before him.

Hapeta's methodology and creative process in the making of *Ngātahi* enabled him and those he met along the way to practise what the films preach by establishing new political and cultural links between communities that, at first glance, appear to have little in common. Hapeta's films, in other words, do more than just represent cultural and political struggle on screen. To borrow from cultural critic Herman Gray, *Ngātahi* also constitutes Hapeta's own 'politics of articulation' (2005), where his extensive travel, informal ethnography, innovative postproduction techniques and grassroots efforts to circulate his films bring together seemingly disparate people, places and movements.

The films are dependent on Hapeta's mobility and travel. Having spent much of the first decade of the 2000s on the road, Hapeta follows a *Ngātahi* trail that is at heart a process based on building human relationships through shared love for hip hop and global justice activism. While much of Hapeta's emphasis is on hip hop, it is the politics of popular culture and activism, rather than their form, that drives *Ngātahi*. In fact, in Hapeta's films many scenes don't have much to do with hip hop at all, including those in Whitehorse, Toronto, Havana, Manila, Sydney, Kingston, Free Derry and Belfast. Each of his encounters, however, does illuminate antiglobalization, anticolonial or antiracist struggle. Describing the segments he filmed in Northern Ireland, for example, Hapeta explained, 'That's the thing. There's no Irish hip hop in here. There is Irish hip hop, I just didn't end up connecting with Irish hip hop kids. That's just how it goes. Calling it a rapumentary, people just think it's about hip hop everywhere. Well, not really, it's about rhyme and percussion. And I'm using r-a-p as an acronym' (2008). Wherever he goes and whatever he finds, Hapeta presents interviews, performance and activism in ways that blur the boundaries between politics, music and art. While it may be hard to tell where one begins and the other ends, it is easy to see that music and art are the vehicles for people to share their politics with him and others in ways that might not be possible otherwise.

Hapeta ultimately reveals a kind of globalization from below in which people articulate their utopian visions via their art, music and activism. With a global scope that remains embedded in local places, Hapeta's method of tracing cultural politics and performance supports anthropologist James Clifford's contention that travel enables 'reflections on conditions for human connection, alliances cutting across class, race, gender, and national locations' (1997: 18). Like Clifford, Hapeta seems to intuitively understand ethnography as a series of travel encounters where movement creates contacts at the same time that it sustains ideas of home, dwelling and discrete regions. Both the 'roots' (with a double *o*) and the 'routes' (with an *ou*) that Clifford describes are very much alive in *Ngātahi* (ibid).

With such travel and encounter, Clifford reminds us, comes the need for cultural translation if people are to make sense of how they might make and learn from political connections with those different from themselves (ibid). In the case of *Ngātahi*, translation and mobility take on the most literal of meanings. Remarking on a portion of his travels, Hapeta notes: 'Leaving Palestine and coming here to Ireland, 'cause that's the order in which I did it, Ireland was like easy in a way. 'Cause everyone's speaking English. And I can get on a bus and go here or on a bus and go there. And get the general idea of the environment'(2008). If translating language and meaning from place to place was among the stiffest challenges in making *Ngātahi*, it is not one Hapeta shied away from. He concludes that translation, both during his travels and in the post-production process, was 'about as big as making the thing' (ibid).

As much as his travel and translation, it is Hapeta's free-flowing ethnography and production, described by one critic as 'guerilla filmmaking', which connects the performances, interviews and protests from city to city (Sweetman 2003). Hapeta explained his easygoing if slightly unorthodox methods, which usually consisted of grabbing his camera and walking the streets of whatever city he found himself in, regardless of his familiarity with the place: 'Yeah, I definitely feel that I'm guided 'cause I just turn this corner and went that way instead of going the other way and bang! I bump into someone. Yes, yeah, it's like writing songs as well. I feel that with song writing as well. If I come up with a line, I just feel like I'm guided. It's not just my physical self that's doing this. I think all artists feel that in some way' (2007a; Te Kupu Profile). He recalled his visit to Rio de Janeiro, for example: 'All the tourist books tell you don't walk around Copacabana with a camera. You gonna get jacked. First night I get there, [I] go down with my camera' (ibid). Though his visit to Rio coincided with that of several other Aotearoa-based musicians, Hapeta combed the beaches and favelas while his colleagues worked in the recording studio. 'I like talking to the locals you see,' he continued. 'And, uh, so I just do, I just talk to them. I just sort of walk around looking for the hip hop scene. Knowing that there'll be conscious rappers inside that. I don't even have any big long questions—I just say police brutality. And, ah, they just went on and on about it, you know, cause it's just so bad there' (ibid). It is not hard to see that Hapeta promotes an openness, comfort and reciprocity. The way he embodies those ideas fuels the form and content of his films so much that he feels, 'like I can go and see any of these people in ten years' time' [and the links will remain strong] (Hapeta 2008).

More than simply shooting from the hip, Hapeta's interview, ethnography and travel style constitute a rhizomatic politics. Contacts and travel opportunities pop up unexpectedly; no one place, struggle or community is privileged over others; there is not necessarily a set plan; and his research and filmmaking are shaped by a malleable and decentered approach that values the experience and process as much as, if not more than, the end result. Practising what the Zapatistas have called the politics of 'preguntando caminamos' (asking we walk) Hapeta understood there was a range of possible paths to take and as much is to be learned from failure as success (Holloway 1996). This was evident in the ways Hapeta found contacts in each of his destinations. For example, he connected with the rap group Ramallah Underground in Palestine after he found their email address on the Internet during his first night in a backpacker's hotel in Jerusalem. He sent them a message, received a response the next morning and met with the band the following day. He described how many of his encounters grew from moments when he 'just heard some music through this door. I said, "Oh, what's going on in there?" I just sort of walked on in there [. . .] . I says, "You know what, I'm making a film about this and that"' (2008). In one instance, Hapeta even received help from the New Zealand ambassador to the Philippines who, despite knowing of Hapeta's leftist politics, helped him meet folks in the Philippines and avoid travel problems (ibid). Hapeta came to understand his network of contacts around the world as the result of a shared politics and openness to aiding others involved in similar struggles. 'Activists are the best people on the planet,' he says. They 'give up contacts no problem, not like the music business! [. . .] With activism it's about something greater than your career, greater than the music industry. It's about people's lives for real. People living and dying. So people are all too willing to share their links' (ibid).

Despite the fact that he rarely appears on screen himself, some might argue that the *Ngātahi* films rely too much on him and his individual talents. Hapeta, however, thinks otherwise; he firmly believes that the people he meets in his films are responsible for *Ngātahi*. He noted that the responses to Parts 1 and 2 included demands from viewers, film festival organizers and television executives in Aotearoa that he appear in more scenes. His response was: 'From the beginning it was never my idea to be in it anyway. What the hell you need to see my face for? There's no need!' (ibid). Accordingly, he has considered creating additional films in the series by soliciting videos from around the world without him ever leaving Aotearoa. He explains that he is 'thinking of doing another six parts after this, but not in the way I've done this. But, other people doing it and contributing to the whole project' with a song, political commentary or 10-minute historical piece that they would send to him for inclusion in the new films (ibid). By approaching *Ngātahi* without preconceived ideas of what it should be, embracing the possibility of the unknown and accepting the results, Hapeta brings variant struggles from around the world into conversation, even if the links between them are not easily translatable into any cohesive social movement. Through *Ngātahi* he suggests a political movement *of* movements that are loosely connected through shared networks of support, friendship and popular culture.

Just as his travel and ethnography encourage viewers to follow the *Ngātahi* trail and link each local struggle with the next, so too do Hapeta's slyly effective postproduction techniques. Virtually every scene includes moments where he connects strangers and seemingly disconnected places by splicing, juxtaposing and interspersing music, images and interviews. The soundtrack accompanying political speeches and cultural performances often contains beats and lyrics from local rappers and singers or Hapeta's own band, Upper Hutt Posse. Graffiti, murals, ordinary street activity and urban scenery serve as central features, immersing viewers in each place while simultaneously drawing parallels with others. The movement of bodies and politics, from Hapeta's globetrotting to the physical bodies of the dancers and performers he captures on film, are central to *Ngātahi*. As one reviewer commented, 'everyday movement from walking to surfing is displayed as if it was break dancing' (Collins 2004: 95).

While mobility is central to *Ngātahi*, the circulation of the films themselves raises the question of who actually sees them. Though a festival cut of Parts 1 and 2 was shown at the 2004 Sundance Film Festival, Hapeta never approached film festivals or television companies to solicit screenings. Assuming that they would just turn him down, he figured that it was not worth the effort. While Parts 1 and 2 were screened on Maori television in Aotearoa, Parts 3 and 4 were not accepted for TV in his home country, leading Hapeta to exclaim, 'Ah, fuck TV in New Zealand! [. . .] I don't even care to do that. But people have always said to me, "Man, it should be on TV! People should be seeing it!" And I says, "Well, I didn't make it for those clowns!"' (2008). He preferred to 'just put it into stories and let it find its audience', largely through cyberspace and by word of mouth in international hip hop, Indigenous and progressive activist circles (Reid 2003). Like many of the cultural workers he meets along the *Ngātahi* trail, Hapeta rejects much of the conventional movie, music and pop culture industry and remains committed to a kind of decommodification of hip hop, film and the politics embedded in them.

The prospect of circulation, or noncirculation, of *Ngātahi* raises another potentially troubling question: Who cares about the art, the people or politics in *Ngātahi* if there is no audience? While viewers see the political transformation of those on screen, let us imagine for a moment that the films were never seen. In that case, Hapeta's creative process, extensive travel and improvisational ethnography still circulated political struggle and made *Ngātahi* something real *off screen*. By practising his unique form of rapumentary, Hapeta linked different struggles for dignity around the globe by constructing new social relations and political formations with those he met and with whom shared dance floors, festival stages and political marches. There are important lessons in the making of *Ngātahi*, ones that suggest that popular culture does not simply reflect already existing politics but can ignite new politics; that one person or community's struggle is integrally connected to that of another; and that the process of imagining and struggling for a better world is as important as any end goal or finished product.

Ngātahi and a Theory of Dignity

In another scene from *Ngātahi*, viewers hear the sound of the wind whistling and traffic passing by as Hapeta and John McCuster stroll along the street in front of the International Wall in Belfast,

Northern Ireland. McCuster, an Irish Republican and pro-Palestine activist, explains how longstanding historical efforts by the Irish for freedom from British tyranny are mirrored in the Wall's ever-changing murals of other struggles for autonomy and independence around the world. From Cuba to Palestine and from Frederick Douglass to the Manchester Martyrs, the Wall's images, quotations and affect connect the very different and vast battles of folks from Ireland, the Americas and other distant places and times in their message that a better, more just world is possible. As McCuster says to his Maori companion,

> Every one of us who ha[s] been enslaved, occupied or invaded should never forget the lessons that come with that. That freedom is an inherent right for everybody and justice is an inherent right. And we have to help these people struggle for it as well, as well as fight our own struggles. There's a common struggle for everybody and it's the right to be free. And that's one of the underpinning concepts of Irish Republicanism. That it abhors any type of occupation, enslavement, any type of privilege, that everybody has the inherent right to be free on equal terms (Hapeta 2008).[5]

With Hapeta behind the camera and McCuster walking along the Wall, this *Ngātahi* scene underscores Irish claims to dignity against centuries of English imperialism. At the same time, it suggests that Irish dignity is dependent on recognizing that of others—that struggles for Irish dignity are strengthened by learning from and connecting with those of others around the world and throughout history. *Ngātahi* reveals dignity as a constant struggle embedded in cultural expression, including the production of the murals on the Wall, in which people craft political critique, challenge their dehumanization and, sometimes, if only for a moment, create utopian spaces by putting their visions of the future into practice.

In Hapeta's films, dignity functions as a struggle against its own denial. It is less a static quality or state of being worthy, honoured or respected and more the lived struggle for pride, hope and humanity against poor life chances in the face of neoliberal globalization. Dignity in the *Ngātahi* films is both a politics of refusal and a politics of encounter (Holloway 1998; Callahan 2005). It is an effort to expose, reject and refuse the humiliation, dehumanization and displacement that too often shapes the history of aggrieved communities' contemporary experiences with capitalism and colonialism. Yet dignity in *Ngātahi* is also incumbent upon building points of exchange among different people and political struggles, both in human interaction and more discursive solidarity. It is not an accident that this point is made so dramatically in the Northern Ireland scenes of *Ngātahi*. Perhaps in part because of his own whiteness—his mother is white and father Maori—Hapeta argues, 'And, also, I wanted to have some white people in *Know the Links*! I said, "Well, shit, I'm going to Ireland then!" Fucking hell!' (2008). The dignity of Hapeta and others in *Ngātahi* is not limited to formal political organizations or bound by race, ethnicity or region.

Dignity in the *Ngātahi* films also works as a diaspora, one defined less by shared connections to place or ethnicity and more by people's shared refusal against neoliberalism and colonial legacies. The films chart a diaspora of dignity that is as much looking forward toward possible connections among a range of activist impulses and performances as it is looking backward to any shared home or ancestral land or any appeal to common kinship or race (Clifford 1997; Gilroy 1993). Much as Vivek Bald describes overlapping ethnic diasporas in the early twentieth-century United States, *Ngātahi*'s diaspora of dignity includes 'movements and relations between multiple locations'; it moves 'away from an overdetermining focus on "homeland"' and departs from 'a singular emphasis on particular racial, ethnic or national groups' (Bald 2006: 7). For Bald and Hapeta, diaspora operates more as 'a process of encounter, intermixture, and the negotiation of difference across all these lines' (ibid). These connections are at once historically rooted and utopian in their dreams of a better future, growing from vibrant exchanges about how diverse people from different places survive, navigate, challenge and even thrive in the face of great odds.

Against the violence of Indigenous land loss, the growth of industrial tourism and corporate greed and the ongoing racism, poverty and poor life chances of so many, people in the *Ngātahi* films reclaim dignity and humanity through artistic, political and cultural expression and protest. In the films we see the dehumanization and stripping away of dignity spawned by the corporate greed of mining interests from the Yukon to South Africa; police brutality from Los Angeles to Manila; and land loss from Palestine to Wounded Knee. While some might describe such scenes as portraying a diaspora of misery, exploitation or dystopia, Hapeta's travels reveal a wide-ranging and informal matrix of activists and artists who are continuously at work to build new and powerful alternatives. What we are left with after viewing the *Ngātahi* films is a global cartography where activism and performance are not as isolated as we might think; where the multiplicity of local struggles reinforce one another; and where people seem to be less concerned with their small political acts leading to something bigger than they are with generating as many small acts as possible (Gilroy 1994). Within dignity's diaspora are also numerous contradictions. It is not hard to see in the films that one person's dignity is another's indignity, and that dignity is as contested along racial, gender, sexual and class lines as any other marker of struggle and politics. The *Ngātahi* films thus help us think in terms of dignities in the plural—a recurring theme in Hapeta's project that encourages working through difference and thinking of difference as something that can bring people together as much as pull them apart (Hall 1989).

Ngātahi and the Circulation of Struggle

Part 4 of the *Ngātahi* series includes extensive footage from Cape Town, South Africa, where just hours after his arrival Hapeta discovered an underground rap gig, connected with a number of local artists and began a whirlwind grassroots tour of the South African hip hop and spoken word scene. Included in the Cape Town segments is Hapeta's informal interview with Shaheen Ariefdien of the hip hop group Prophets of da City. Filmed casually on a living-room couch, Ariefdien eloquently and powerfully describes the influence of US urban-based rap and hip hop culture on his own politics and life experience in apartheid and immediate post-apartheid South Africa.

> I guess growing up under apartheid when you've been brainwashed to believe that you're not shit, you never will be shit, it doesn't matter what you do. Hip hop came at a time for a lot of people, you know, where it was almost a kind of alchemy, the way I see it. That it tapped into people's potential, turned base metal into gold type of thing. That potential to say, 'We don't have shit, we don't own shit, no musical instruments, kick a fucking beat box!' You know what I mean? 'I got a cardboard, I don't have a dance studio, do a fucking head spin!' You know, stuff like that. And I think that that potential of hip hop was fucking brilliant for me.

Ariefdien continues, 'Because you know at some point hip hop to me was like African tradition with Japanese technology processed by kidnapped Africans on stolen land' (Hapeta 2007b).[6]

Along with his stops in Los Angeles, New York, Rapid City, Bogota, London, Paris, Arusha and the West Bank, which focus on rapping, break dancing and graffiti, Hapeta's interview with Arief-dien reminds us that hip hop—and, more broadly, pop culture—can create new political relationships among the folks who make, purchase and perform it (Lipsitz 1997). Perhaps more than any other parts of *Ngātahi*, the hip hop–centred segments showcase how pop culture's commodity form facilitates the movement of its political content, often shifting or distorting its meaning as it travels the globe.

Ngātahi shows that hip hop circulates critical politics and utopian possibilities. Though often considered a uniquely US cultural expression since its creation in the late 1960s and early 1970s by African American, Caribbean and Latino youth in the South Bronx of New York, the sounds and styles of hip hop have quickly become both a trans-American and a global phenomenon. More than just a mimicking of commercial hip hop in the United States, burgeoning scenes of highly politicized and social justice–oriented hip hop have sprouted around the world. It is not surprising that Hapeta, as a rapper and musician himself, filmed scenes at a house party in Mexico City where he recorded a freestyle rap against North American Free Trade Agreement (NAFTA) and interviewed another rapper about Zapatista struggles for autonomy. In Los Angeles, he hung out with Chicano rappers who voiced seething critiques against the racist nature of public education in Southern California. In Rapid City, South Dakota, he chilled with native youth who rap against the history of genocide and anti-Indian violence. In Arusha, Hapeta came across scores of Tanzanian youth invested in rap as a forum to protest the long history of colonialism in Africa. In Paris, he met with Afro-French rappers and graffiti artists who likened their battles against police brutality to those of black and Indigenous folks across the globe. In all of these segments, Hapeta focused on young people's use of hip hop to articulate both their displeasure with conditions of inhumanity and their ability to undermine those conditions, if even only for a few moments during a politically inflected rap or head spin while break dancing.

The Cape Town scenes especially show hip hop's movement from the United States and how it became a primary register for young South Africans to claim dignity and make sense of apartheid, colonialism and the impact of globalization in their home country. In many cases, hip hop fuelled their antiapartheid and antiglobalization politics. In the 42-plus minutes of Cape Town footage in *Ngātahi*, for example, we see Hapeta on a walking tour of the Guguletu Township where he films local rapper Koriander performing a five-minute, single-take freestyle rap on racism and poverty in postapartheid South Africa. We also see an impromptu music video of dancehall reggae and rap group Chronic Clan's song 'Ghetto Life' about growing up in the townships. Hapeta captures on film the spontaneous performances of a number of hip hop–inflected artists, including digital artist Mustafa Maluka (who shares his anticapitalist, interactive online art with Hapeta from his home computer, illustrated in part by his line 'I fart in the face of commodification'); spoken word artist Marlon (whose nighttime poetry performance in the middle of the street in front of Cape Town's government quarter says, in part, that the 'only problem with revolution is the rebels bruising end up musing in the very groove where they started their movement'), and poet Shameema of the group Godessa (who shares her thoughts and rhymes on being black in South Africa from her dining-room table). In his bedroom with Bob Marley and Malcolm X posters on the walls, rapper Shamiel X confirms hip hop's power for younger generations of South Africans and its uniquely US origins when he tells Hapeta:

> I was politicized through hip hop. Malcolm X didn't exist until I heard 'Don't tell me that you understand until you

> hear the man.' Which was Public Enemy referring to Louis Farrakhan. And we wanted to know what man is he talking about! Who, what was going on? So, a lot of that stuff came through, in fact, the hip hop. And I got, I'm proud to say, my politicization not from the ANC, not from any of the political shit that was going on here. It came through hip hop (Hapeta 2007b).

If the Cape Town clips emphasize how the mobility of pop culture often carries razor-sharp political ideas across time and space, they also alert viewers that when music transports anticapitalist, anticolonialist and antiracist images and content, they do so through the very networks of capitalism, politics and society they seek to critique. Without pretending to resolve these contradictions of what we might think of as capitalism-fuelled anticapitalist, anticolonial and antiracist cultural politics, Hapeta and most of the artists and activists in *Ngātahi* recognize the inherent limits—as much as the possibilities—of their cultural and political work. Hapeta works this recognition into the film's form: in one typical *Ngātahi* segment, for instance, Hapeta splices bits of his Cape Town interviews with Ariefdien and poet Emile of the group Black Noize with Marlon's performance of his 'Revolution' poem at the gates of the South African parliament. Hapeta's editing moves among the three, presenting powerful condemnations of both the commodification of hip hop and the failures of postapartheid South African politics. From Ariefdien's passionate explanation of South African hip hop as a 'thing that essentially comes from working-class people' and risks coming apart at the seams when 'corporations get a hold of it,' Hapeta moves to Emile, interviewed alongside an unnamed dirt road. Emile argues that the music industry 'won't push the revolutionary hip hop or the real hip hop that exists in every township, favela, ghetto around the world. They'll never push that because they realize it's not part of the agenda to generate income for a handful of people' (Hapeta 2007b, Part 4). From Marlon's scathing critique of the ANC as a 'puppet show' and postapartheid selling of South African natural resources as part of getting 'fucked in stages' in the political name of 'constructive engagement', Hapeta returns to Ariefdien's conclusion that apartheid combined 'the worst of the British and the worst of the Dutch that gave us this kind of racist capitalism' (ibid). Hapeta then goes back to Marlon's stanza 'Revolutions got us going around in circles like hour hands' (ibid). Hapeta's skill as filmmaker and editor underscores that hip hop, art and activism draw the cast of *Ngātahi* characters together at the same time as their cultural expression and politics are anything but exempt from the forces they critique.

If the *Ngātahi* films show how people use popular culture to share hopes for social change, they also reveal something special about the rapumentary form's ability to circulate struggle. Like a few other existing documentaries on recent antiglobalization movements, Hapeta's films draw from a spectacular range of places and people. They leave it to the viewer to draw parallels between seemingly decentered and different struggles and movements, and are unconventional in their presentation and circulation.[7] This apparently haphazard format gives rise to fresh possibilities of how *Ngātahi* might strike a chord with viewers and how they might connect to the broader political project Hapeta's films seem to call for—that we all practise *Ngātahi* in our own local contexts.

Ngātahi and the Utopian Imagination

In the initial moments of the Medellín scenes in Part 1 of *Ngātahi*, we see images of street protests and graffiti against US economic intervention in Colombia and for workers' rights, accessible education, and proper health care intermixed with the sounds and scenes of cumbia music, street vendors and everyday life in the city. This transitions into Hapeta's experience at the International Poetry Festival in the same city. Onstage in front of thousands and dressed in a Colombian national team football shirt, Hapeta shares a poem of his own titled 'The Maori Green Sun'. In his native Maori language, mixed with elementary Spanish, Hapeta feeds off the crowd's feeling of togetherness, solidarity and optimism. Another performer encapsulates the vibe of the festival when he says to the crowd,

> In a city that has become a symbol of death, massacres and car bombs that have astonished the world, the International Poetry Festival is an alchemy of poets and political projects from all over the world, with the objective of defending the life of the people, internationalizing the profound voice of poetry and its destiny on earth to globalize the struggle of an imagination in search of human liberty (Hapeta 2003).[8]

Like the parts of *Ngātahi* that detail Hapeta's visits to First Nations festivals in Whitehorse, Tahiti and Hawaii, and other big festivals in Northern Ireland, the Philippines, New York, San Francisco and elsewhere, the shots from the International Poetry Festival in Medellín have much to say about the cultural work of global justice and the utopian imagination. The Colombian scenes, like the rest of *Ngātahi*, challenge us to consider how the flows and scales of globalization shape people's most immediate hopes and dreams for a better future. Hapeta and many others in the films experiment with the emancipatory possibilities of global justice politics. In doing so, they remind us that globalization works from the bottom-up in the form of local and small politics at the same time it maintains a top-down, transnational and vast reach.

The folks in Hapeta's films share ideas of global justice and a utopian imagination that are based on cultural and social labour. In *Ngātahi*, global justice and utopia are hard work. A contentious and slippery idea, global justice often serves as shorthand for diverse struggles around the planet seeking full and universally realized socioeconomic and civil-political rights (Kurasawa 2007: 1). The 'full' and 'universal' aspects of such a notion of global justice are tricky because they elide difference and diversity for the sake of homogeneity and cohesion. Rather than an abstract set of morals or ethics, an institutional or legislative fiat or even solidarity between distinct social movements or NGOs, *Ngātahi* offers an alternative sense of global justice. Hapeta and the folks in his films practice what political theorist Fuyuki Kurasawa calls 'the work of global justice' (ibid). Global justice—some might say the utopia of global justice—is made up of hard cultural and social labour that includes difficult decisions by those involved and extraordinary levels of commitment, time, energy and resilience. Just as Stuart Hall observed that 'hegemonizing is hard work' (1989), making global justice is hard work too. Global justice in the *Ngātahi* films is thus more of a long-term war of position that rarely entails big victories over the 'powers that be' (Kurasawa 2007). It is the labour of organizing a political rally or festival; the work required to write a poem, song or speech for such an event; the effort to paint a mural on the side of a public building; or even the spontaneous decision to break out in song or dance that fuels the kind of global justice movement evident in *Ngātahi*. By sharing countless examples of these seemingly small efforts, no matter how isolated they may appear, Hapeta shows that global justice as an 'inter-struggle struggle' is alive and well. The social and cultural labour in *Ngātahi* projects a global justice that is splintered and local, but also multiple and dialogic. Global justice is based on cultural practices that involve specific acts of aid, forgiving, redress or solidarity and enables us to see the human action in global justice (ibid: 17). Rather than assuming that global justice is a utopian goal that will never be reached (utopia, after all, means 'nowhere'), *Ngātahi* suggests that the utopian character of global justice is something that can be and is routinely attained in the work of many artists, activists and musicians.

Hapeta's films suggest that the utopian imagination is embedded in the everyday and always part of a job unfinished. *Ngātahi* echoes what cultural theorist Jill Dolan calls 'utopia in performance'. Dolan argues that utopia is made of those 'small, but profound moments' with which we have 'fleeting contact', that it is 'always in process, always only partially grasped', and that its importance is 'as an index to the possible, to the "what if," rather than a more restrictive, finite image of the "what should be"' (Dolan 2005: 8, 13). Hapeta and those in the *Ngātahi* films do not reach some world-changing moment of transcendence, but seek to be a part of and help create many such small moments. *Ngātahi* explores utopia as struggle. Rapping, dancing, poetry, organizing and freestyle philosophizing in the films bear witness to how the politics of small things challenge the power of big things (Goldfarb 2006). Hapeta docu/rapuments how people around the world make global justice for as long as they can, making unequal relations of capital, race or colonialism unworkable on the ground in creative, if often temporary, ways.

Ngātahi reveals a politics of the possible evident in the ways people excavate the past to make sense of the present and imagine a different future. As if acknowledging cultural critic José Esteban Muñoz's contention that utopia and 'hope as a critical methodology can be best described as a backward glance that enacts a future vision' (2009: 4), *Ngātahi* illustrates that histories of police brutality, poverty and political powerlessness give rise to people's struggles and hopes for the future. Hapeta's historical method recognizes the cultural expressions he observes as what cultural critic George Lipsitz calls the 'alternative archives of history, the shared memories, experiences, and aspirations of ordinary people' (2007: *xi*). At Indigenous festivals in Whitehorse, Manila, Tahiti and Hawaii, as well as urban visits to San Francisco, Los Angeles, New York, London, Kingston, Detroit, Washington DC and Belfast, people share historical counter-narratives against colonialism, genocide and racist legacies. Such narratives serve as the fulcrum for current struggles to transform culture, reclaim land and garner new political power. At a First Nations festival in Whitehorse, Canada, for example, Hapeta meets children and elders who speak poignantly of how their understanding of the past animates their vision of the future. Phil 'Sun Dog' Gatensby of the Tlingit Nation, waxed poetically: 'When I think about north, south, east and west,' he said, 'we've all been through the same shit. The native people have been stepped on, abused, but from a people who almost got wiped out, we're coming back, we're getting back on our feet, we're gathering strength' (Hapeta 2007a).[9] Out of disaster and oppression come hope and possibility. This is a familiar story of the last century, to be sure. Eric Hobsbawm called it the 'age of extremes', when catastrophic war, ecological disaster, totalitarianism from the Left and Right and the deepening poverty of the Global South left dystopian cynicism and unbridled utopianism as diametrically opposed poles of political thought (Kurasawa 2007: 1, citing Hobsbawm 1994).

The *Ngātahi* films also raise questions about the seductive and limited nature of small cultural politics for global justice that emerge from, within and against the long history of capitalism and colonialism. If the strengths of the cultural politics Hapeta uncovers include mobility, adaptability and multiplicity, such features may also be among their weaknesses. Can such politics lead to substantive change or are they simply a way of living? While there is no guarantee of the former, *Ngātahi* does suggest that the kinds of performances and everyday activity Hapeta documents are at once bigger and smaller than the nation-state, an avenue for short-term politicization and seeds of hope for change in the long term. If, as Immanuel Wallerstein argues, significant work towards a lasting radical democracy must take place in the middle run between the short and long term, *Ngātahi* reminds us that the immediacy of hard labour for utopia in the here and now is equally important (Wallerstein 2008).

If the utopian imagination in *Ngātahi* is defined in part by the labour of global justice, it is also deeply gendered. The message of togetherness in Hapeta's films is fuelled by an underlying masculinity that raises important questions about the possibilities and limits of dignity's diaspora and utopian struggles as *Ngātahi* portrays them. From the scenes of the young black male Parisian hip hop crew and their battle against Paris police violence in Part 1 to Hapeta's interviews with Tanzanian young men about their anti-colonial rap in Part 5, it is evident that the political and cultural links in *Ngātahi* are often, though not always, male and masculine. This mirrors the hypermasculinity evident in much of the pop culture industry and, more generally, some Indigenous, immigrant and aggrieved communities. It may, however, also grow from the history of Hapeta and his own band, Upper Hutt Posse (UHP). At the forefront of the rebirth of cultural nationalism among Maori youth in the mid 1980s, UHP, like many other Maori and South Pacific rap and reggae artists since, invested heavily in lyrics, performances and cultural discourse about warriorism that equated resistance with manliness (Alvarez 2008). Though not explicitly in UHP's case, much 'island boy' rap and reggae identifies Indigenous women as hypersexualized or as protectors of the old ways, and speaks to a broader presumption by many male cultural performers to know what women want or how they behave (Bucknor 2004). The longer history of the hypermasculine character of hip hop across the globe is evident in *Ngātahi* and helps determine who has the privilege of participating in the films and the cultural performances they rapu/document.

Despite the open-ended and flexible nature of Hapeta's ethnographic methods, there is an unexamined and deeply gendered framing of how and where he talks to men and women and the kinds of conversations he has with them. In the more hip hop–oriented cuts, including scenes filmed at house parties, underground gigs and public performances, most of the performers featured are male and virtually all of the lengthier interviews are with young men. Young women are usually featured in their performance pieces only, with very few featured in longer monologues or interviews. Hapeta includes the most women in the Indigenous, First Nations segments on sovereignty struggles, redressing claims and cultural maintenance. Save for a brief discussion with two preteen Indigenous girls at the festival in Whitehorse, most of these are with women well past their teen years and are filmed as part of larger community protests or cultural festivals. This may very well have to do with the gendered limitations of Hapeta's ethnography. He noted, for instance, that in his travels he had 'to work a bit harder' to find women. 'I really do go out and look for women as well', he said. 'But as a guy it's easy for me to find guys. No doubt. I start rolling up on women in places, "Oh, this guy's trying to pick me up." That's the thing. I don't care actually, I would roll up on a lot of women' (Hapepta 2008). Hapeta's openness in talking about the gendered nature of his films is laudable and, ultimately, suggests that masculinity plays a critical role in both the production of the *Ngātahi* films and the diaspora of dignity and utopian imagination they help foster.

Ngātahi reveals that political links across geography and racial difference are often made on the terrain of gender. If people often experience assaults against their race, class and national identities in gendered ways, it stands to reason that they also strike back on gendered ground. Dignity is deeply gendered and assaults upon individual bodies and communities are often interpreted as attacks on manhood. This is a much longer historical phenomenon, but *Ngātahi* shows how specific places and people mobilize in a manner suggesting that sometimes masculinity and hypermasculinity may be the shortest way through to the togetherness, the *Ngātahi*, that helps make up new coalitions and social movements. Rather than celebrate the embedded masculinity of the cultural politics in *Ngātahi*, it is incumbent upon viewers to do what Hapeta at least begins to do in his discussion of his own production process: acknowledge the deeply gendered nature of dignity's diaspora, the utopian imagination and movements for social change. Following Hapeta's self-critique when it comes to gender politics, it is crucial to identify the blind spots of *Ngātahi* as much as celebrate its many possibilities.

Concluding Thoughts

Ngātahi contains at least three key lessons for those of us interested in social change and the utopian imagination. First, the films propose a number of critical tools and pedagogical approaches for connecting apparently unrelated political struggles. Flexibility, listening and willingness to alter course midstream are important tools for contemporary social movements and for building dignity's diaspora. These are among the practices that help generate new social relations and political possibilities, even from the depths of dystopic conditions and poor life conditions fostered by neoliberalism across the globe. *Ngātahi* is as much about pedagogy, the production of shared knowledge, and the regeneration of political struggle as it is about art or activism. It emphasizes the value in political processes and multiple experiences of struggle more than any cohesive movement or political endgame. Inhabiting these micro scales of globalization, Hapeta, the people featured in the films, and many who may view them qualify as what Gustavo Esteva and Madhu Suri Prakash call 'incarnate' intellectuals, those who move beyond a politics of representation and solidarity to share and build new forms of struggle, movement and encounter in non-vanguardist ways (Esteva and Prakash 1998). *Ngātahi* is a movement of movements that encourages participation of a diverse range of experiences and voices, all engaged in reclaiming dignity in their own way and locales.

A second important lesson to be learnt from *Ngātahi* lies in its reframing of the utopian imagination as an everyday struggle, made up of the small politics of cultural and social labour. Rather than think of utopia as that ever-elusive ideal society or some big moment of transcendence that solves all of our problems, Hapeta and his films remind us that utopia is as much an imaginative process as anything else and that there is great benefit in participating in little moments of transcendence. In the *Ngātahi* films utopia is fleeting and momentary, grounded in everyday activity, yet also rooted in how people make sense of alternative histories to reveal new possibilities for the present and future. *Ngātahi* reminds us that the utopian imagination is not a privilege afforded only to those with great amounts of monetary wealth and power. In fact, along with Hapeta's own Maori identity and sense of indigeneity, the films demonstrate that it is the folks with the least money and political pull that might have the most to teach about how to imagine a better world.

A third and final lesson is that despite its seductive exploration of dignity's diaspora and the utopian imagination, *Ngātahi* is not without warnings about how we might fail to realize social change. Though the films emphasize travel and encounter as central to connecting different struggles, it is not always clear how we move from 'knowing the links' to more substantial and deep analyses of the structural and material conditions of neoliberalism, differential colonialisms and uninterrogated nationalisms that both spawn and inhibit these links. While we might celebrate the alternating rupture and flow of the cultural expressions and political activism in *Ngātahi*, to borrow cultural critic Tricia Rose's still-apt description of hip hop (1994), how do we account for the privileging of certain voices, male voices in particular? Moreover, if *Ngātahi* celebrates ordinary people in struggles for global justice, it does so with no guarantees of radical, leftist, progressive or even liberal politics. There are uneasy moments in the films when the reinforcement of essentialist, nationalist or hypermasculine politics—not to mention the fetishization of anything or anyone deemed critical of globalization—raises questions about whose struggles for dignity may not be included in *Ngātahi*'s diaspora.

Still, *Ngātahi* gives us reason to be optimistic about the future. Rather than being depressed and hopeless about the prospect of people's struggles against the seemingly overwhelming forces of neoliberalism and colonialism, one cannot help but feel inspired and uplifted after viewing the films. Hapeta's informal conversation with his friend Brent Clough, longtime music and radio producer in Aotearoa and Australia, makes this point. When Clough asks him about his sense of optimism in making *Ngātahi*, Hapeta responds, 'I feel happy about it. I feel inspired by the films. Yeah, I'm an optimist. Although, you know, I'm always talking about the bad shit.' Clough, in turn, elaborates the point: 'Optimism born of the worst things, tragedy and death and murder, but through it all people come up with, you know, music and art.' In agreement with his friend, Hapeta captures the spirit of *Ngātahi* when he adds, 'Shit, man, if there wasn't optimism there'd be no use in doing this. I wouldn't do it' (Hapeta 2008).

Notes

This work was originally published in *Kalfou: A Journal of Comparative and Relational Ethnic Studies* 2(2) (Fall 2015) under the title 'Building Dignity's Diaspora through Rapumentary Film: Learning from Ngatahi.' Reprinted with permission.

1 This section describes the chapter of the film titled 'No More Prisons', set in Los Angeles, California (Part 3, 2007).

2 For each of the five parts of the *Ngātahi* series completed between 2003 and 2008, Hapeta garnered $10,000 dollars ($50,000 in total)

from the Screen Innovation Production Fund, at least half of which went towards airfare for his travels around the world. Part 6 was completed in a similar manner in 2012.

3 Like the *Ngātahi: Know the Links* films, this essay is something of a freestyle and flowing series of analytical takes on why we should care about rapumentaries such as *Ngātahi* and what we might learn from them. I would like to think that borrowing from the form of the films in this way offers commentary on their pedagogy, presentation and production of knowledge, as much as it reflects my inability to fully capture the power and depth of the films as they appear on screen. To be truthful, however, it is probably a bit of both.

4 My thinking about small politics is especially informed by Robin D. G. Kelley (1994); James Scott (1985); and Jeffrey Goldfarb (2006).

5 This section describes the chapter of the film titled 'The International Wall', set in Belfast, Ireland (Part 5, 2008).

6 This section describes the chapter of the film titled 'Concerned about the State of Hip Hop', set in Cape Town, South Africa (Part 4, 2007).

7 See, for example, *The Fourth World War* (2004); Michael Franti (2006); and Fermin Muguruza (2009).

8 This section describes the chapter of the film titled 'Colombia, Medellín' (Part 2, 2003).

9 This quote is from the chapter of the film entitled 'Separation Blues'.

Works Cited

ALVAREZ, Luiz. 2008. 'Reggae Rhythms in Dignity's Diaspora: Globalization, Indigenous Identity, and the Circulation of Cultural Struggle'. *Popular Music and Society* 31(5): 574–97.

BALD, Vivek. 2006. 'Overlapping Diasporas, Multiracial Lives: South Asian Muslims in US Communities of Color, 1880–1950'. *Souls: A Critical Journal of Black Politics, Culture, and Society* 8(4): 3–18.

BUCKNOR, Michael. 2004. 'Staging Seduction: Masculine Performance or the Art of Sex in Colin Channer's Reggae Romance *Waiting in Vain*?' *Interventions* 6(1): 67–81.

CALLAHAN, Manuel. 2005. 'Why Not Share a Dream? Zapatismo as Political and Cultural Practice'. *Humboldt Journal of Social Relations* 29(1): 6–37.

CLIFFORD, James. 1997. *Routes: Travel and Translation in the Late Twentieth Century*. Cambridge, MA: Harvard University Press.

COLLINS, Francis Leo. 2004. Review of *Ngātahi: Know the Links, Parts 1–2* by Dean Hapeta. *Graduate Journal of Asia-Pacific Studies* 2(1): 95–6.

DOLAN, Jill. 2005. *Utopia and Performance: Finding Hope at the Theater*. Ann Arbor: University of Michigan Press.

ESTEVA, Gustavo, and Madhu Suri Prakash. 1998. *Escaping Education: Living as Learning within Grassroots Cultures*. New York: Peter Lang.

FOURTH WORLD WAR, THE. 2004. Narrated by Michael Franti & Suheir Hammad. Big Noise Films, New York.

FRANTI, Michael (director). 2006. *I Know I'm Not Alone: A Musician's Search for the Human Cost of War*. Studio Epitaph / Ada, San Francisco.

GILROY, Paul. 1993. *The Black Atlantic: Modernity and Double Consciousness*. Cambridge. MA: Harvard University Press.

——. 1994. *Small Acts: Thoughts on the Politics of Black Cultures*. London: Serpent's Tail.

GOLDFARB, Jeffrey. 2006. *The Politics of Small Things: The Power of the Powerless in Dark Times*. Chicago: University of Chicago Press.

GRAY, Herman. 2005. *Cultural Moves: African Americans and the Politics of Representation*. Berkeley: University of California Press.

HALL, Stuart. 1989. 'Ethnicity: Identity and Difference'. *Radical America* 23 (44): 9–20.

HAPETA, Dean (director). 2003. *Ngātahi: Know the Links, Parts 1–2*. Kia Kaha Productions, Wellington, New Zealand.

——. 2007a. *Ngātahi: Know the Links, Part 3*. Kia Kaha Productions, Wellington, New Zealand.

——. 2007b. *Ngātahi: Know the Links, Part 4*. Kia Kaha Productions, Wellington, New Zealand.

——. 2008. *Ngātahi: Know the Links, Part 5*. Kia Kaha Productions, Wellington, New Zealand.

HOBSBAWM, Eric. 1994. *The Age of Extremes: A History of the World, 1914–1991*. New York: Vintage.

HOLLOWAY, John. 1996. 'The Concept of Power and the Zapatistas'. *Common Sense* 19: 20–7. Available at: https://goo.gl/iCJBli (last accessed on 11 February 2016).

——. 1998. 'Dignity's Revolt' in John Holloway and Eloina Peláez (eds), *Zapatista! Reinventing Revolution in Mexico*. London: Pluto Press, pp. 159–98.

KELLEY, Robin D. G. 1994. *Race Rebels: Culture, Politics, and the Black Working Class*. New York: Free Press.

KURASAWA, Fuyuki. 2007. *The Work of Global Justice: Human Rights as Practices*. Cambridge: Cambridge University Press.

LIPSITZ, George. 1997. *Dangerous Crossroads: Popular Music, Postmodernism, and the Poetics of Place*. London: Verso.

——. 2007. *Footsteps in the Dark: The Hidden Histories of Popular Music*. Minneapolis: University of Minnesota Press.

MARCOS, Subcomandante. 2001[1999]. 'The Fourth World War'. La Jornada (23 October). English translation available at: http://goo.gl/c5XbyA (last accessed on 11 February 2016).

MUGURUZA, Fermín (writer, director). 2009. *Checkpoint Rock: Canciones desde Palestine* (2009). Filmanova, A Coruña, Spain.

MUÑOZ, José Esteban. 2009. *Cruising Utopia: The Then and There of Queer Futurity*. New York: New York University Press.

REID, Graham. 2003. 'The Real People Have Their Say'. Review of *Ngātahi: Know the Links, Parts 1–2* by Dean Hapeta. *New Zealand Herald* (16 September), p. 16. Available at: http://goo.gl/ok4Lok (last accessed on 11 February 2016).

ROSE, Tricia. 1994. *Black Noise: Rap Music and Black Culture in Contemporary America*. Hanover, CT: Wesleyan University Press.

SCOTT, James. 1985. *Weapons of the Weak: Everyday Forms of Peasant Resistance*. New Haven, CT: Yale University Press.

SWEETMAN, Simon. 2003. Review of *Ngātahi: Know the Links, Parts 1–2* by Dean Hapeta. *Dominion Post* (24 October). Available at: www.tekupu.-com/Ngatahi-review.1.html (last accessed on 27 October 2010).

WALLERSTEIN, Immanuel. 2008. 'Remembering Andre Gunder Frank while Thinking about the Future'. *Monthly Review* 60(2): 50–61. Available at: http://goo.gl/NoQpf6 (last accessed on 15 February 2016).

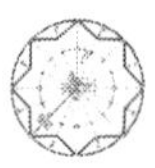

Chapter 2

'INDIANS ON PARADE'
Spectacular Encounters in the Canadian West

Lisa Doolittle and Anne Flynn

We live and work as university professors in Western Canada. This is our home, but not our native land.[1] Our home is built on an unstable foundation of the unequal encounter between Indigenous people and European settlers. The encounter resulted in a spectacular expansion of power and privilege for those who arrived, and a spectacular reduction of the same for those who had been here all along. Maintaining and rationalizing the inequitable outcomes has required similarly spectacular deployment of physical and imaginative energy. Disembodied government policies and laws to ensure settlers' permanent establishment as residents here were enacted corporeally—people were massacred, jailed, confined on reserves and infected with deadly, unfamiliar illnesses. Yet the presence of the First Nations and their cultures continued. In addition to direct, physical methods of oppression, achieving and sustaining the colonial project of illegal and unethical occupation required the continuous performance of imagined Native disappearance and colonial dominance, often taking the form of festive stagings of Indigenous and colonial identities. In this essay, we will look at photographs of Indigenous, settler and colonial people together. This mutual presence is crucial. Typically, accounts of the history of Canada's western lands infer that the displacement of Indigenous communities happened long before the arrival of serious settlement[2] when, as these images demonstrate, coexistence was ongoing. The photographs depict or refer to staged celebrations where colonial personalities and settlers encountered, organized, observed and often danced with Indigenous people. Our investigation of these images, and the embodied experiences they memorialize, complicates our understanding of this home, its natives and the land we call Canada.

Spectacles, Nations and Bodies

Spectacles are not only utopian imaginings of nation states, argues Margaret Werry, in her study of tourism and race in New Zealand, but actual embodied performances of state power, especially 'where national hegemony is forged across deep (racial or ethnic) disparities in power or entitlement' (2011: 95). Following Werry, we take spectacle to be not just 'representational but also as performative, as a form of "poetic world-making" that works across the terrain of fantasy and materiality' (ibid.: *xiv*). The need for participation and witnesses make large-scale performances inherently open systems, unstable moments where many different agents influence their effects. From the perspective of our home discipline, dance studies,[3] embodiment is key. Corporeal experiences link to identities in deeply contextual ways, each dancer's experience informed by their own complex cultural realities. But also, dancing is doing, experiencing that can disrupt or connect the dancer to these cultural realities—or do both simultaneously. When bodies participated in transcultural spectacles in the West, opportunities arose for identities to be in flux despite and alongside the dominant discourse, which aimed to legitimize white hegemony.

Stagings of 'Indian' spectacles in the Canadian West were frequent and the resulting images ubiquitous. Ideals of colony and empire—utopias that required the disappearance and/or assimilation of

Indigenous peoples—were imagined, represented, controlled, resisted and consumed in such spectacles. Photographs of spectacle encounters included meetings of Indigenous subjects with colonial dignitaries and settler audiences, on festive occasions invented by settlers, or in staged 'Indigenous' ceremonies captured by the cameras of colonial/settler agents and entrepreneurs. Using these moments as opportunities to observe enactments of power and public policy, we consider how such performative intercultural moments may reveal the tensions between processes of containment, protest and accommodation. Overlapping containment strategies mobilized over time include late-nineteenth and early-twentieth-century legislation such as the banning of dancing and traditional celebrations and confining Indigenous populations to reserves and limiting children to residential schools, enacted through the Indian Act of 1876 (see Titley 1986). The less direct but no less powerful commodification of Indigenous identities, places and objects into nostalgic curiosities for tourists in order to entrepreneurially exploit this renewable resource is another kind of containment strategy.[4] Some argue that Canadian multiculturalism as developed in the 1970s and 80s was another strategy for disappearance and containment, in its management of difference without transforming power, where embodiments of immigrant identities, for instance, in 'Heritage' festivals, masked colonial relations based on appropriation of Indigenous lands.[5]

While pointing out these oppressive tactics, we simultaneously work to acknowledge and investigate the agency of Indigenous participants, by interpolating their own (usually absent) accounts and experiences into and around the performative events. Our analysis casts the spectacles in these photographs not as images of utopia but, rather, as heterotopian spaces, 'space(s) of alternate ordering [. . .]. Heterotopias organize a bit of the social world in a way different to that which surrounds them' (Hetherington 1997: *viii*, cited in Tomkins 2012: 105). When the colonials and settlers meet

First Nations communities in these images, we glimpse a what-if space, where a complicated choreography both supports and destabilizes power and authority. Particularly relevant to this examination of culturally diverse moments of dancing together is the reality that all the performers must improvise as they deal with unfamiliar sensations and ideas through their movements in every performance. Encountered in spectacles, colonial processes of erasure, containment and appropriation dance with Indigenous strategies of protest and persistence.

Notes on Method

The process of selecting these particular images to begin a conversation about embodiment and history also contained elements of improvisation as we sorted through dozens and dozens of photographs, swapping and rearranging, seeing new connections in different configurations. What we offer the reader is one choreographic interpretation of a complex history of staging colonial expansion into the vast landscape of southern Alberta. Over the past 10 years, we have investigated the process of Canadian nation-building from the 1870s to the 1970s in staged performances of 'traditional' dancing. We have collected the stories of dozens of dancers and observers of dance through conversations and formal recorded interviews (see Doolittle, Twigg and Flynn 2005), and we have attended all kinds of dance events as participants and observers. We have encountered hundreds of photographs and archival materials, and we have used the theoretical tools of dance and performance studies to engage with all these data to provide analyses of how dance performance and participation function in the invention of Canada.

The images in this essay represent only a few moments in a centuries-long story of geographies and identities colliding in festive settings, drawn from a truly vast store of similar images archived in institutions across the West and beyond. We find it more productive to view each photograph in this small collection as a system of contradictions rather than as a connected chronological narrative. When we 'reorient history away from narrative [. . .] it decenters the notion of a "source" [. . .] and reconnects documents to the cultural systems that produce them' (Nye 1983: 21). Instead of being authoritative documents, these photographs become 'structured fields of meaning' (ibid.: 16). As such, we briefly situate them in context—who took the image, in what geopolitical context, for what reasons—public or private, and speculate about what effect the display of the image might have. Along with considering 'the bureaucratic intentionality that gives rise to these images' (Williams 2007: 35), we mark the often-unremarked experience of Indigenous participants in the photographed event by drawing upon interviews we conducted with Blackfoot elders in 2005–06. We selected images and events that featured First Nations, settlers, and colonials participating in ceremonies and spectacles together. Most of these images are publicly archived, and all were taken by non-Natives from a range of professions and identities: commercial photographers, journalists, government personnel (North West Mounted Police, Indian agents) and tourism entrepreneurs (Stampede, Indian Days). We take into account the control of the archive, in which we see the organization of 'others' into white subjects' frames of reference. Along with this evidence from public archives, it is useful to imagine photographs not taken, and the inaccessible personal photos. It is worth considering, too, that while First Nations communities are just beginning to be invited by museums to participate in colonial/settler archive projects about themselves, Indigenous subjects have long continued to enact power, knowledge and memory—contained in the repertoire of song, story and dance (see Taylor 2003)—in traditional and hybrid events within and outside the photographic frame.

FIGURE 2.1. **'Indians on Parade'**
Photographed by Rafton Canning. Galt Museum and Archives (19750101001).

This parade is posed in a prairie landscape that evokes the primeval freedom of the plains in the settler imaginary of Canada's West (Figure 2.1). Yet, dimly visible in the distance behind the impressively decked-out line-up of Indigenous people on horseback, we can see the booming city of Lethbridge, the largest city in the province at this time. The description attached to this image by Charles Magrath in 1944 reads: 'A large group of Blood Tribes people visited Lethbridge for the fair and exhibition events.'

To the colonial government, and by extension to settlers at the beginning of the twentieth century, the Indigenous people constituted a problem if not a threat. The 'problem' was their longtime residency on lands that settlers sought to appropriate for the extraction of resources and for personal and imperial enrichment. In addition to legal and policy moves like the series of treaties[6] and the Indian Act, to achieve and sustain the colonial project, festivals like the Lethbridge Exhibition could offer opportunities to perform the imagined dominance of the settlers. Spectacle and celebration, exhibitions of identities, embodiments of hierarchies—parades are public performances of the nation-state served up as entertainment.[7] The festivals typically began with a parade through town. The parade's linear choreography embodies ideas of containment (spectators frame the participants) and of progress (it moves relentlessly forward). As choreographed by the colonizer and settler organizers, parades, which typically featured both settler and Indigenous performers, imaginatively demonstrated how the nation-state may contain many identities marching under a single purposeful and preordained direction, planned in ways that implied hierarchies of leaders and followers.

This photograph is an arresting image of Blackfoot grandeur unlike later city-parade images that typically show the spatial containment of urban environments and the objectifying dynamics of the settler spectator's gaze. Here, the absence of parade spectators allows us to better imagine the meaning of this large gathering for the performers themselves—a shared experience that surely offered many opportunities for interaction among the members of the tribe, and a way to present a powerful image of collective identity. We are reminded of the settler presence only in the barely visible distant city, and in the form of the photographer, adventurer Arthur Rafton-Canning,[8] behind the camera, controlling the frame, taking this image as part of a long-term project of his to document Lethbridge city events over time. Such a project assumes change, seizing events before they evaporate into history. Rafton-Canning's probable intention here is to capture these 'Indians' on film before the presumed inevitability of their disappearance. Right next to this parade line-up in his archived fond are images of settlers lining up at the land titles office—snaking around whole city blocks—waiting to obtain title to 'free' land, homesteads on Blackfoot territory appropriated and surveyed by the Canadian government.

FIGURE 2.2. **'Indian Agency' and 'Indian Agents'.**
Blackfoot 'pow-wow' near Blackfoot Agency, Southern Alberta, 1900. Glenbow Archives (NA 3164–375).

In contrast to the parade's linear choreography previously discussed, here we catch Indigenous dancing and singing in a choreographic spatial form that seems more traditional—a circle (Figure 2.2). The circular choreography, common to participatory dancing, constructs a cohesive, inwardly focused group space, tending to create a sense of community and equality. When a community's dancing is uprooted from its original contexts and re-choreographed for entertainment/display, one of the most common choreographic strategies is to create outward-facing formations, especially front-facing lines for the stage and, as we have seen, forward-facing lines for parades and processions. One could derive interesting information about traditional dancing from this photo, but our gaze takes us to the edges of the frame. Differing from anthropological/ethnographic depictions of traditional or sacred Blackfoot dance in its inclusion of white spectators, here evidence of settlers' intervention is manifest. This 'pow-wow', as the photographer has labelled it, is a moment of dancing—social rather than sacred—on ground within the Siksika Reserve, lands designated by treaty negotiation as held in trust by the Crown for this tribe. The dancers are in their 'home' territory, yet this location within the reserve is more colonized than any other bit of reserve land—in front of the dominating building of the Indian Agent.[9] We can see Blackfoot, settler, colonizer men and women along with police. Another photograph, of the three in the archive that depict this event, documents the presence of Governor General Lord Minto and his wife, British dignitaries whose visit provoked the celebration.[10]

At the time of this photograph, the Blackfoot's main source of sustenance, the buffalo, had been virtually extinct for 25 years and Treaty Seven was just 23 years old. To the impoverished Blackfoot, Treaty Seven promised education, cash, reserve land and hunting rights among other concessions in return for the Blackfoot 'ceding' their traditional lands to the Crown, enabling mass settlement and resource extraction. Also, the Canadian government's Indian Act ban on ceremonial dancing had been in effect on the prairies since 1894,[11] part of the project of assimilation and eradication. Anti-dance sections of the act targeted the aspects of Plains ceremonies—their long duration, unpredictable timing, 'nudity', torture and giveaways—that were an anathema to colonial ideals of capitalist entrepreneurship, agricultural production and puritanical Christianity.

The photograph reveals dozens are dancing, apparently at the colonials' request. What is going on? According to Kainai elder Roland Cotton, there could be several motivations for celebratory dances inside Blackfoot communities, including the pow-wows[12]—social dances which were never banned. For instance, Blackfoot people traditionally celebrated with dancing any visit of a person who brought wealth to the community. As signatory to the treaties, did the visits of British royalty go beyond pomp—were they seen as opportunities to cement allegiances outlined in the treaties, with the British representing a force to counteract local settler and Canadian federal oppression and corruption? For the dancers, then, is this a choreography that strategically shores up alliances, that enacts their enduring occupation of the land? For the settlers and British colonials, does it embody an imagined superior civilization contrasting with 'Indian primitiveness', a superiority that rationalizes colonial/settler dominance and presages the Native's disappearance?[13] Dancing and watching at cross-purposes, colonial royalty, police, settlers and First Nations are united in the moment of the spectacle.

Imagine the engine of Canadian corporate development, the Canadian Pacific Railroad—mythic unifier of the nation[14]—hurtling towards the tiny whistle stop of Gleichen near the Siksika Reserve east of Calgary, Alberta, bearing Imperial Press Association representatives

FIGURE 2.3. **Trains and Transvestites.**
Visit of Lord Burnham, Imperial Press Association, Gleichen, Alberta, 19 August 1920. Glenbow Archives (NB–16–113).

of every nation in the British Empire on a trans-Canada tour. The Imperial Press Association's mission—to collect and disseminate accurate, 'unbiased' and first-hand information—intersected with imperial agendas of political control of the far-flung regions of a declining empire.

This photograph (Figure 2.3), taken at Crowfoot near Gleichen, documents another ceremonial encounter between colonial dignitaries, in this case British Lord Burnham, director of the Imperial Press and his wife, and local Blackfoot chief Yellow Horse, who is bestowing upon Lord Burnham the honorary name of his ancestor, Chief Old Sun.[15] The image captures the imperial Burnhams masquerading as Indigenous chiefs, gamely sporting ill-fitting ceremonial buckskins,[16] while the real chief stands, with a stoic expression, behind them, in formal British dress.[17] The official proceedings note: 'It was unanimously agreed by the delegation that Mr. Woods and his committee had provided a most notable programme for the short stay at Gleichen, and the novelty and informality of this picturesque interlude were greatly enjoyed' (Donald 1920: 69).[18] This patronizing description diminishes any importance the occasion may have held for the Blackfoot hosts. Meanwhile, the jarring visual artificiality foregrounds the fundamental absurdity of the spectacularized endowment of chieftainship, rendering it a tragicomic image of cultural transvestism. How curious the colonial imaginary of Natives as 'doomed primitives' seems when juxtaposed to this image of colonials in traditional Native deerskin and feathers alongside Natives in dapper, colonial formal dress and top hats. In this awkwardly captured moment, do we gaze, transfixed, at the spectacle of an imperial utopia of domesticated and disappearing colonized peoples, or do we glimpse, more fluidly, the dignity and persistence of the Blackfoot as they weather this onslaught?

Let us briefly juxtapose to this another image and contextual description to widen the frame. The years 1920 and 1921 saw the peak of prosecutions for violations, on the prairies, of the federal ban on dancing ceremonies (Indian Act Section 149) (Titley 1986: 178). Furthermore, struggling with truancy at all federally sponsored and church-run Indian schools, the Department of Indian Affairs made it compulsory in 1920 for Native children to leave their families for extended periods to attend residential schools; it no longer supported industrial or day schools on reserves. In an innovation to the existing law that made attendance compulsory—in effect since 1894—an amendment gave truant officers the authority to convict parents if they withheld children from schools (Roberts, Boyington and Kazarian 2012: 207). In the context of these policies that aimed at cultural erasure or—euphemistically and officially—'assimilation', we present a description of a photo that we cannot locate in the archive. Elder Frank Weaselhead told us why, as a young schoolboy, he hated it when photographers asked him to dress in traditional buckskin.

> In [residential] school I couldn't wear my feather or a beaded vest . . . when I moved to school I couldn't wear any of those . . . I couldn't paint my face, my grandmother couldn't paint me. But then there was going to be a [news] story on the residential school. And the principal had a buckskin outfit, hawked to him . . . I had to put it on, get on a horse and be photographed [. . .] . So you see why I hate it, I couldn't do that [. . .]. it was all a lie (2005).

Two photographed performances, both arranged for the press. A young vulnerable and powerless Frank, immobilized on a horse in an abusive and foreign institution on his ancestral territory, wearing a colonizer's buckskin outfit to advertise the success of the very institution that was robbing his people of their culture and destroying their families. A pair of British royals, decked out in ceremonial Indian outfits, receives Indian honorary names as '[t]he Canadian Parliament has not (yet) withdrawn the privilege from the native races of conferring titles on distinguished visitors' (Donald 1920: 68). The parenthetical 'yet' is key, punctuation that gestures to an inevitable future full stop, an enclosure that enshrines imperial powers by diminishing Indigenous cultural practices as erasable privilege, and assumes settler and colonial ascendancy.

We encounter these mid-century Indigenous performers in a theatrical space (Figure 2.4), a semi-permanent structure of bleachers

FIGURE 2.4. **Playing and Paying.**
Dancers at the Banff Springs Hotel, Banff Indian Days, 1939. Glenbow Archives (NA1241–571).

with the Rockies and a glamorous Canadian Pacific Railway (CPR) hotel as setting. Nearby, an encampment of tepees and a rodeo grounds complete the festival offerings. Fifty-five years after the founding of Banff Indian Days, a touristic economy of Indian performance is firmly entrenched. With the certainty of an audience, there is investment in building infrastructure. This was an all-Indian performance event, all-white spectator event. The sublime natural setting, accessible transportation, ritzy accommodations and authentic local performers made the event a distinctive tourist draw.

The construction of the CPR ensured that the small town of Banff, Alberta, nestled in the Rockies and Canada's first established national park, in the heart of Stoney sacred lands, would become a centre of tourism. The beginning of Banff Indian Days is an emblematic story about Indigenous dance and frontier entrepreneurship:

> On June 1884, the Bow River flood washed out several miles of track and stranded guests at the Banff Springs Hotel. Tom Wilson, 'Canada's foremost mountain man' who had worked for CPR and then provided independent guiding services for tourists, is credited with inventing Banff Indian Days. [. . .] Realizing the fascination of tourists with Indians, Wilson suggested that the neighboring Stoneys be asked to participate in a series of contests for prizes to be put up by the CPR. He travelled to the Stoney reserve at Morley as the company's emissary and convinced the Indians of the benefits of his plan. A large contingent followed him to Banff, where the braves competed in horse races, bucking and roping competitions and traditional dancing while the women vied to outdo each other in horse packing and tepee (sic) pitching. The hotel guests were so taken with the performance that the CPR, with the assistance of local businessmen, sponsored Banff Indian Days as an annual event (Hart 1983: 59).

It is also a story of the meshing of corporate and political interests. The CPR had always been an important factor in empire and nation building. In order to accomplish the settlement of the west, the federal government granted the CPR the authority to manage immigration, which also allowed it to recruit workers.[19] In addition, the CPR was responsible for advertising Canada abroad as an attractive destination for both visitors and settlers, and this marketing project meant that the 'Indian problem' had to be managed. CPR cleverly chose an advertising strategy that converted the 'problem' into an 'attraction'. This required, and enabled, the 'mining' and packaging of heritage like Indigenous dancing.[20] These white men took charge of selling Canada via representations of nature and Indigenous peoples, using 'the paradoxical process by which the discourses of the nation require the remarginalization of some of its subjects even as they call for assimilation' (ibid.: 91). Events such as Banff Indian Days were of course not marketed as exercises in marginalization and assimilation. Instead, advertising suggested that organizers' praiseworthy presentation of this 'exotic' dancing conserved vestiges of a 'noble yet vanishing civilization'—in a trope anthropologists now call 'the salvage paradigm' (see Williams 2003: 81).

The photograph is one of over a thousand images made by Fern Gully,[21] who was, for several decades, dedicated to producing portraits of Stoneys, images of rodeos and 'Indian' dancing and festivals. The exhaustive, almost encyclopedic nature of his work (which parallels that of Lethbridge's Rafton-Canning and many others) suggests the influence of the salvage paradigm. The relationship of trust with the people he portrayed—he was made a blood brother of the Stoneys in 1942—suggests his documentation was welcome.

A comment from Beverly Hungry Wolf about such touristic performances offers a Blackfoot perspective on their participation in Banff Indian Days:

> Sometimes they would be invited up to . . . ah . . . Banff, to perform, [and they'd say] *Taakitawatato' kwa'kinnawa*—we're going to go play at the holy springs. And they would go and put up their camps and have dances for the tourists that came to the lodge but it was considered playing. And . . . they got paid (2005).

We can surely assume that as a kind of 'migrant worker', the Native performers were not the main beneficiaries of the economic success of the festival. But there were other compelling motivations for their participation. During the 1930s, Canadian Natives remained heavily regulated—often confined on reserves and in abusive situations in ineffective residential schools[22]—and impoverished by the very systems that purported to assist them towards 'modernization'. In these circumstances, the festival setting, by bringing members of different tribes together, became sites where embodied culture was enacted and acknowledged. The environment of touristic festivals continued to provide opportunities for First Nations individuals and groups to exercise agency.[23]

Pictured next (Figure 2.5) is the central moment in the ceremony of transfer of a chieftainship, the Capture Dance, in which the recipient of the honour is literally captured into the tribe. The leader of this capture dance is Horace Quesnelle, a decorated veteran of the Canadian armed forces, dressed in his formal veteran's uniform with medals on his chest, entwining military and Native histories. Charles, Prince of Wales, is dressed informally in shirtsleeves and a cowboy tie. He later dons a massive feathered headdress and deerskin outfit, and receives gifts including a pinto horse and saddle. Notably, this unpublished photograph—one of hundreds taken by the photographer on this day—captures the significant media presence at the event.

FIGURE 2.5. **Headdresses and Crowns.**
Prince Charles with Second World War veteran elder Horace Quesnelle in the Capture Dance portion of the Induction into the Blackfoot Chieftainship ceremony 8 July 1977. Photograph by Rick Ervin, *Lethbridge Herald* fond, 1991–1076 Galt Museum and Archives.

In 1977, Treaty Seven, which had been signed by chiefs of the Blackfoot confederacy and representatives of Queen Victoria, was 100 years old. For the empire, such treaties helped to open the floodgates of settlement and resource exploitation; for the First Nations, they seemed to offer protections for their traditional way of life (land, hunting rights) and access to modernization, including education, which would help them cope with the disappearance of the buffalo and could ensure their continued healthy existence. A royal visit to the site of the original signing of the treaty at Blackfoot crossing on the Siksika reserve was the centre piece of the centennial celebrations. Among additional honorary events, the Kainai chose to induct Prince Charles into Blackfoot chieftainship, giving him the name Red Crow, or Mekaisto, the same as the Kainai chief who signed Treaty Seven with representatives of Queen Victoria.

We draw on archived articles from the *Lethbridge Herald*, the National Film Board's documentary *A Pinto for the Prince* (1979) and an interview with Kainai elder Adam Delaney.[24] The *Herald* quotes Chief Jim Shot Both Sides welcoming the prince as an official member of the tribe: '[W]hat has happened here today was not just invented for the occasion. What you have seen has been part of our religion and culture. Everything has its meaning and we have done it to bring good fortune and a long life to our royal chieftain . . . ' (1977). Calling attention to the persistence and depth of their culture, Chief Jim Shot Both Sides invokes the historic allegiance of the Blackfoot and the British Crown. The documentary also casts the event as an encounter between equals; in the voice-over narration, the lineage of Jim Shot Both Sides and Prince Charles are presented as parallel and equally high-status biographies. On the Kainai reserve, Canada is cast as witness, not actor in the proceedings. The colonial government (represented here by, for example, former prime minister John Diefenbaker, the current representative of the Queen, Governor General Roland Michener, and current provincial premier Peter Lougheed) becomes passive, immobile onlooker. In reality, these governments held most of the cards in the game of 'whose land is this anyways', but the rhetoric speaks to a telling moment in the relationship between the Canadian government and the First Nations people.

This event occurs in the context of Canadian First Nations and federal government revisiting Indian policies. In 1968–69, the Canadian government held consultation meetings with Indian representatives in recognition that the Indian Act was outdated, and First Nations negotiators hoped that special rights would be honoured and land treaty claims settled before the act was to be revised. Instead, Prime Minister Pierre Trudeau's government presented policy proposals (the White Paper) in June 1969, ignoring First Nations priorities and suggesting abolishment of the Department of Indian Affairs and of the Indian Act within five years, and elimination of Indian status. In effect, the importance of Indian treaties and First Nations claims was downplayed. The Indian response to the proposed government policy was hostile and sustained. This was the beginning of a comprehensive national network of contemporary First Nations political organizations (Taylor 2006). It was also the beginning of intensified activities within First Nations communities around reviving traditional ceremonies. In 1972, three years after the White Paper fiasco, Kainai elder Adam Delaney helped re-establish the Horn Society on the Blood Reserve and began to work with others to demand repatriation of sacred objects from museums back to the Kainai.

Delaney recounts the story of the prince's visit with a mixture of defiance and humour, emphasizing his sense of conspiring with royalty to puncture bureaucratic pomposity and questioning the ability of the colonial government to completely control events and their outcomes. His account registers both the embodiment and the limited scope of Blackfoot agency. To accommodate the royals' schedules, the chief had asked Delaney, who was in charge of spiritual ceremonies, to delay the Sun Dance. In a planning meeting with high-level government and police representatives, Delaney draws the battle lines among three levels of authority—white government, tribal council (a tribal authority invented by the Indian Act) and traditional spiritual and political leadership—as he recalls the events leading up to and including the centennial ceremony:

> You federal government, provincial government, and solicitor general and RCMPs and you big shots in here . . . remember one thing, both governments, you're on Blood Indian reserve! The rest of the land you guys took away from us, but this is Blood Indian reserve you're on now! My chief right here runs the reserve plus twelve councilors, but that spot at the Sun Dance area, I'm in charge of that. My chief here he had to ask me permission. So, I'm not gonna . . . change my . . . rules, regulations through our ceremony, all on the count of one person—no, I don't have to do that! (2005)

Delaney did eventually agree to the delayed Sun Dance schedule that accommodated the royals, and reveled in his status during the ceremony itself.

> You should of seen the security there—oh gosh, talk about security. So then my chief knew that we have rights, you know! So he invited them in his tepee, so . . . even some of the security wanted to go in there. Our Chief told 'em, 'No the rest of you stay out there.' . . . [During the dance] Prince Charles was standing in-between us, so we dance around in the arbour while the rest of the big shots, and both governments [are] behind us . . . (ibid.)

Delaney's humorous description of the ceremony's closing moments gives a sense of the conspiratorial connection between traditional tribal authority and the Crown:

> And the plane was quite a ways from the camp . . . so he's supposed to ride this horse over there and get on the plane . . . that was a really funny part there . . . . He got on the horse, then people was taking pictures of him. And he told me himself, Prince Charles, he bend down on his horse and he says, 'I'm gonna run away from everybody,' so he gave his horse [a whip] and he rode it. You see, see those security following close and running (*laughs*) . . . (ibid.)

Perhaps Charles' informality and renegade actions undermined the political power of the ceremony, or perhaps, for Delaney, Charles, by subverting protocol, aligned himself against external forces of control in support of the Kainai. In the glare of the media spotlight, Delaney and his colleagues enact their authority through insisting on Blackfoot protocol and subverting outsider protocol. The dancing ceremony that has always connected them to the land sidelines the governmental forces that continue to seek to sever this connection. At this point in Canadian–British histories, the actual political power of the Crown is negligible, yet the performance of the alliance resonates through the media with a message of tradition meeting modernity and a positive assertion of continued Blackfoot presence.

The commemorative pin of the Young Canadians of the Calgary Stampede (Figure 2.6) is the portable and permanent reminder of 'Tribute to the Indian', the theme of the 1977 Calgary Stampede to honour the centenary of the signing of Treaty Seven. Displayed on jean jackets, cowboy shirts and dance bags belonging to the members of this official Stampede performance group (ages 7 to 21), the image of a Plains Indian dancer in action travelled around the city and beyond carrying with it the mythology of the West and the mystique of the Indian. It also lives on in perpetuity as a symbol of Canada's multicultural ideals in action: dancers and singers trained

FIGURE 2.6. **Signing (Treaty Seven) and Signing (Indian Sign Language on Stage).**
Young Canadians of the Calgary Stampede Salute to the Indian commemorative pin. Photograph courtesy of Russell Moore Images.

in ballet, jazz and musical theatre rehearsing with Native elders to learn sign language for the finale of the 1977 Grandstand Show, the large-scale stage production that caps off every evening of the 10-day Calgary Stampede performed to 16,000 international spectators.

This finale featured the Young Canadians, over 60 First Nations performers representing the tribes who signed Treaty Seven in 1877 (Blackfoot Nation: Kainai, Piikani, Siksiki; T'suu T'ina Nation; Stoney-Nakoda Nation: Bearspaw, Chiniki, Wesley) and the Royal Canadian Mounted Police.[25] Despite its size and the historical significance of its theme, we found little media or archived information—only a few newspaper clippings and a newspaper review. We contacted Young Canadians dancers and the choreographer Margot McDermott, who worked on the piece titled 'On the Threshold of Decision' with Grandstand Show producer Randy Avery. In our written correspondence, she recalled a portion of the production that featured Indigenous performers:

> The Opening Pageantry was a parade of members from each tribe in their colourful, fringed, beaded clothing and magnificent feathered head dresses. A formal introduction was given to each Tribal Chieftain followed by dancers, singers and drummers performing a sequence of traditional dances culminating to thunderous applause with the world champion Hoop Dancer weaving his story as he accumulated 24 hoops to form the final tableau of 'eagle wings.' The sequence of traditional dances included the circle dance, grass dance, buffalo dance, chicken dance, shawl dance and fancy dance performed to the vibrant rhythm of the drums and the haunting chants of the singers (2012).

McDermott recalled the involvement of Native elders in the creation process:

> The rehearsals were a magical affair as the natives always sat in a circle as they shared ideas, traditions and folklore. A very special part of rehearsal process was when the Young Canadian Dancers were taught how to use native signing. Even for rehearsal purposes the native singers and dancers had to be in full dress before they were allowed to perform. The finale was a picturesque and moving tribute to Treaty Number Seven featuring the (non-native Young Canadian) dancers signing to the words of an original poem 'On the Threshold of Decision' written

> by Randy Avery and accompanied by a stirring and pulsing underscore (ibid.).

McDermott and the dancers all spoke fondly of this finale tribute. They experienced it as a quiet and sincere moment of acknowledging and honouring First Nations people, and of embodying their undeniable presence in the story of settlement in Canada's west. White teenage girls in buckskin dresses, standing with hands in prayer position, eyes lowered, closed the evening's extravaganza before the fireworks swept the audience's attention upwards to the vast prairie sky.

Calgary Herald reviewer Brian Brennan had a totally different experience of this finale choreography:

> The Indians take part in what is described as a 'dedication' to the Treaty Seven Indians and it seems peculiar that an elaborate dance routine in this sequence is done by female members of the Young Canadians. The extravaganza ends with Randy Avery's self-composed song to Canadian unity, a clumsily crafted hymn entitled 'On the Threshold of Decision' which adds a mock solemn dimension to what is essentially a loud entertainment spectacle (Brennan 1977).

Views from inside the artistic production are filled with sincerity and reverence, and signal to Canada's multicultural utopia where difference is visible, acknowledged and celebrated. Comments from the local high-art theatre and music critics describe a very different choreography from McDermott's and the dancers' 'moving tribute', ridiculing the attempt at 'artistic' interpretation and betraying the unspoken prejudice that demands that only 'authentic' First Nations can embody Indigenous performances—how could white female performers and white male composers create a meaningful tribute? While criticizing the move outside the Vegas genre, Brennan simultaneously mocks the low-art, Vegas-style framework of the show as a whole. For Brennan, the intercultural collaboration of the performers and its potential for transforming their concepts of, and actual relationship with one another—potential embedded in the process of creating the art—remains invisible. Only the newspaper review remains archived as the permanent record available to researchers, while the parallel stories of the both Native and non-Native participants—stories that might chronicle a new stage in the representation of the Indian in Western Canada—exist only in personal memory.

Without the names of the Indigenous participants in the performance and rehearsals, we can only speculate about their perspective on their representation in the Grandstand Show. The only Indigenous voice we hear in the archive is that of Benjamin August Calf Robe (b. 1890) who had worked as a North-West Mounted Police interpreter and scout. A Calgary bridge bears his name, honouring all the bridging he did between Indigenous and settler communities. Speaking to a *Calgary Herald* reporter, Calf Robe, who had attended every Stampede since it began in 1912, said: '[O]ne of the good things (the Stampede) has done is have us in the grandstand show' (Richardson 1977). His positive reference to the inclusion of First Nations performers (presumably an infrequent occurrence) points again to the multilayered perspectives on these encounters.

For another highly ironic perspective on the 1977 Stampede's Indian theme, we turn to a Kainai artist, writing in a Kainai publication a few short weeks before the exhibition opened.

FIGURE 2.7. **'Rather Odd . . . '**
Cartoon by Everett Soop, 1977. Glenbow Archives (M–9028–909).

Everett Soop was an artist, a writer and a regular cartoonist who created a series of satirical and political cartoons between 1968 and 1983 for the *Kainai News* (Figure 2.7). His cartoons and writings are noted for satirizing not only government agencies and their treatment of First Nations peoples but also the foibles of his own people. Moving from the spectacularly conceived Grandstand Show to the everyday encounter, what Soop highlights is the Native observation of, and humorous comment on, the non-Natives' disrespectful and racist reactions that continued to mark encounters between whites and Natives in Calgary, the very relationships, negative attitudes and actions that the official theme of 'Salute' presumably sought to address and transform.

Conclusion

In what is an ongoing choreography of Indigenous–colonial/settler contact, we have interrogated the effects of the circulation of performances and representations/images of performances. When assessing the power of First Nations participation in events that were apparently orchestrated entirely by and for the benefit of colonials, we have endeavoured to take embodiment into account.[26] Our analysis of the embodied participation that gave rise to these images aims to disrupt the colonial/settler interpretation of their own arrival as either dystopian (devastating Indigenous populations) or utopian (heroically salvaging Indigenous cultures) or simultaneously both. Looking beyond the photographed moment, we notice the work of imagination, creation and rehearsal of events prior to their documentation. We imagine the myriad workers—women who made the outfits, singers who prepared the soundtracks, fed the horses and argued about protocols. We acknowledge the contributions of First Nations ancestors whose ceremonies could be flexibly adapted to events they could have never foreseen. And while the power inequalities remain tremendously problematic, awareness of the foundations of those inequalities in colonial/settler actions can be built through ongoing examination of such performative moments of intercultural contact.

James Clifford proposes a theory of cultural contact that he calls articulation, which suggests that it is perhaps time to debunk the all-or-nothing, fatal-impact notions of change, that is, when people representing different cultures make contact, one has to always lose. Indigenous dancing and 'indigenous societies have persisted with few, or no, native language speakers, as fervent Christians, and with "modern" family structures, involvement in capitalist economies, and new social roles for women and men' (2006: 182). Spectacular encounters in Canada's west are examples of articulations in Clifford's sense. Settler participation in the spectacles we have described—behind the lens or in front of it—betrays attempts to control, appropriate and repress. First Nations participation in the spectacles described throughout this chapter demonstrates ways that communities can and must always assert their presence and reconfigure themselves in the face of relentless assault, exercising persistent and creative agency.

As contemporary dancers living in the foothills and the Northern Great Plains, regions 'far outside' the internationally recognized artistic centres of central Canada (Toronto and Montreal), we have been able to learn particular things about the meaning of creative agency as we apply it to our work as dancers, educators, scholars and community activists. Operating from these margins has sharpened our awareness of what is missing from dominant discourse, the actions that vanish unremarked, the endless labour of dancing that goes unrecognized and remains absent from historical record. Our off-centre positioning also been our best teacher of research methods, prompting us to look carefully for clues in places right around us, and directing us to the stories of people who live ordinary lives in the same place we inhabit. Conversations with Blackfoot co-researchers at traditional ceremonies and speculations watching archival film footage in the local archive create personable relations that highlight our awakeness, our ignorance and our hopefulness. Warmth, laughter and goodwill have become our most reliable research tools as we attempt this leap across cultural divides and divergent histories in a glaringly uneven landscape of power relations. Knowing that we will never 'get it right' has finally stopped paralysing us and, instead, we are progressing, putting our best foot forward, palm up, ready for the next partner.

Notes

1 This references the opening lines of Canada's national anthem 'Oh Canada, Our Home and Native Land', which tries to perform a kind of 'indigeneity' for all who sing it.

Our chapter includes several terms referring to First Nations peoples, including 'Native', 'Indigenous', 'First Nations' and 'Indian'. Each of these terms emerges out of specific historical and political contexts in Canada and globally, and we endeavour to retain context-specific usage. Current usage favours 'Indigenous' and 'First Nations' which is seen to better express self-determination. Use of 'colonial' is not meant to be historically specific (as in neocolonial, imperial, postcolonial) but, rather, generic, referring to authorities and processes that initiated and continue the occupation of formerly First Nations-occupied territories of North America. Canada is one of Great Britain's settler colonies (sharing historical similarity with Australia and New Zealand). 'Colonial' refers to British envoys and administrators and to British royalty. 'Settler' refers to immigrants who remained in Canada; some colonials became settlers. Incomplete documentation means it is not always possible to distinguish 'colonials' from 'settlers' of some archival photographs, although it is likely that often both were present.

2 'The popular Canadian vision of migration to the West, one that emphasizes migration as a creative drive with beneficial and productive personal, cultural, economic, and political effects. Central to this vision is the multifaceted figure of the migrant him- or herself as a nation builder who is both "rescued" by and labors within the project of "making Canada." The settler-centric chronology of "making the west Canadian" frequently infers substantial temporal distance between First Nations dispossession and European migrant arrival in the West, attempting to disconnect these often historically simultaneous processes' (Bertram 2011: 160).

3 Dance studies adapts research methods and theories from many fields, placing dance in a wider landscape of human ideas. Dance studies concepts important to this essay include:

(a) Dance is part of 'repertoire'—practices and knowledge that cannot be stored in a conventional archive. Scholar Diana Taylor demonstrates that some human knowledge is stored by writing it down in documents and storing it in archives, while other knowledge is stored by performing it. Bodies remember knowledge by enacting it, by dancing it (2003). See also Lisa Doolittle and Anne Flynn (2004).

(b) Dance can awaken emotions or affect. Moving one's own body, and watching bodies dancing, connects feelings with ideas, performers with spectators. Once ignited, emotions can motivate powerful action beyond the moment of dancing. Susan Leigh Foster's elaboration of empathy and embodiment in relation to power is illuminating for our project: 'The history of sympathy/empathy when placed in parallel with the history of colonization helps to explain how the British evaluated and responded to the foreigners whom they encountered in North America [. . .]. It also helped to rationalize how and why they could relate to one another as they did, exercising forms of political and social control, punishment and torture, and enslavement' (2011: 129).

(c) Dance can embody utopian societal visions. Many governments have harnessed performances to convince or convert populations to their vision. Also, in many communities, performances like dancing go beyond the function of creating cohesion and identity. They can open the way to envisioning new futures.

4 It has been argued that settlers declared newfound national identity 'by presenting those they have displaced as their symbolic surrogates, nostalgically borrowing the authenticity of indigenous images and property, and buttressing the racial distinctions between primitivism and modernity that undergird the whole edifice of nation' (Werry 2011: *xiv*). See related arguments in Christopher Bracken (1997) and Jacqueline Shea Murphy (2007).

5 In their 'Introduction: Labours, Lands, Bodies' to *Home and Native Land: Unsettlling Multiculturalism in Canada*, May Chazan et al. question 'Canadian multiculturalism's generally blind and potentially cynical posture towards colonial relations' and 'how the complicated logics of multiculturalism have contributed to the colonization of Aboriginal peoples and ongoing contests over land and resources' (2011: 2).

6 Treaties were intended to unite the interior of Canada and formally recognize these as territories of Canada. They also gave clear title of lands to the Crown for building a railway that would facilitate the extraction of resources. All treaties were initiated by European settlers and colonial representatives. They negotiated the sale of lands and mineral rights for the benefit of First Nations communities; land was to be surrendered only to the Crown; annexed to each treaty was a schedule of reserves held in common by the Crown and tribes; annuities in cash were promised to signing members, and the First Nations communities retained full hunting privileges. Treaty Seven

was signed by chiefs of the Blackfoot Confederacy. For a concise description of the numbered treaties signed in Canada between 1871 and 1921, see John Roberts, Darion Boyington and Shahe S. Kazarian (2012: 185–6).

7 Ngũgĩ wa Thiong'o describes the ways in which externally imposed governments, as in colonization, enact power by relentlessly performing its own being 'through its daily exercise of power over the exits and entrances, by means of passports flags and visas' (1997: 27). We argue that parades and festivals similarly perform national 'being'. Analogous to the banning of Indigenous dancing under the Indian Act, Ngũgĩ describes how British colonial authorities in Kenya exercised power through widespread attempts to ban or limit open-air performances like the traditional *ituika* ceremony of the Agikyu in Kenya (ibid.: 12) in which power was transferred ceremonially over a period of 6 months, every 25 years. This was stopped by the colonial state in 1923. An annual British military-type parade at the opening of new sessions of the legislative assembly replaced *ituika* type performances. See also Ngũgĩ (1986: 37–8).

8 When Arthur Rafton-Canning came to Canada from the UK, he became an officer of the Royal Canadian Mounted Police. He later established the British & Colonial Photographic Company in Lethbridge in 1907 and operated it until 1913 when he moved out of southern Alberta. Rafton-Canning recorded an encyclopedic array of life in Lethbridge, returning again and again to the same locations, taking images from the same perspectives to illustrate the changes that occurred over time.

9 The 'Indian Agent' was the government-appointed intermediary between government, settlers and reserve Indigenous people. The agent's job was to hand out money and goods as promised in treaties, maintain discipline (he could, for instance, remove and replace band council chiefs), control sales of goods produced, arrest, detain and eventually convict reserve members of violations of the Indian Act. Essentially, he was an agent of Indigenous dependency.

10 The archive suggests that this photo is by Edward Blake 'Curly' Curlette (1872–1952) who moved to Alberta from Ontario in 1899, and joined his uncle's (Snider) photographic business.

11 Just eight years after the proclamation of the Indian Act in 1876, a section was added that expressly forbade the cultural practice known

as potlatching, a giveaway type of ceremony that included dancing. In 1894 the prohibition was extended to dances of the Plains Indians. Amendments of various kinds ensued (many of which remained as part of policy until 1951) to contain amounts of time spent dancing, control the spaces for dancing and dictate the purposes and practices of the dance. For example, the chest-piercing part of the Sun Dance ceremony was forbidden as a practice of torture. Gatherings for the purpose of ceremonial dances were suspected of political agitation. Administrative enthusiasts of the dance ban attempted to prohibit dancing at exhibitions but it was a major tourist attraction and exhibition organizers ignored prohibitions. See Titley (1986: 165–7).

12 Pow-wow was at this time perhaps a label that whites used to refer to Indigenous dancing practices in general. Among the Blackfoot, pow-wow dancing was a social dance, and while it was performed during multi-day sacred ceremonial events like the Sun Dance, the dancing carried no sacred meanings. 'We have never heard of pow-wows until just recently, within the last 30 years. We've adapted to this word. Before it was *paskhahn. Paskhahn* means "time to flirt" [. . .]. You might see when they celebrate a dance, when they celebrate something like a dignitary or somebody has brought back wealth, they dance, they celebrate, they come together in their own regalia and they celebrate and then they'll begin dancing [. . .]. The leisure dances were never forbidden' (Roland Cotton, personal interview, May 10, 2005).

13 See, for instance, Christopher Bracken's illuminating analysis regarding the contradictory impulses of the colonial/settler powers towards Indigenous populations (1997: 231).

14 The Canadian Pacific Railway (CPR) was built between Eastern Canada and British Columbia between 1881 and 1885, fulfilling a promise extended to British Columbia when it entered the Confederation in 1871. It was Canada's first transcontinental railway, and was instrumental in the settlement and development of Western Canada. CPR became one of the largest and most powerful companies in Canada, a position it held as late as 1975. Under the initial contract with the Canadian government to build the railway, the CPR was granted 25 million acres.

15 'The christening of a new chief is not settled until the head of the tribe sees the subject, so that he may choose a name which fits. Lord Burnham's cheerful countenance and genial smile at once suggested

to Yellow Horse that *Nat-o-Sapi*, "Chief Old Sun," was the appropriate designation. It was a special compliment. The Blackfeet were sun-worshippers before a third of them became Catholics, and another third became Protestants, while the rest remain in a state of doubt as to their future faith. Yellow Horse's predecessor, a famous brave, was also named "Old Sun"' (Donald 1920: 68).

16 The customized robes that had been prepared for them had been stolen by an enterprising tribesman and sold across the border.

17 Probably Chief Yellow Horse. Chief Weasel Calf was also in attendance.

18 We were not able to determine whether the Siksika received payment for their efforts, other than the medals given to them commemorating the press visit. The proceedings note that the event included two processions (press officers, RCMP and natives), the investiture 'behind a screened enclosure' and a 'cowboy stampede', including Native and RCMP participants of steer roping, racing and breaking in wild horses.

19 The Railway Agreement of 1925 allowed the two national train companies—Canadian Pacific Railway and Canadian National Railway—to recruit cheap labour under the guise of importing European agriculturalist immigrants.

20 'Alexander Begg's Emigration Department had launched its campaign to sell CPR lands in western Canada as early as 1881 with the distribution of the settlement guide *The Great Prairie Provinces of Manitoba and the Northwest Territories*. Soon afterwards it began to distribute tens of thousands of maps, folders and pamphlets in ten languages to agencies all over Britain and continental Europe. Coordinating its activities out of its London office, the department published ads regularly in 167 British and 147 continental journals and newspapers' (Hart 1983: 22).

21 William Fernley 'Fern' Cose Gully (1892–1951) emigrated from England and became chief accountant at the *Calgary Herald* newspaper. He was a well-known amateur photographer and was a member of the Calgary Photo Forum. His portraits of Natives were widely shown.

22 In 1932, only 100 out of the enrolled 17,163 students reached sixth grade (Milloy 1999, cited in Roberts, Boyington and Kazarian 2012: 47).

23 See the illuminating discussion of agency for Indian performers in shows such as *Buffalo Bill's Wild West* in Jacqueline Shea Murphy (2007: 57–80). She argues that governments used the 'theatrical disciplinary system' as part of ongoing strategies to contain and eliminate the power of Indian spiritual practices, which performed their connections to the land. Yet these theatrical productions did not effectively contain Native American agency.

24 Several reports appeared in the local newspaper (see Scarth 1977a, 1977b; *Lethbridge Herald* 1977). *A Pinto for the Prince* (1979) was directed for the National Film Board of Canada by the celebrated Canadian documentarian Colin Low, who would go on to extensively document the maintenance of Kainai culture with the films *Circle of the Sun* (1960) and *Standing Alone* (1982).

25 We hunted for photographic images, but none were sufficiently high resolution for reproduction.

26 Jacqueline Shea Murphy (2007) is a notable exception. Two works about First Nations and photography that integrate First Nations agency and aspects of embodiment in their analysis are Carol J. Williams (2003) and Alison K. Brown, Laura Peters, with Members of the Kainai Nation (2006).

Works Cited

BERTRAM, Laurie K. 2011. 'Resurfacing Landscapes of Trauma: Multiculturalism, Cemeteries, and the Migrant Body, 1875 Onwards' in May Chazan, Lisa Helps, Anna Stanley and Sonali Thakkar (eds), *Home and Native Land: Unsettling Multiculturalism in Canada*. Toronto: Between the Lines, pp. 157–74.

BRACKEN, Christopher. 1997. *The Potlatch Papers*. Edmonton: University of Alberta Press.

BRENNAN, Brian. 1977. 'Ted Knight No Anchorman for Lavish Grandstand Show'. *Calgary Herald*, 9 July, n.p.

BROWN, Alison. K., Laura Peters, with Members of the Kainai Nation. 2006. *'Pictures Bring Us Messages': Photographs and Histories from the Kainai Nation*. Toronto, University of Toronto Press.

CHAZAN, May, Lisa Helps, Anna Stanley and Sonali Thakkar. 2011. 'Introduction: Labours, Lands, Bodies' in May Chazan et al (ed.), *Home and*

Native Land: Unsettling Multiculturalism in Canada. Toronto: Between the Lines, pp. 1–14.

CLIFFORD, James. 2006. 'Indigenous Articulations' in Bill Ashcroft, Gareth Griffiths and Helen Tiffin (eds), *The Post-Colonial Studies Reader*, 2ND EDN. London: Routledge, pp. 180–3.

DELANEY, Adam. 2005. Personal interview, Cardston, Canada, 11 July.

DONALD, Robert. 1920. *The Imperial Press Conference in Canada*. London and New York: Hodder and Stoughton. Available at: http://goo.gl/BF8lGm (last accessed on 17 February 2016).

DOOLITTLE, Lisa, and Anne Flynn. 2004. 'Not Like a Document: Like a Dance' in Naomi Jackson (ed.), *Right to Dance: Dance and Human Rights*. Banff: Banff Centre Press, p. 269–91.

——, Troy Emery Twigg and Anne Flynn. 2005. *Videotaped Interviews with Blackfoot about Dance*. Lethbridge: Blackfoot Digital Library. Available at: http://goo.gl/4BmV63 (last accessed on July 31, 2012).

FOSTER, Susan Leigh. 2011. *Choreographing Empathy: Kinesthesia in Performance*. London: Routledge.

HART, E. J. 1983. *The Selling of Canada: The CPR and the Beginnings of Canadian Tourism*. Banff, Altitude.

HETHERINGTON, Kevin. 1997. *The Badlands of Modernity: Hetreotopia and Social Ordering*. London: Routledge.

HUNGRY WOLF, BEVERLEY. 2005. Personal interview, Cardston, Canada. 11 July.

LETHBRIDGE HERALD. 1977. 'A Prince of a Fellow: Charles Welcomed into Kainai Tribe'. *Lethbridge Herald*, 7 July, p. 47.

LOW, Colin (director). 1979. *A Pinto for the Prince*. National Film Board of Canada, Montreal.

MCDERMOTT, Margot. 2012. Personal correspondence with Lisa Doolittle and Anne Flynn, 13 June.

MILLOY, John S. 1999. *A National Crime: The Canadian Government and the Residential School System, 1879–1969*. Winnipeg: University of Manitoba Press.

NGŨGĨ wa Thiong'o. 1986. *Decolonising the Mind: The Politics of Language in African Literature*. London: James Currey.

——. 1997. 'Enactments of Power: The Politics of Performance Space'. *TDR: The Drama Review* 41(3): 11–30.

NYE, David. 1983. *The Invented Self: An Anti-biography from Documents of Thomas A. Edison*. Odense, Odense University Press.

RICHARDSON, Jean. 1977. 'Calf Robe's Memory Covers Every Stampede'. *Calgary Herald*, 8 July, n.p.

ROBERTS, John, Darion Boyington and Shahé S. Kazarian. 2012. *Diversity and First Nations Issues in Canada*, 2ND EDN. Toronto: Emond Montgomery.

SCARTH, A. 1977a. Charles Welcomed within the Circle of the Sun. *Lethbridge Herald*, 8 July, p. 1.

SCARTH, A. 1977b. Prince Charles Visits South: Schedule Allows 10 Royal Glimpses. *Lethbridge Herald*, 6 July, p. 9.

SHEA MURPHY, Jacqueline. 2007. *The People Have Never Stopped Dancing: Native American Modern Dance Histories*. Minneapolis, University of Minnesota Press.

TAYLOR, Diana. 2003. *The Archive and the Repertoire: Performing Cultural Memory in the Americas*. Durham, NC: Duke University Press.

TAYLOR, John Leonard. 2006. 'Aboriginal People: Government Policy' in *The Canadian Encyclopedia*. Toronto: Historica Canada. Available at: http://goo.gl/LqzOM5 (last accessed on 25 February 2016).

TITLEY, E. Brian 1986. *A Narrow Vision: Duncan Campbell Scott and the Administration of Indian Affairs in Canada*. Vancouver: University of British Columbia Press.

TOMKINS, Joanne. 2012. 'Theatre's Heterotopia and the Site-Specific Production of *Suitcase*'. *TDR: The Drama Review* 56(2): 101–12.

WEASELHEAD, Frank. 2005. Personal interview, University of Lethbridge, Cananda, 16 June.

WERRY, Margaret. 2011. *The Tourist State: Performing Leisure, Liberalism, and Race in New Zealand*. Minneapolis: University of Minnesota Press.

WILLIAMS, Carol J. 2003. *Framing the West: Race, Gender and the Photographic Frontier in the Pacific Northwest*. Oxford, Oxford University Press.

WILLIAMS, Carol. 2007. 'Beyond Illustration: Illuminations of the Photographic "Frontier"'. *Journal of the West* 46(2) (Winter): 29–40.

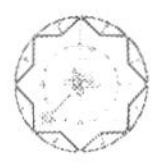

Chapter 3

QUADRILHAS CAIPIRAS

Encountering Difference and the Making of Creative Communities in Festas Juninas, São Paulo, Brazil

Pegge Vissicaro

In June 2010, the Fédération Internationale de Football Association (FIFA) World Cup took place in South Africa. The event was broadcast in every country of the world, reaching over 3.2 billion people; almost half the world tuned in to watch. Approximately 7,100 kilometers west, the people of Brazil, comprising nearly 6 per cent of those viewers, were glued to every possible form of media—radio, television, Internet, newspaper—hoping and praying for their national team to become six-time champions. While such an extraordinary achievement would be unprecedented, Brazilians assumed this utopian quest to be attainable. Brazilian *futebol*[1] players often rise to a rock-star, god-like status. To mere mortals, the World Cup team or *Seleção Brasileira* is one of the modern wonders of the world. Their physical talent is virtuosic but their unique style exemplifies Brazilian *jeitinho*, an informal 'problem-solving strategy' to get things done (Ferreira et al. 2012: 336). Sometimes this entails bending the rules, which in *futebol* often means discovering or inventing an unusual method to pass the ball and score goals.

Jeitinho demands ingenuity; such emphasis on improvisation may be observed among Brazilians as an ideal skill to seamlessly accommodate new environments, new people and new ways of moving. This aspect of creativity shared by *futebol* and dance, specifically samba, an Afro-Brazilian music and dance form reflects spontaneity and individual expression. The phrase *jogo de cintura*, or 'play of the waist', a reference to the twisting, articulated pelvis characterizing many West African dance forms, is synonymous with *jeitinho* and also describes the way *futebol* players transfer their weight to manoeuvre on the field. In 1959, Brazilian anthropologist Gilberto Freyre wrote:

> The Brazilians play football as if it were a dance. This is probably the result of the influence of those Brazilians who have African blood or are predominantly African in their culture, for such Brazilians tend to reduce everything to dance, work and play alike, and this tendency, apparently becoming more and more general in Brazil, is not solely the characteristic of an ethnic or regional group (1963: 111–12).

Freyre's statement, based on sociological theory that perceives Brazil as a nation built on assimilation and miscegenation,[2] juxtaposes sociocultural binaries of unity and diversity to each other. The confrontation of opposites is a ubiquitous theme throughout the country, observed on the Brazilian flag itself, which proclaims *ordem e progresso* (order and progress)—structure and dynamism.

It is this theme of how contrasting elements intersect that frames my (auto)ethnographic account of research focusing on Festas Juninas, the annual June parties that are a significant part of Brazilian popular culture. Suggestion of the account as a self-study comes from the belief that all ethnography is rooted in and shaped by one's personal emic perspective.[3] Through cross-cultural processes people relate familiar and unfamiliar information to find similarities and differences. Connections formed through comparison may lead to consonance or understanding at least temporarily until something changes. Then the process repeats. That fleeting balance point in the liminal space between known and unknown provides the jumping-off point for my analysis of the Quadrilha Caipira, a rural quadrille dance exclusive to Festas Juninas in São Paulo and neighbouring regions. Quadrilhas Caipiras are a momentary alternative reality in which participants encounter and embody difference. Interactions with otherness catalyse creative communities to form during Festas Juninas, reflecting humanistic utopian values.

The activity of knowing opposites may assuage, at least transitionally, the disproportionate socioeconomic class structure evident in Brazil. Like the dualism yin and yang, poverty and wealth exist together as two parts of the whole. However, for dancers performing Quadrilhas Caipiras, the body becomes a site where the familiar and unfamiliar meet, producing conditions in which *jeitinho* can flourish. Expressive movement is a tool for blurring boundaries, mediating difference and linking dissimilar elements. This premise for my research investigating Festas Juninas is set against a backdrop of the 2010 FIFA World Cup—two activities that consistently overlap every four years.

Primeiro Tempo[4]

São Paulo, the capital of São Paulo state, is the largest city in Brazil, the largest in the western and southern hemisphere, and the seventh most populous worldwide. On Tuesday, 15 June 2010, I am flying into São Paulo from the United States. The excitement of arriving in Brazil slowly transforms into frustration as fog delays landing at Guarulhos International Airport. Diverted to Rio, I sit for hours at the gate, waiting for clearance to travel to my intended destination. Today is Brazil's first World Cup match against North

Korea. I had planned to see the televised game at a hotel in Santos but quickly realize things are going to be different. Eventually touching down in São Paulo, I recognize that it will be a race against the clock to reach my final stop near the beach and see the match before it ends. As my anxiety increases I am struck by the realization that the World Cup has given my travel to Brazil another level of significance. The original reason for being in this place at this time was to further research Festas Juninas, a centuries-old tradition with pre-Christian origins. However, since *futebol* pervades the national consciousness, it becomes obvious that the World Cup competition will play an unexpected role in my investigation of Festas Juninas. Seasonally, it is also the beginning of winter, characterized by drier weather and the harvesting of major crops, such as coffee and sugarcane. The range of sounds, smells and tastes that reflect Brazil's diversity find common ground during this period emphasizing farm production and country life. It is also a time for sharing Brazil's distinctive foods, most involving corn. As the world's fourth-largest producer, Brazil's obsession with corn means that roadside stands, grocery stores, street markets and all Festas Juninas events feature foods such as *milho verde* (boiled corn on the cob), *bolo de milho* (corn cake), *canjica* (sweet corn pudding), *pipoca* (popcorn) and the most classic of all, *pamonha* (a sweet corn and milk paste boiled in its husk, described as a dumpling, often resembling a tamale).

Until now, I studied Festas Juninas exclusively in a rural setting where persistence of practices formed a thread connecting past, present and future. Previous research conducted from 1999 to 2007 during annual family visits to the village of Guaraná, located approximately 1,000 kilometres north-east of São Paulo in the state of Espírito Santo, sparked a personal interest in Quadrilhas Caipiras, similar to square dance with couples and a caller cueing movement patterns. Performances of Quadrilhas

Caipiras exist almost exclusively throughout the states of São Paulo, Rio de Janeiro, Minas Gerais and Espírito Santo. The states of Minas Gerais and Espírito Santo border São Paulo and Rio de Janeiro respectively. Local variation in the dance is impacted by the knowledge exchange that occurs when family members who work in the industrial centres travel home on special occasions.

Contrary to São Paulo, the small, tight-knit community of Guaraná is practically unknown even in Brazil and generally subsists apart from mainstream society, similar to other rural communities. Isolated from major urban areas and relatively self-sufficient, residents have minimal contact with people outside the municipality, limiting the influence of new ideas and information. Insular attitudes likely affect the lack of civic engagement, educational reform and modernization. Over the past decade of researching Festas Juninas in Guaraná, I have noticed relatively minor variations influencing participants as well as how, when and where events of the festival occur. Yet temporary modifications are usually forgotten over time, perhaps pressured by dominant provincial views to return to the comfort and familiarity of convention.

Guaraná and São Paulo could not be more contrary in terms of continuity and tradition versus change and innovation. What the two have in common is the incorporation of special events, such as *futebol* matches, into day-to-day activities. Sitting in a school classroom, working at one's job, doing housework, cooking, eating, socializing in the *barzinho*—all mix with the play-by-play broadcast emitting from television and radio sets to become one integrated soundscape. The quotidian and wondrous coexist. Interactions with varied stimuli heighten the sensory experience, each contrasting and complementing the other. For Brazilians, polychronicity[5]—the ability of people to engage in several things happening at the same time—is automatic[6] and cognitively consonant;[7] again it may be related to the idea of *jeitinho*, characterized by an ease to negotiate change as well as embrace diverse views, people and activities. In polychronic contexts such as Brazil, I observe yet another layer of potentiality: the contemporaneousness of extraordinary and hyper-extraordinary phenomena, manifest in my study of Festas Juninas during the 2010 FIFA World Cup. The linking of these two special events, one annual and the other every four years, can be observed in the street decorations that transform neighbourhoods into festive sites. Instead of the strings of small solid-coloured *bandeirinhas* (swallowtail flags) that fly high above everyday movement during the Festas, this year there are mini Brazilian flags, which combine national pride for the *Seleção* with the popularity of the June parties. They move my eyes from one side of the street to the other, forming a nexus between locales.

Bandeirinhas are also used to create *arraiáis*, the thatched-roof tents where traditional Festas Juninas celebrations occur. *Arraiáis*, perhaps the most recognizable sign of Festas Juninas, are usually constructed several weeks in advance to publicize the approaching event. This structure creates a place in which people converge and generate energy, igniting purposeful interaction among the various performing bodies. Additionally, *arraiáis* may be reminiscent of customs that involve communities working together with mutual support to plant and harvest crops. These activities demonstrate a human–nature relationship and emphasize the continuum that situates past practices in a contemporary context. *Arraial* construction in both rural and urban environments also encourages greater inclusivity; it is an ideal performance venue for Brazil's pluralistic society.

The *bandeirinhas* usually extend outward from a central hub, like spokes of a wheel, to invite participation by people of all ages, abilities, ethnicities and socioeconomic status. While the Quadrilha Caipira performance structure imposes some limitations —for example, cooperating with a partner to perform specific movement patterns within the *arraial*—every other festival component welcomes unstructured involvement. In this open setting, individuals freely navigate their own unique sensate journey, personalizing rhythm, tempo, spatial position and direction. Variances include lingering by the food *banca* (booth) a few moments longer to savour the extraordinary taste of *cural* (sweet corn pudding), jumping rhythmically to the ambient sound of *marcha* (lively accordion-based music that accompanies Quadrilha Caipiras and is played only during Festas Juninas), discovering the quickest path to the *pescaria* (a game using fishing poles) with hopes of winning a prize, and maintaining equilibrium due to the effects of drinking the seasonal specialty *quentão* (made with *cachaça* or fermented sugarcane, ginger, cinnamon, nutmeg and citrus juice).

Today, the annual Festas Juninas, which nowadays means large numbers of people gathering in expansive outdoor or indoor settings, may intentionally be designed to heighten the senses to evoke mind-body transformation, a quality of ritual. However, unlike rites of passage that mark an individual's transition from one phase of life to another, the festival rite of intensification[8] highlights values and ideals that most benefit the group. Importantly, these rites generate a shared ethos and intensify the collective experience.

Historically, Festas Juninas derive from rituals that acknowledge the natural world. These ceremonies originated in Europe and took place during the midsummer season or summer solstice, a reference point marking one extreme orientation for Earth's orbit around the sun. Fire, which the ancient Greeks considered to be one of the four primary elements, played an integral role in midsummer rituals, signifying both creation and destruction. The use of fire primarily for heat as well as for cooking and light led to the colonization of Europe, beginning over 800,000 years ago (Balter 2004). Conversely, the devastating affects of fire have continued to threaten human existence; certain practices also incorporate fire to purge evil spirits, associating it with magic (Pyne 2001). By simultaneously exterminating and propagating, fire is a connection point for the polarities of past and future.

Fire rituals, such as jumping over bonfires during Festas Juninas, spread throughout the world and were later assimilated into Christian beliefs, reaffirming religious faith and identity (Burke 1978). In particular, they were used to pay tribute to Saint John whose feast day is 24 June. This timing closely aligns with the first day of summer in the northern hemisphere, which takes place on or around 21 June. The Feast of Saint John, also known as Midsummer's Day, was and continues to be the most important time when Festas Juninas occur.[9] Biblical texts link Saint John with fire, portraying him as filled with the Holy Spirit or the incarnation of fire while in the womb of Elizabeth, cousin to Mary, mother of Jesus. This familial bond supports the selection of John, cousin of Jesus, to perform the holy baptism. Additionally, Christ himself describes Saint John as a burning and shining lamp or light, words that seem to symbolize the sun. Stated in the Gospel of Luke (Luke 1:36, 1:56–7), John was born about six months before Jesus. Thus the Feast of John the Baptist was fixed on 24 June, six months prior to Christmas, one of the few saints' days to commemorate a saint's birth rather than a death. The first association between the pre-Christian midsummer fire celebrations and Saint John probably happened around the fourteenth century in England; however, by the sixteenth century, they were common in Northern Europe (Hutton 1996).

The Festas Juninas season in Brazil consists of celebrations for Saint Anthony on 13 June and Saint Peter on 29 June. Including the Saint John celebration, there are usually several weeks of nonstop festivities. Flexible scheduling means that Festas Juninas can begin in early June and last into July, the latter sometimes called Festas Julinas. Events happen throughout that timeframe without any particular hierarchy, except for those honouring specific patron saints on a particular day and set in the church named for that saint. It is interesting that grouping commemorations of multiple saints also occurred in much of Europe. Since Saint John's Day was one of the most important yearly events, it was frequently celebrated in two instalments, combining with the feast days of Saint Peter and Saint Paul as a strategy to repeat effective festivities and to have the option to cancel one in case of bad weather (ibid.).

Padre Fernão Cardim, a Portuguese colonist who settled in Pinorama, São Paulo, brought the tradition of honouring saints' days to Brazil as early as 1583 (Câmara Cascudo 1972[1954]). Influenced by other European contact, they probably transferred the bundling of Saint John and Saint Peter (and Saint Paul) along with Saint Anthony, venerated among the Portuguese, specifically in Lisbon. However, Brazil's location in the southern hemisphere meant that the festivals coincided with the winter solstice. Following the autumn harvest, Festas Juninas celebrations became a display of respect and gratitude for *terra madre*, her bounty and those who farmed the land. The 'time out of time', a term anthropologist Alessandro Falassi uses to describe festivals (1987), encouraged both attitudes and behaviours that accommodated two contrasting but interconnected worlds during Festas Juninas: the natural and supernatural. These annual events were also a welcome change from the relentless everyday routine of hard work in the field and an opportunity to mitigate conflicting ideologies and adapt to the new-world context.

Agriculture, the major theme around which Festas Juninas are based, was the impetus for further colonization of Brazil by the Portuguese. After unsuccessful attempts at harnessing Indigenous labour, African slaves were imported to work the sugarcane plantations and later mine precious minerals. More than 3 million people representing numerous ethnic groups from many countries —in particular, Angola, Congo, Mozambique, Nigeria, Ghana and Benin—brought their respective music and dance cultures. Brazil was the largest importer of African slaves, transporting seven times more than the United States, and the last to abolish slavery in 1888. Miscegenation was widespread, which is reflected in today's population; 2010 census statistics indicate that the majority of Brazilians are black or mixed race, also referred to as *pardo*. This is not to say racial prejudice and discrimination did or does not exist in Brazil yet there is a sense of pride among many Brazilians of openness to new ideas and liberal interaction among different peoples.

Although the Festas Juninas do not feature the dance styles representative of African traditions that typically influence other Brazilian movement forms, such as samba and capoeira, there is, particularly in the north-east, the convergence of Festas Juninas and *candomblé*, the syncretic belief system that fuses Christian and African religious practices. Conflation occurs between *orixás*, supernatural beings ranked in hierarchies modelled on the pantheons of the Yoruba people of West Africa, and Roman Catholic saints. For example, Saint Anthony may be associated with Ogum, a classical warrior and deity of metal work (Assunção 2002). Affiliation of Xangô with Saint John is seen in depictions of a child with a ram, Xangô's sacrificial animal (Tishken, Falola and Akínyemí 2009). Also, the *orixá* Exu, considered to be Satan, becomes Saint Peter and Saint Anthony in the Festas. As Saint Peter, he 'opens and closes doors, opens the gates of heaven with his heavy bunch of keys, and acts as keeper of candomblé fraternities' (Murrell 2009: 171). *Candomblé* merges opposing beliefs and embodies the notion of duality in which two parts exist symbiotically.

Unlike *carnaval*, Festas Juninas engage all Brazilians, either directly or indirectly; church membership no longer matters, despite the 2010 census declaring that 65 per cent of the country subscribes to Catholicism. Festas Juninas is one of the few transnational practices in Brazil, although it must be recognized as context-specific in terms of regional variations. For example, some people most closely associate Festas Juninas with the north-east since colonization took place there first. That area along Brazil's Atlantic coast, including the states of Pernambuco, Bahia, Alagoas, Maranhão, Sergipe, Ceará and Paraíba became the base of Brazilian economy and society. This region also had special significance for Festas Juninas as a rite of intensification, which aligns with the rainy season. The arid north-east was and is particularly susceptible to drought; so prayers to Saint John for rain afford additional protection for good crops and ultimately a better quality of life. Two north-eastern towns have competed with each other for the title of Biggest São João Festival in the World—namely, Caruaru in Pernambuco State and Campina Grande in Paraíba State. Their annual events are highly commercialized, professionalized and competitive, attracting millions of tourists from other parts of Brazil and around the world. Numerous personal conversations with Brazilians affirm that these locations are ideal to experience Festas Juninas, especially the dance form known as *quadrilha.*

Quadrilhas, whose origins may be based on the French version of the stately quadrille, are performed only during Festas Juninas. Introduction of this dance to Brazil was a result of interactions between the French and the Portuguese beginning in the mid-eighteenth century. After Brazil's independence from Portugal in 1829, sociopolitical and economic ties with France continued to strengthen. One relevant account of the dance's origins in Brazil describes the 1836 visit of France's Prince de Joinville, when he organized and invited family members of Brazil's constitutional monarchy[10] to dance the quadrille on his ship after arriving in the port of Rio de Janeiro (Brown 1945). Joinville's marriage to the sister of Brazil's emperor Dom Pedro II in 1843 solidified the link between the French and Brazilian governments, facilitating exchange of goods and services. One other less prominent theory on how French customs came to Brazil is known among stringed-instrument bow makers worldwide. Knowledgeable in musical-instrument history, they affirm the existence of active trade routes between France and Brazil during the mid-eighteenth century to transport *pau brasil*, a reddish wood highly sought for clothing dye and for making violin bows (Vissicaro 2012).

Upper-class decorum related to quadrille's aristocratic history is most pronounced in the north-east Quadrilhas. In this context, one may observe trained, skilled dancers moving with precise steps, performing rehearsed routines, displaying 'proper' etiquette and clearly defined gender roles and judged according to rigorous standards. The Festival de Quadrilha in Caruaru, Pernambuco, features groups that range from 50 to 80 participants, competing over a two-week timeframe. Quadrilhas are evaluated on: how they enter the *arraial*, their animation, the musical repertoire, innovations and choreography, costumes and characterization, performance, scenery, make-up and how they leave the performance venue. Additional research about the continuity of Festas Juninas practices and more classically codified examples of Quadrilha in the north-eastern region may provide further insight into Brazil's colonial past.

Intervalo

The interval that separates *futebol* matches into two parts offers a physical, mental and/or emotional break from out-of-the-ordinary engagement. Players and spectators momentarily return to an everyday reality, allowing for rest and reflection. This shared recess consists of predictable activities; however, as people anticipate the second half, intermission may actually alter awareness. Expectancy of what could happen next leads to quickening pulse rates and other biological changes that signal a different state of consciousness, making the familiar seem unfamiliar. Extended pauses further accentuate such feelings, most noticeable between rounds in the tournament. As the entire nation endures an interminable wait for the *Seleção* to play Chile, I too experience the unsettled emotions of anxiety, excitement and hope, which disturb my daily patterns. Even the clothing, decorations and paraphernalia displaying Brazil's colours seem to intensify, heightening the senses. With each passing day, increased optimism about winning the World Cup is like a virus that infects our routine, prosaic lives.

Similarly, the period leading up to Festas Juninas animates the mundane. For Brazilians, preparing for this annual celebration evokes childhood memories of eating seasonal foods and playing games. Nostalgia, a sentimental longing for happy times associated with Festas Juninas, is in fact key to understanding its widespread popularity. Both reminiscing about the past and imagining the future divert attention away from the ordinary present, which helps many to cope with day-to-day struggles. Dancing is yet another way that the usual becomes unusual. Drawing from pedestrian movement as the basis for its vocabulary, dance is the transformation of behaviours that no longer exclusively function as run-of-the-mill activities. Less familiar patterns of rhythmic walking, turning and swaying affect physiology and, consequently, experience.

The dancing body, as a site where sameness and difference meet, plays a critical role in negotiating that convergence. During Quadrilhas Caipiras participants wear typical farm clothes and move according to circumstances that more likely happen in a rural environment. Yet performing in a dance context means exaggerating the ordinary with ill-fitting, patched clothes as well as overly emphasizing gestures such as '*olha a cobra*' (look at the snake), which cues everyone to scream loudly. Quadrilhas Caipiras further increase social interaction among people not otherwise connected.

Group efficacy enables teamwork to relate to each other in close proximity at a prescribed tempo and form spatial designs with coordinated gestures and steps. By exceeding the demands of everyday life, this activity develops and strengthens community ethos as a rite of intensification.

The process of uncommoning the common in Quadrilhas Caipiras initially happened through the recontextualization of Festas Juninas. Transmission of rural practices to urban sites at the beginning of the twentieth century was a result of industrialization in metropolitan São Paulo. By the 1950s, encouraged by economic expansion led by President Juscelino Kubitschek, internal migration doubled in comparison to the previous decade (Graham 1970). This nationwide population shift of some 20 million people constituted one of the largest in history. New arrivals to the city, especially São Paulo, included former slaves and immigrants or their descendants, all attempting to negotiate the unfamiliar and survive in the strange setting. These people coming from the countryside often were called *caipiras*, a word attributed to the Tupí-Guaraní language family spoken among many Indigenous people of Brazil, indicating a person of the *roça* (fields). Even today the term has pejorative connotations, depicting someone as uneducated, sickly, lazy and/or poor. One source for this negative image was the character Jeca Tatu, introduced in the work of Monteiro Lobato, best known for writing children's literature. His 1918 book *Urupês* stigmatized *caipiras*, synonymously referred to as *caboclos* or 'ticks of the land' (Matos 2010). Lobato explicitly criticized the rural lifestyle, which he experienced growing up in rural Taubaté, 123 kilometres east of São Paulo. Later, through the appropriation of the character to boost sales of the *biotônico fontoura* tonic,[11] Jeca Tatu became part of a successful advertising campaign promoting better health practices. Over several decades, the image of the *caipira* continued to evolve and further various agendas, even political ones. The Partido Comunista Brasileiro (Communist Party of Brazil) used Jeca Tatu as their poster boy for oppression and inequality, associating him with their socialistic ideals.

Most relevant to my research is the characterization of Jeca Tatu by actor-director-producer Amácio Mazzaropi, who portrayed the *caipira* in theatre, film and, later, television. Mazzaropi saw Jeca Tatu as the everyday family man, intelligent but without education, innocent yet wise, a beloved figure (ibid.). Sayings voiced by Jeca Tatu, such as *é melhor ser pobre honesto de que falso rico* (it is better to be poor and honest that rich and false), resonated with ordinary people. In his own life, Mazzaropi travelled between both urban São Paulo and rural Taubaté, although he claimed not to have personal or literary contact with Lobato. During this escalating period of internal migration, Mazzaropi observed how the transplants, driven by their desire for economic productivity, longed for happiness in a place so different from their accustomed surroundings. They coped by bringing traditions of the *roça* to the city, such as raising small animals and growing crops in country-like *bairros* (neighbourhoods) on the edge of town; adapting—characteristic Brazilian *jeitinho*—which included recycling and jerry-rigging parts to invent and/or fix whatever was necessary to survive. It is likely that Festas Juninas practices, also relocated from agricultural settings to the city, gained in popularity and made the metropolis more familiar with each new transplant.

Mazzaropi's first Jeca Tatu film in 1959 was a major force for disseminating *caipira* cultural knowledge to the masses. As the antithesis of Lobato's character, Mazzaropi restored dignity, freedom and solidarity to rural migrants and other simple folks who saw themselves through Jeca—the people's hero. The film inverted real life so that, instead of being a helpless victim of the powerful, Jeca was a source of inspiration, the example of how to satisfy the collective desires for progress and happiness (Museu Mazzaropi 2013). This counternarrative, set against a backdrop of urbanization and the external threat of imperialism that still loomed in the

1960s, catalysed a nationalistic spirit, united by a belief in democratic values that advanced human rights, which Jeca embodied. Although Mazzaropi's films blatantly critiqued political suppression, they were never banned as other films were; many artists—including musicians, writers, and actors—were exiled between 1964 and 1985 during Brazil's military dictatorship. Over the course of 21 years, the company, Produções Amácio Mazzaropi (PAM), made seven Jeca Tatu films.[12] Each successive one more deeply implanted the simple *caipira* in Brazilian popular culture.

Mazzaropi's films represented the realities of a hierarchical, corrupt and class-controlled country, with Jeca Tatu symbolizing both subjugation and resistance in and towards a society that he naively subverted as he met the difficulties life brought him. His attitude, adapted by Brazilians, was expressed in the phrase *seja como for*, 'it is as it comes' (Botelho 2013). The *caipira*, with his backwoods wisdom and low-key attitude, confronted modernity wearing mismatched clothes in stark contrast to the cosmopolitan *paulistas* rushing about in their tailored business suits, an overt critique of economic inequality. Not only was this exaggeration humorous but it also generated sympathy for Jeca who mirrored the audience's own awkward attempts to adjust to increasing industrial change. Through his comedic persona, Jeca Tatu enacted ways to confront the anxiety that surfaced when opposing worlds clashed, blending traditional and contemporary realities. For example, in Mazzaropi's classic 1959 film, Jeca used money he received for helping a politician win the popular vote to dress his chicken in pants and shoes to fit into modern society as part of the family. Similar creative, albeit odd, solutions to make sense of urban living reflect the improvisatory and idiosyncratic qualities of *jeitinho brasileiro* for which *caipiras* became known (Dos Santos and Silva 2009). This strategy to connect the familiar and unfamiliar is a prime catalyst motivating development of creative communities for those who perform the Quadrilha Caipira in Festas Juninas.

Segundo Tempo

The excitement is palpable as Brazilians visualize celebrating a World Cup victory by their invincible *Seleção* in less than four weeks. World Cup fever is ubiquitous, infiltrating all aspects of daily life. The image of the championship trophy in their team's hands empower Brazilian *torcedores* (team supporters) who crazily blow green and yellow plastic *vuvuzelas*[13] that blast the eardrums of those nearby. For many *futebol* fanatics, this four-year championship cycle seems to feed the utopian dream of a globalized, idealized world without borders, joining all people under the banner of solidarity and cooperation.

It is Saturday, 19 June and I have planned to attend Colégio Santa Maria's annual Festas Juninas event in Jardim Taquaral, São Paulo. Established in 1947 by the Sisters of the Holy Cross ministry, the school has over 2,900 preschool, primary and secondary students united through the mission of creating a 'society seeking sustainable development, where there is room for all, and open to different identities' (Colégio Santa Maria 2008).[14] The themes for the dance presentations, including Quadrilhas, reflect the mission: each grade chooses a region or movement style to study as part of their curriculum. For instance, eighth graders focus on gumboot to learn about South Africa; first graders explore *frevo*, most closely associated with *nordestanos* (north-easterners), comprising one of the largest percentage of Brazilian migrants lured to industrialized centres; and seventh graders practise the *linguagem contemporânea* of hip hop. Dance as a way to know others and investigate unfamiliar practices resonates deeply with my own work. I imagine a perfect world for the Earth's seven billion people to move in polychronic synchrony. This utopian thought dissipates upon hearing the audience wildly yell for the last group of dancers entering the Colégio Santa Maria *arraial*. Now it is time for the granddaddy of all country quadrilles with over 100 participants dressed in a melange of outfits.

At this private school, characterized by privilege and opportunity, it is the alumni who return to perform the Quadrilhas Caipiras as the day's climax. Amid the multiple activities of people at food and games booths, several large, flat-screen television sets located throughout the Colégio's beautifully landscaped property project a live feed of the dancing inside an open-air gymnasium transformed into a gigantic *arraial.* A standing-room-only crowd greets the Quadrilha participants with a unanimous deafening roar. Ranging in age from approximately 15 to 19, these teenagers and, in some cases, young adults enter in pairs, holding hands and skipping in a double-line formation from opposing sides. They deliberately try to surpass one another as the most eccentric-looking *caipira* with their incongruous clothing combinations. Looking more closely as I count the couples—at least 50 fill the space—I quickly realize that all the men are dressed as women and the women as men. Cross-dressing is not common among the rural practices that I know in the village of Guaraná; however, in this contemporary urban setting, Quadrilhas Caipiras clearly reflect more liberal attitudes towards personal expression. It is hilarious to watch the men in dresses, pantyhose and high heels, completely unaccustomed to their new attire. Discomfort and awkwardness is obvious as they tug at hemlines and wobble while walking. The couples improvise as the women (dressed as men) carry their partners through the choreographed floor patterns, adjusting to compensate for the difficulty the men are having with their shoes, which prevents them from keeping pace. In this situation, *jeitinho* is an inventive solution to avoid disrupting the flow of motion. The women have transformed to become Jeca Tatu, with charcoal-painted moustaches and beards, straw hats and patched pants. It is a topsy-turvy world, like Bakhtin's carnival—reversal of social hierarchies and gender roles are normal. I observe the performing body as a place where binaries (upper and lower class; male and female) merge into one physical, tangible reality. The country quadrille epitomizes the moment when opposites collide, mixing customs of the farm and the royal court into a unified dance. So too, the World Cup is a 'time out of time' when players from different countries, social classes, ethnicities and backgrounds amicably come together to participate in the single largest international sporting competition.

Children and the elderly alike delight in the bizarre and ridiculous, the celebrated and magical; their expectations realized as the illogical turns logical in this make-believe rural environment. Strangely, everything seems rational as I witness a series of theatrical vignettes featuring Lady Gaga, Ricky Martin as well as Snow White and the Seven Dwarfs (wearing Brazilian *futebol* jerseys) that appear out of nowhere and momentarily interrupt the dancing. The presence of these extraordinary characters seems to be not only accepted but also appreciated. Emotion heightens as the Quadrilha finale approaches. It is the *pièce de résistance,* that part of the dance event that resists or defies orthodox practices. In this scene, the socially recognized convention of the *casamento,* or marriage ceremony, in the Quadrilha Caipira is a debauchery: the bride is pregnant, the father has a shotgun, and the priest is drunk. For the community, ritual catharsis challenges norms as comic relief shaped by contradictions.

The bride and groom enliven the discourse with their embodied sociopolitical commentary on current events and popular media. With her bulging belly, the alumna bride wears a bright pink short skirt, impersonating the 20-year-old female student recently expelled from a private institution in São Paulo for allegedly acting in a provocative and disrespectful manner. While skimpy clothing is commonplace in Brazil, this conduct, according to officials, was incompatible with the university environment. An Internet uproar followed, and hundreds of protesters marched nude; within hours the decision was reversed. The student's lawyer claims she suffered personal humiliation at a school already stereotyped as lower class. During one scene, a mob aggressively chanted 'whore' to further discriminate and set her apart from the other students. Similar to Jeca Tatu, she became a poster girl for human rights, victimized for being different and sparking supporters to rally in her defence.

Similarly, Quadrilha Caipira groom further emphasizes atypical behaviour within the typical marriage model. Like the pink-skirted girl, this groom is hardly ordinary. With painted blue skin, a waist-length braid and wearing a loincloth, in him I recognize the image of *Avatar*'s main character dancing with his bride, their arms linked. In the 2009 blockbuster film,[15] the protagonist is a paraplegic former marine called to mission on the distant planet Pandora, which is inhabited by the 10-foot-tall cyan-coloured Indigenous Na'vi. Futuristic technology allows him to use his mind to remotely control a genetically engineered Na'vi avatar. In this temporary state, he learns about their utopian lifestyle, which harmoniously connects with the land and all living creatures. The story changes when instead of fulfilling his assignment, which would lead to the destruction of Pandora, he becomes a trusted member of their community and rebels against his fellow humans. In gratitude, the Natives achieve the impossible by helping him permanently transform into his Na'vi avatar.

This bride and groom might create a dissonant visual configuration in another context, yet their strange appearance and outrageous performance at the Colégio Santa Maria is normal and probably not unique in relation to other urban São Paulo Festas Juninas. Unlike the characters they represent, their presence does not generate negative reactions and, instead, ignites enthusiastic cheers from the audience who encourage the extraordinary union. It seems that this year's *casamento* reflects the congregation's mission to 'support universal human rights, advocate economic justice, preserve all life on the planet and create a culture of peace' (Sisters of the Holy Cross 2014). More than tolerance, their vision of inclusivity reveals itself in the collective dancing body. That medium, extending self as other, communicates a positive message of unity through diversity and calls attention to change.

Structure produced by a set sequence of recurring movements modulates such dynamism. Repetition, a choreographic technique, effectively transmits knowledge, which may deepen insight, connect information and create patterns that enable groups to share meaning in heterogeneous festive settings. The efficacy of repeated exposure heightens the communal experience and strengthens this rite of intensification. At the Colégio Santa Maria, the power of so many participants moving repetitively and simultaneously reinforces mutual values, establishing a communion through individual expression within a group. Since duplication is never exact, there is much room for idiosyncratic interpretation. The recorded and looped *marcha* accommodates these variations in timing. Spatial designs like circles and rows as well as directions (forward-backward and clockwise-anticlockwise) and turn taking (men dressed as ladies go first) also ensure organization. An additional component that helps to preserve order in the midst of otherwise complete chaos is the *marcador* or caller. As at a square dance, the caller instructs participants to do predetermined figures or shapes, facilitating the progression of the event.[16] Some of the calls are reminiscent of the dance's origin. One of the most frequent of these modified French terms is *balancê (balancé* in French), meaning 'to swing'.[17] Language hybridization is yet another example of how contrasting elements intersect in Quadrilhas Caipiras. The foreign term is almost identical in pronunciation to the Portuguese word; the only difference is spelling, which has little impact on the vocalized instructions. *Balancê*, called in Quadrilhas throughout Brazil, restructures the dance and refocuses participants.

Just as the choreography of dance recontextualizes ordinary movement as extraordinary, the activity of dancing becomes a strategy for knowing the unknown. Partners switch throughout Quadrilhas Caipiras so they are continually investigating *balancê* in new ways. For every change, the familiar swinging facilitates transition to the next unfamiliar pairing. People engage with one another's differences to collaborate as couples, aligned within the larger group. Dance in many cultures acts as a bridge to connect naturally diverse bodies moving through time and space. For Quadrilhas Caipiras participants, the more individual physicalities and perspectives contrast, the more challenging and fun it is to dance together. Improvisation, which involves unplanned responses, is one tool that helps dancers discover the range of options in a given situation. Like the rural migrants who adapt to urban settings using *jeitinho*, the dancers evolve highly perceptive improvisatory skills to encounter new information. *Balancê* also embodies this negotiation process: the swinging movement, a balanced giving and receiving, is a back-and-forth exchange of energy between partners. However, at the Colégio Santa Maria, most of the alumni deliberately pull and push one another to create imbalance and disorder. The exaggerated movement requires even greater effort to execute the steps and avoid falling, which adds to the overall chaos, applauded by performers and viewers alike. Those dynamics fuel the formation of creative communities.

Community, a basic human social organization, involves purposeful behaviour among its members to achieve common goals.[18] Like any assemblage of people, Quadrilhas Caipiras participants reflect biological and sociocultural variation. Differences prompt interaction as individuals attempt to share meaning and contribute to the good of the group, which, over time, creates trust. Colégio Santa Maria alumni exemplify this idea since many have established relationships developed from as early as age 6 and extending to age 14.[19] Like the *intervalo*, separation may even strengthen ties among these former students who anticipate the annual reunion that includes planning their Quadrilha Caipira performance. Trust is a major reason why interacting with difference happens more easily in communities (Vissicaro 2010). Reciprocity, respect and support raise comfort levels to enable members to take risks and explore new opportunities that benefit all. Importance placed on each person's unique knowledge, skills and abilities further empowers individuals, giving them confidence and a sense of duty to fulfil their Quadrilha Caipira roles. The desire to produce a successful event that reflects the best interests of staff, students and families motivates preparation and implementation. Their *esprit de corps* and loyalty to realize this mutual objective also validates the ministry's core value of a community that 'commits to journey together [. . .] to live in solidarity with one another' (Sisters of the Holy Cross 2014).

Community members work jointly as a system in which interdependent components form an integrated whole, greater than the sum of its parts. Inclusivity, an overall organizational goal for the Colégio Santa Maria, strengthens and sustains such synergism. As the community expands with new members and resources, so does the shared network. This idea resonates for many Brazilians and highlights their polychronic nature. In that lifestyle, fluid interactions enable encounters with difference as integral to the larger context. The eclectic Quadrilha Caipira alumni community manifests inter-connectivity through the *grande roda*, a call that signals the group to form a large circle. Similar to the stabilizing tactic of *balancê*, the *grande roda* is performed several times during the dance. All participants hold hands with the dancer to their right and left and move in a large circle that starts anticlockwise, then reverses to create symmetry. Further, the *grande roda* movement symbolizes the Earth and the Sun and their cycles during this solstice. Its configuration connects each person to experience other performers as equals. The all-embracing circle, which epitomizes community, forms a locus for unity that cultivates an emergent web of relationships. In the Colégio Santa Maria, it is this power of place that grounds the increasingly heterogeneous, polychronic city of São Paulo, Brazil.

Since Brazil's historic twentieth-century population shift began, people from nearly every region of the country and the world have continued migrating to São Paulo at a relatively steady rate. The clustering of multicultural human capital is a major force behind the economic growth of cities (Florida 2002). Considered the industrial and financial centre of Brazil, São Paulo offers a wide range of employment and culturally enriching experiences. It is a modern city filled with potential and openness for change where greater contact with more people, practices and ideas allow creative processes to flourish. This aligns with creative capital theory in which concentrated diversity in cities speeds the flow of knowledge, leading to higher rates of innovation (ibid.). So many things happen at once that the prospects for what will take place, where, when, why, how and with whom are boundless, catalysing inventive and spontaneous problem solving. In such an unpredictable environment, engaging with information that is similar and different is equally probable. Citizens of São Paulo, highly accustomed to random encounters on mass transit or in any dense public area, often develop relaxed attitudes towards interacting with others. As interaction becomes familiar, so does difference, successively encouraging more interaction with difference. This perpetual feedback loop expands the available resources with which to connect and broaden thinking that may inspire imagination.

My vision of these interactions resembles a moving spiral in which the progressively larger concentric circles form patterns within smaller circles. As the spiral expands from its centre, the outer edge meets 'uncharted' territory, which adjoins to the whole. New encounters previously beyond the spiral are brought into contact with prior or known territory, as the spiral curves around the inner core. This path illustrates temporality[20] —the unity of time described as 'coming toward itself in its possibilities of being by going back to what has been' (Korab-Karpowicz 2009) in which the future opens by bending towards the past, a reflexive action that is both subjective and intersubjective.

It is not surprising that Quadrilhas Caipiras include spirals, a pervasive design in nature, which usually happen at least once during the dance and often signal the end. That movement, known as *caracol* or snail, coils inward towards a central axis and then circles out, reversing direction. A leader directs the group, all holding hands, and determines how the curved space contracts and expands. These fluctuations impact proximity to others as well as directional orientation, size of movements and tempo. As the *caracol* weaves outside-in and inside-out, interactions between self and other stimulate intersubjective awareness, performing reflexivity. Individual differentiation through constantly varied responses also makes more explicit the effect any one person has upon a setting. The making of community reflects that perpetual process as dialectic cooperation (Sennett 2012). This utopian notion situates the other as an interlocutor, inviting conversations that may engage discovery, spark imagination and encourage invention. Encounters with difference ignite the fire for creativity. Communities emerge from the recognition that each person has something different to offer; positive acknowledgement of those contributions motivates a willingness to work together. Through dialogic exchange differentiation affirms the distinctive value of individuals, which can diminish competition and promote cooperation (ibid.).

The Colégio Santa Maria annual Festas Juninas is a microcosm of São Paulo. It provides an opportunity to seek and accommodate increasing heterogeneity. Within the dance itself, becoming *caipira* synchronously expresses an idealized past rooted in the natural world, a present critique of modernity and a future sustained by the production and distribution of diverse knowledge resources as creative capital. Quadrilhas Caipiras participants use dialectic and dialogic exchange to make visible the invisible process of embodying difference.

Minutos Adicionais

For *futebol* spectators, lengthening the second half with additional minutes expands possibilities for the game. Teams have the opportunity to score goals that may thrust them ahead to win or simply strengthen their lead. In the days following my experience at Colégio Santa Maria, anticipation is high as the World Cup theatre continues to permeate daily life. Approaching the eve of Saint Peter's Day on Monday 28 June, Brazil demolishes Chile 3–0 in the round of 16 and is advancing to the quarterfinal game against the Netherlands. By now I have travelled from the fast pace of São Paulo to Guaraná. Even in this country town, I am aware of the positivity and hopefulness for Brazil's next victory, reflected in people's actions and conversation. The shift in location abruptly changes my energy, which slows considerably along with the winding down of Festas Juninas events. Feeling unusually relaxed, I sort through boxes filled with family photos and letters, and in doing so come across an old paperback written by Acrísio de Camargo, an early-twentieth-century poet and folklorist from rural São Paulo. In his collection of writings, entitled *Lorotas*, he describes a *caipira* village with few people and little movement (*pouca gente; pouco movimento*).[21] He could have been referring to Guaraná.

While holding this relic of time's passage, I suddenly realize that it is 2 July and the quarterfinal game is on television. Although a weekday, the nation has stopped all work to watch their beloved *Seleção*. Just 10 minutes after the start, Brazil scores, dominating possession of the ball. As the team scores, an announcer's voice calls out 'GOOOOOOOOOOOOOAL.' The communal roaring response spreads throughout the village. However, tables turn in the second half and complete silence falls as the Netherlands rallies back, scoring two goals. Watching this happen, I sense something different as others around me complain in Portuguese that the team chemistry is missing. *Futebol criatividade* (creative soccer) or *jogo bonito* (beautiful game) are terms Brazilians use to describe their team's playing style, hardly evident in this game. Analysts later criticize the *Seleção* coach's technical, European-influenced approach, which is linear, monochronic and predictable. While precise, it lacks the individuality that showcases each player's talent, stifling the polyrhythmic and variable conditions in which *jeitinho* thrives.

Unfortunately, the Brazilian team loses; yet fans are already looking forward to the return of 'authentic' *futebol brasileiro* in the 2014 World Cup, which would take place in Brazil.[22] Breathing a sigh of frustration and relief, I walk outside along the main road by the town centre and up the hill past the church and cemetery where little white-faced monkeys play on avocado trees and vultures swarm above the eucalyptus in the forest ahead. Immersion with the non-human other deepens my understanding of connections between nature and Festas Juninas practices. I realize that *jeitinho*—a way to negotiate unpredictable circumstances—actually plays an important role for Festas Juninas. In the natural world, survival means life or death, so *jeitinho* must be automatic and instinctual. However for Brazilians, *jeitinho* has a more deliberate and altruistic quality. Bound by emotional ties within the group, Colégio Santa Maria alumni demonstrate this learnt strategy to intentionally encounter difference by humanizing the other. The 'tension' of diverse bodies moving in unfamiliar ways necessitates improvisation and openness to unknown changes. That capacity for alterity in the extraordinary situation of *jeitinho* (Borges 2011), exemplified by Quadrilhas Caipiras, makes creative communities possible, which I suggest is symbolic of contemporary urban São Paulo and a harbinger of Brazil as a more democratic society.

Notes

1 *Futebol* is Portuguese for football or soccer, also spelt *futbol* or *fútbol*.

2 In the mid-twentieth century, focus on *mestiçagem* gave the impression of a harmonious nation poised for modernization. The hypocrisy of that claim, likely a tool for social control, was backed by census data in the late 1970s, revealing the 'reality of racial mystification: Brazil was a majority Black nation, yet this majority suffered inequality and marginalization' (Alberto 2011: 267). Freyre, most responsible for constructing and disseminating this vision, later changed from 'progressive defender of *mestiçagem* to reactionary apologist of a fictitious racial democracy' (Cleary 1999: 12).

3 The term 'personal emic' (Vissicaro 2003) originates from linguist Kenneth L. Pike's important contribution to social science, particularly comparative studies. Pike identified two perspectives for investigating cultural systems. 'Emic' refers to culturally-specific insiders' perspectives; however, 'through the "etic" lens the analyst views the data in tacit reference to a perspective oriented to all comparable events (whether sounds, ceremonies, activities), of all peoples, of all parts of the earth' (1954: 41). As cross-cultural research developed, anthropologist Marvin Harris identified the starting point for comparative analysis as the researchers' or observers' emic views, which he distinguishes from those of the participants in the system under study (Harris 1990). His idea inspired me to identify the 'personal emic', an approach used by the individual conducting ethnographic study that shapes understanding of her object of study.

4 *Futebol* matches are 90 minutes in length, divided by two 45-minute periods—*primeiro tempo* (first half) and *segundo tempo* (second half)—and a 15-minute halftime or *intervalo*. Almost every game has *minutos adicionais* (additional minutes), extending the second half by approximately three to four minutes. This accounts for time lost due to injury, substitutions and/or other interruptions since the clock continues running throughout the entire game.

5 In 1959, anthropologist Edward T. Hall introduced the concept of polychronicity. It contrasts with monochronicity, which emphasizes doing one thing in one place at a time, most often in linear sequence. While monochronic behaviour suggests more efficient task management and compartmentalizes interactions, it does

alienate people much the same way as 'looking through a cardboard tube narrows vision' (Hall 1959: 20).

6 'Automatic' refers to a type of cognition that social anthropologist Roy D'Andrade investigated and which shaped the field of cognitive anthropology. Automatic cognition, a kind of routine or everyday cognition, is implicit, unverbalized and rapid; whereas deliberative cognition is explicit, verbalized and progressive, occurring as attention shifts to a problem or issue (D'Andrade 1995). Deliberative cognition forces one to stop and think critically and reflexively, involves the motivation to override existing schemata and allows the variability of time for knowledge processing to occur.

7 The term 'cognitive consonance' evolves from the research of social psychologist Leon Festinger. His focus on 'cognitive dissonance' led to the realization that forced or accidental exposure to new information may create cognitive elements that are dissonant with existing cognition (Festinger 1962). In a state of dissonance, people may feel disequilibrium, frustration, dread, guilt, anger, embarrassment, anxiety, etc. Thus people tend to seek consistency in their beliefs and perceptions, which initiates change in order to reduce the variance or disagreement.

8 Eliot Chapple and Carleton Coon differentiate 'rites of intensification' from rites of passage as group- (rather than individual-) centred ceremonies, such as those aimed to renew and intensify the fertility and availability of game and crops. Ritual techniques enable individuals to build up interaction rates needed to restore equilibrium of the group (1942: 528). Anthony Wallace further categorizes (communal) rites of intensification as both technological and ideological. 'Ritual as technology' includes hunting and gathering rites of intensification 'that purports directly or indirectly to control the availability and fertility of game (fish, fowl, insects, mammals, or whatever), of flocks and herds, or of wild and cultivated vegetable crops' (1966: 107–8) and thus transform 'man's external environment into states favorable to man' (ibid.: 112). Ideological rites of intensification revitalize a community of people to 'its attachment to the values and customs of its culture' (ibid.: 130). These reminders are 'corrective measures' that reaffirm religious beliefs and mythologies as well as strengthen social relationships. Both technological and ideological rituals function to promote task performance and group cooperation,

evident in Festas Juninas, which directly reflect the group's ability to manipulate the growth and harvest of crops.

9 'Midsummer represented the end of a solstice, the period in which the sun ceased to move for a short period, but rose and set at the same points on the horizon at the extreme end of its range. Now, however, it was at the height of its strength, and light at its longest, and Midsummer's Eve represented the culmination of that period of apogee, just before the days began to shorten again as the sun moved southward. In response to the swelling of heat and light, foliage and grasses were now likewise at their fullness, before the time of fruiting approached. No wonder that it seemed to be a magical time to ancient Europeans' (Hutton 1996: 312).

10 Portugal's King João VI was living with his family in Brazil after fleeing Napoleon's invasion of Portugal in 1808. When he returned to Portugal in 1821, his son Dom Pedro I remained as regent of Brazil. One year later, Pedro led the secession of Brazil from Portugal, assuming its head as Emperor Pedro I of Brazil. After his abdication in 1832, he also returned to Portugal, leaving behind his five-year-old son, Emperor Pedro II, who ruled until 1889 when he was ousted by a coup d'état.

11 Monteiro Lobato gave the name *biotonico fontoura* to a medicinal tonic created by his friend Cândido Fontoura in 1910. To increase sales, Monteiro wrote the *Almanac Fontoura*, an annual 'advertisement' available for free at pharmacies throughout Brazil, which also included such information as moon phases to determine good days for fishing. Monteiro's marketing strategy suggested the tonic cured the hookworms 'afflicting' Jeca Tatuzinho (the diminutive form of Tatu). First published in 1920, the almanac's first run was over 50,000 copies. As circulation grew, over 100 million copies were distributed of the last edition in 1982 (Machado, Rossi and Neves 2012).

12 PAM created 24 films in 22 years (1958–80). One theory explaining the success of these films in escaping censorship was to avoid direct confrontation or 'a revolutionary way' by not calling attention to resistance, often disguised as conformity (Bueno 1999).

13 This South African two-foot-long horn used to cheer on teams at football matches is now common paraphernalia after its TV debut to audiences around the globe at the 2010 World Cup.

14 The Sisters of the Holy Cross Roman Catholic ministry came to Brazil from the United States. They are affiliated with the Congregation of the Holy Cross established in France in 1837. With an admission fee of R$25 per person (about US$12) and a crowd of over 5,000 people, as one of their main fundraising events, the school likely collected a large amount of money.

15 *Avatar* continues to be the highest-grossing film of all time; its Brazilian release was only months before the 2010 Colégio Santa Maria Festas Juninas event. Director James Cameron and actress Sigourney Weaver promoted the movie's release in São Paulo by planting the first of over one million trees as part of an Earth Day Network / Fox Home Entertainment effort. Interestingly, the first tree was *pau brasil*, an endangered species, the same tree exported by French traders in the 1700s for its red dye and to make violin bows, as mentioned above.

16 Some of the many calls include *damas à direta e cavalheiros à esquerda* (ladies to the right and gentlemen to the left), *travessê geral* (everybody cross), *preparar para a cesta* (prepare for the basket), *preparar o grande túnel* (prepare the long tunnel) and *grande roda* (big circle).

17 Common calls that are adapted from French or are actual French words include *anavantur* (*em avant tout*: forward everyone), *anarriê* (*em derrière*: backward), *otrefoá* (*autrefois*: again), *retournê* (return), *changê* (change) and *retirê* (retreat).

18 Sociologist Ferdinand Tönnies defines community (*Gemeinschaft*) as characterized by an underlying, organic or instinctive driving force or will (*Wesenville*) that embodies the collective consciousness of belonging together and affirms the condition of mutual dependence (1957). It is interesting that Tönnies understood community and society (*Gesellschaft*) as dichotomous since they mutually complement and explain each other.

19 Fundamental education (*ensino fundamental*) in Brazil is mandatory for children aged 6 to 14. Grades are designated as years 1 to 9.

20 Temporality, which philosopher Martin Heidegger refers to as *Dasein*, explores the unity of time. In everyday German language, the word *Dasein* means life or existence (Korab-Karpowicz 2009).

21 My copy of *Lorotas* does not indicate a publisher. Material was probably distributed by the magazine *Atalai* or in the weekly *Ituanos* sometime in the 1920s and 30s.

22 Since this writing, the 2014 World Cup occurred. Brazil lost 1–7 in the semifinals to Germany, who went on to win the championship, beating Argentina 1–0.

Works Cited

ALBERTO, Paulina L. 2011. *Terms of Inclusion: Black Intellectuals in Twentieth-Century Brazil*. Chapel Hill: University of North Carolina Press.

ASSUNÇÃO, Matthias Röhrig. 2002. *Capoeira: The History of an Afro-Brazilian Martial Art*. London: Routledge.

BALTER, Michael. 2004. 'Earliest Signs of Human-Controlled Fire Uncovered in Israel'. *Science* 304(5671): 663–5.

BORGES, Fernanda Carlos. 2011. 'A Improvisacão no Jeitinho Brasileiro' (The Improvisation within Brazilian *Jeitinho*). *Revisita Trama Interdisciplinar* 2(1): 134–43.

BOTELHO, Pamela. 2013. Personal interview with Museu Mazzaropi staff member, Taubaté, São Paulo, Brazil.

BROWN, Rose. 1945. *American emperor, Dom Pedro II of Brazil*, New York, New York: The Viking Press.

BUENO, Eva Paulino. 1999. *O Artista do Povo: Mazzaropi e Jeca Tatu no Cinema do Brasil* (The People's Artist: Mazzaropi and Jeca Tatu in Brazilian Cinema). Maringá: Editora da Universidade Estadual de Maringá.

BURKE, Peter. 1978. *Popular Culture in Early Modern Europe*. Surrey: Ashgate.

CÂMARA CASCUDO, L. Da. 1972[1954]. *Dicionário do Folclore Brasileiro* (Dictionary of Brazilian Folklore), 10TH EDN. Rio de Janeiro: Ediouro.

CHAPPLE, Eliot Dismore, and Carleton Stevens Coon. 1942. *Principles of Anthropology*. New York: Henry Holt.

CLEARY, David. 1999. *Race, Nationalism and Social Theory in Brazil: Rethinking Gilberto Freyre*. Cambridge, MA: David Rockefeller for Latin American Studies, Harvard University. Available at: http://goo.gl/8bLNJC (last accessed on 26 February 2014).

COLÉGIO SANTA MARIA. 2008. 'Missão e Visão' (Mission and Vision). Available at: http://goo.gl/-lU5SDX (last accessed on 12 July 2013).

D'ANDRADE, Roy. 1995. *The Development of Cognitive Anthropology*. New York: Cambridge University Press.

DOS SANTOS, Patrícia Gomes, and Cristina Schmidt Silva. 2009. 'A Cultura Caipira no Cinema Brasileiro: Um Estudo da Filmografia de Mazzaropi'

(The Caipira Culture in Brazilian Cinema: A Study of Mazzaropi Filmography). Paper presented at UNITWIN/Cátedra UNESCO de Comunicação, para o Desenvolvimento Regional, Folkcom 2009. Universidade Metodista de São Paulo, São Paulo. Available at: http://goo.gl/zPGZEX (last accessed on 1 March 2014).

FALASSI, Alessandro. 1987. 'Festival: Definition and Morphology' in Alessandro Falassi (ed.), *Time Out of Time: Essays on the Festival*. Albuquerque: University of New Mexico Press, pp. 1–10.

FERREIRA, Maria Cristina, Ronald Fischer, Juliana Barreiros Porto, Ronaldo Pilati, Taciano L. Milfont. 2012. 'Unraveling the Mystery of Brazilian Jeitinho: A Cultural Exploration of Social Norms'. *Personality and Social Psychology Bulletin* 38(3): 331–44.

FESTINGER, Leon. 1962. *A Theory of Cognitive Dissonance*. Stanford, CA: Stanford University Press.

FLORIDA, Richard. 2002. *The Rise of the Creative Class*. New York: Basic Books.

FREYRE, Gilberto. 1963. *New World in the Tropics: The Culture of Modern Brazil*. New York: Alfred A. Knopf.

GRAHAM, Douglas H. 1970. 'Divergent and Convergent Regional Economic Growth and Internal Migration in Brazil, 1940–1960'. *Economic Development and Cultural Change* 18(3): 362–82.

HALL, Edward T. 1959. *The Silent Language*. Garden City, NY: Doubleday.

HARRIS, Marvin. 1990. 'Emics and Etics Revisited' in Thomas N. Headland, Kenneth L. Pike & Marvin Harris (eds), *Emics and Etics: The Insider/Outsider Debate*. Newbury Park, CA: Sage, pp. 48–61.

HUTTON, Ronald. 1996. *The Stations of the Sun: A History of the Ritual Year in Britain*. New York: Oxford University Press.

KORAB-KARPOWICZ, W. J. 2009. 'Martin Heidegger (1889—1976)'. *Internet Encyclopedia of Philosophy*. Available at: http://goo.gl/MSc99S (last accessed on 20 August 2013).

MACHADO, Marcelo Oliano, Ednéia Regina Rossi and Fátima Maria Neves. 2012. 'O Discurso Educacional e o Almanaque do Biotônico Fontoura: Por Entre Prácticas de Leitura e a Produção de Uma Representação do Sertanejo (1920–1950)' (The Educational Discourse and the Biotonico Fontoura Almanac: between Reading Practices and the Production of a Backcountry Man's Representation). *Revista HISTEDBR On-line* 45: 78–88. Available at: http://goo.gl/5HqOMd (last accessed on 10 March 2014).

MATOS, Marcela. 2010. *Sai da Frente: A Vida e a Obra de Mazzaropi* (Get Out of the Way: The Life and Work of Mazzaropi). Rio de Janeiro: Desiderata.

MURRELL, Nathaniel Samuel. 2009. *Afro-Caribbean Religions: An Introduction to Their Historical, Cultural, and Sacred Traditions*. Philadelphia, PA: Temple University Press.

MUSEU MAZZAROPI. 2013. Exhibition in Taubaté, São Paulo, Brazil.

PIKE, Kenneth L. 1954. *Language in Relation to a Unified Theory of the Structure of Human Behavior*. Glendale, CA: Summer Institute of Linguistics.

PYNE, Stephen. J. 2001. *Fire: A Brief History*. Seattle: University of Washington Press.

SENNETT, Richard. 2012. *Together: The Rituals, Pleasures and Politics of Cooperation*. New Haven, CN: Yale University Press.

SISTERS OF THE HOLY CROSS. 2014. 'Colégio Santa Maria, São Paulo, Brazil'. Available at: http://goo.gl/98NtKE (last accessed on 10 January 2014).

TISHKEN, Joel E., Toyin Falola and Akintunde Akinyemi (eds). 2009. *Ṣàngó in Africa and the African Diaspora*. Bloomington: Indiana University Press.

TÖNNIES, Ferdinand. 1957. *Community and Society: Gemeinschaft und Gesselschaft* (C. P. Loomis trans.). Lansing: Michigan State University Press.

VISSICARO, Pegge. 2003. 'Emic–Etic Interaction: Processes of Cross-Cultural Dance Study in an Online Learning Environment'. PhD dissertation, Arizona State University, Tempe.

——. 2010. 'The Politics of Extraordinary Possibilities'. *Animated* (Autumn): 27–8.

VISSICARO, Vito. 2012. Personal interview with Arcos Brasil owner, Tempe, Arizona.

WALLACE, Anthony F. C. 1966. *Religion: An Anthropological View*. New York: Random House.

Part Two

UTOPIAN LAUGHTER
FROM MINSTRELSY TO BURLESQUE

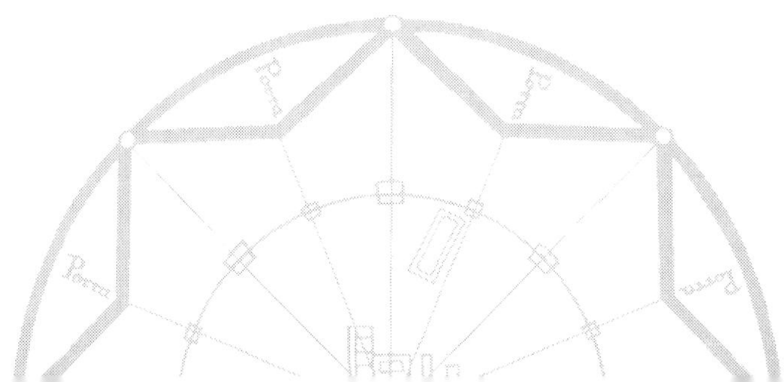

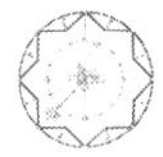

Chapter 4

THE ARIZONA RENAISSANCE FESTIVAL

A Performance in Three Movements

Kevin McHugh and Ann Fletchall

> Is a society with no festivals not a society condemned to death?
>
> Roger Caillois (1988[1940]: 302).

Thirsty Ones

François Rabelais, the sixteenth-century French writer of folk culture and the carnivalesque, begins the first comic epic in Western literature, *Pantagruel*, with the text: 'Most illustrious Drinkers and you, most precious Syphilitics, it is to you, not to others, that my writings are dedicated' (quoted in Boorstin 1992: 288). That drink and dipsomania should headline Rabelais's masterpiece in comic absurdity is fitting, as France was suffering a severe drought at the time. *Panta* in Greek refers to 'all' and *Gruel* in the Hagarene language means 'thirsty'; thus, Pantagruel, son of Gargantua, was named for his destiny: 'Ruler of the Thirsty Ones' (ibid.: 290).

The meaning of Pantagruel is not lost on us as we enter the Arizona Renaissance Festival outside Phoenix in March 2008. Arizona is experiencing a protracted drought, and there is much discussion, debate and consternation about 'watering' (sustaining) an exploding desert metropolis intoxicated on an oasis mentality. Phoenicians thirst for more than water; desires in advanced capitalism are insatiable, whether one contemplates desire born of lack (Lacan 1977), desire as an endless play of floating signifiers (Baudrillard 1981) or repressive forces that thwart liberating desire (Deleuze and Guattari 1983). 'Welcome to the entertaining time machine known as the 20th Annual Renaissance Festival' proclaims the flyer handed to patrons passing through mock-medieval gates. For an admission price of $20, festival-goers are welcomed to 'Fairhaven', a '16th-Century European Country Faire', an experience in 'endless merriment and mayhem' at the largest Renaissance soiree in the western United States. The Arizona Renaissance Festival and Artisan Marketplace springs to life on weekends in February and March each year, occupying 30 acres of Sonoran desert in the foothills of the dramatic Superstition Mountains. Over eight weekends, including the Presidents Day holiday, Ren Fest welcomes approximately 250,000 revellers (Arizona Renaissance Festival 2011).

Our performative analysis of the Arizona Renaissance Festival unfolds in three movements. First, we trace the emergence and proliferation of Renaissance faires in the US, and describe this rebirth as spectacle, a pastiche that jumbles, romanticizes and commodifies history. The spectacle speaks to nostalgia and escape as cultural elixirs manifest in a Rabelaisian landscape of pleasure and excess. In the second movement, we sketch the history of festival and wink to Ren Fest as a sanitized expression of the carnivalesque, a remnant of the transgression and subversion that marked premodern carnivals and festivals. The third and culminating movement is an eruption of festival laughter that reverberates and shakes high-minded seriousness to its bones—laughter that leaves in its dying echoes questions of self, other and relational being in the modern world. Ren Fest, then, is our catapult to that 'little mystery' called laughter, which is, as Henri Bergson calls it in *Le Rire*, a conundrum that has simultaneously intrigued and repelled philosophers and cultural theorists (Bergson 1981: 157; Weber 1987; Bruns 2000). Our entanglement in laughter moves in streams of cultural thought inspired in particular by Georges Bataille, the 'impossible' thinker of overabundance and excess whose laughter smashes representational thought (Bataille 1985, 1992; Noys 2000; Botting and Wilson 1997, 1998; Gill 1995; Borch-Jacobsen 1987; Hollier 1989). We end the performance with a coda that considers eruptions of laughter as vital moments in relational being, moments which trigger possibilities in feeling and thinking differently (Borch-Jacobsen 1987).

Movement I: The Spectacle

The first contemporary reincarnation of a Renaissance festival in the US was held in the Hollywood Hills of Los Angeles in 1963. The Renaissance Pleasure Faire, held over a weekend, was a 'non-profit hippie event' that appealed to the counterculture movement of the time (Ringel 2002: 150). A website promoting the Heart of the Forest Renaissance Faire, a direct descendent of the Renaissance Pleasure Faire, states: 'The first Faires partook of the rich lore and age-old customs of English springtime markets and "Maying" customs' (Heart of the Forest Renaissance Faires 2007). Two additional faires began in California in the 1960s—one in Santa Barbara and another in Marin County—and the idea caught on, stimulating the creation of a dozen modest Renaissance faires around the country in the 1970s (Grendler 2006).

Renaissance festivals flourished in the US throughout the 1980s and 90s. Because of their mass appeal, many festivals were founded and operated as for-profit business ventures. Today, there are over 200 Renaissance festivals and faires operating in 40 states across the US, including 20 'major league' events which run for a month or longer (Siegel, personal interview, 2007). A series of festivals are now owned by a publicly traded company, Renaissance Entertainment Corporation, including Southern California's Renaissance Pleasure Faire, Bristol Renaissance Faire of Illinois/Wisconsin and the New York Renaissance Faire. Another large company, Mid-America Festivals Corporation, operates faires in Minnesota, Michigan, Kansas City and the San Francisco Bay Area (Mid-America Festivals Corporation 2007). From humble beginnings in the 1960s, Renaissance festivals have multiplied in number; many have grown larger in size and scope, longer in duration, and are now permanent features in the American landscape (Grendler 2006).

FIGURE 4.1. **Court Jester, Arizona Renaissance Festival, 2008.**
FIGURE 4.2. **Queen of Hearts, Arizona Renaissance Festival, 2008.**
Photographs courtesy of the authors.

It was in this context that the Arizona Renaissance Festival (Ren Fest) was born in 1989. Situated in the Sonoran Desert on the exurban fringe of Phoenix, the festival's location caters to visitors from Phoenix and Tucson. Over the past 20 years, the festival has grown in size from 5 acres to its present 30 (approximately

20,000 to 121,400 square metres) and from 3 makeshift plywood stages to 12 performance venues, with an increase in visitors from 32,000 to 250,000. In 1996, a jousting arena that seats 4,500 spectators was added and the festival was lengthened to its current two-month winter season (Davis 1998; Myers 1996; The Lord Mayor, personal interview, 2007).

We experienced the Ren Fest on three occasions: twice in 2007 and once again in 2008. As participant-observers, we moved and laughed with the festive throng. We interviewed Jeffrey Siegel, the founder, producer and manager of the festival, as well as performers and cast members known by their faire persona, including The Lord Mayor, Zilch the Storyteller, Contessa Lucretia Noir Morte, Helena Handbasket and Connie Ahrensdahl. We also spoke with shopkeepers and vendors. In March 2007, we conducted an online survey of festivalgoers using SurveyMonkey. The survey was posted on the Arizona Renaissance Festival online discussion board and distributed through the Society for Creative Anachronism, a medieval re-enactment organization. We received 51 (anonymous) posted responses, ranging from one-time Renaissance Festival fairgoers to devotees who participate every weekend during festival season.

How does one describe the spectacle that is Ren Fest? According to its website, 'The Arizona Renaissance Festival is a medieval amusement park, a 12-stage theater, a 30-acre circus, an arts and crafts fair, a jousting tournament and a feast—all rolled into one non-stop, day-long family adventure!' (Arizona Renaissance Festival 2011). Siegel describes the festival as a mixture of 'living history, fairy tale and fantasy, and a dose of a Monty Python movie come to life', reveling in being everything a Renaissance faire might be in the imagination (personal interview, 2007). In short, Ren Fest is a simulacrum (Baudrillard 1994), a pastiche that appeals by jumbling time periods and imploding fact and fantasy under the playful ruse of a Renaissance-era marketplace. Zilch the Storyteller, a popular cast member, describes the simulacrum in telling fashion. 'The festival,' says Zilch, 'has become its own time period' (personal interview, 2007).

The farcical Fairhaven is ruled by King Henry the Only. There are no strict rules in place for costuming cast members; most anything goes. At the faire, there are medievalists of various stripes, including seventeenth-century English and Flemish royalty, jesters and courtiers, Robin Hood types, Spaniards and Italians, gypsies, pirates, sorcerers, wenches, warlocks and wizards (Siegel, personal interview, 2007; see Figure 4.3).

FIGURE 4.3. **Characters at the Arizona Renaissance Festival, 2007: King and Queen, Wench, Pirate Buccaneer.**
Photograph courtesy of the authors.

A popular costume choice we observed on our visits was the pirate, usually in the style of Jack Sparrow as played by the actor Johnny Depp in Walt Disney's billion-dollar *Pirates of the Caribbean* film franchise. Disney is surely apropriate for Ren Fest, where

Umberto Eco's description of Disneyland as hyperreal rings true. The amusement park, writes Eco, makes no claim to represent or authenticate, for 'within its magic enclosure it is fantasy that is absolutely reproduced' (1986: 43).

This 'sixteenth-century Disneyland' (The Lord Mayor, personal interview, 2007) is indeed a simulacrum, fixated on sign value and consumption. This is indicated in the official name of the event: The Annual Arizona Renaissance Festival & Artisan Marketplace. More than 200 shops line the fairgrounds in a giant loop that encourages multiple visits. Vendors pay an annual fee to the management company and occupy their own shops, giving rise to fairytale-inspired architecture that genuflects whimsically to eclectic styles, such as Gothic, Bavarian, Tudor and Tolkienian. A dizzying array of products is on offer for the strolling insouciant, ranging from Renaissance-themed bodily adornments to period weaponry. Shops with names such as Fairytale Fynery, Medieval Metal, Castle Creations and The Perfumed Dragon feed the phantasm, inducing desire for souvenirs as mementos of the Ren Fest experience (Stewart 1993).

For the hungry and thirsty fairgoer, delights abound, including roasted turkey legs of obscene proportion and other medieval faire. Dipsomaniacs quaff ale, beer, mead or enjoy other libations (e.g. medieval margaritas, Da Vinci coladas) at five pubs, sometimes growing tipsy, revelling in a form of play Roger Caillois (1961) terms *ilinx*, a sense of imbalance or whirling (vertigo) inducing merriment and laughter. For gluttons, the ultimate culinary and entertainment experience is the Pleasure Feast, a two-hour dinner show, promoted thus: 'Be treated like royalty while you savor six courses of fine food, ample drynk [sic], and enjoy two hours of raucous Renaissance Entertainment at its best! Let the Feast Master's boisterous serving wenches and tavern knaves dish up a roaring good time!' (Arizona Renaissance Festival 2011). Like some other Ren Fest entertainment, Pleasure Feast comes with the disclaimer: adult humour.

More than three dozen performers and troupes create all-day, nonstop action across 12 stages of entertainment, and at the end of the day the Festival comes to a fitting conclusion with 'A Joust to the Death' in the Tournament Arena. Spectators are welcomed into a sports-stadium-like atmosphere by a pep band playing contemporary arena hits such as 'Tequila' and 'Mony Mony'. The King and Queen of Fairhaven make their grand entrance via horse-drawn cart to preside over the contest. The final joust is the conclusion of a three-act affair chronicling escalating rivalries among several knights. This joust incorporates dramatic dehorsements, sword fighting and fake blood—everything one might hope to see at a joust, if not at a World Wrestling Entertainment (WWE) event. (See Figure 4.4.)

FIGURE 4.4. **Country Wench observes Knight preparing for Joust to the Death, Arizona Renaissance Festival, 2007.**
Photograph courtesy of the authors.

The spectacle that is Ren Fest speaks to *nostalgia* and its twin, *escape*, as potent cultural strains. Three decades ago, the geographer David Lowenthal offered these words: 'Today, nostalgia threatens to engulf all of past time and much of the present landscape'

(1975: 3). Burgeoning industries profiting from invoking nostalgia and memory in many guises—such as heritage tourism, historic preservation and planning, and new residential and community developments genuflecting to the past—lend credence to Lowenthal's prescient remark. Lowenthal draws on the California Renaissance Faire in articulating estrangement and escape as bedfellows with nostalgia:

> What nostalgia requires is a sense of estrangement; the object of the quest must be anachronistic. Like Renaissance devotion to the classical world, the remoteness of the past is for us part of its charm. 'We want to relive those thrilling days of yesteryear,' says a critic, 'but only because we are absolutely assured those days are out of reach.' The return to the past is usually fleeting, as at California's 'Pleasure Faire', a sixteenth-century recreation where hippie craftsman quaff mead and 'hot elixir'. 'Most of us identify more with Renaissance times than with the present,' explained a young potter. 'This is our annual escape into a better world' (ibid.: 4).

Similar to the young Californian potter, an online participant in our study commented that 'the Renaissance is the time period that I wish I had grown up in', a wish expressed precisely because, like utopia, it can only be imagined, not fulfilled. Nostalgia thrives on the fact that the past as past is beyond our grasp. Nostalgia breeds fantasy and the desire to escape the doldrums of daily life. What is desirable and attainable is recreating or recasting an imagined past in the present. We asked in our online survey: Did you enjoy your experience at the festival? Why or why not? Responses (anonymous) tapping fantasy and escape were common, such as these four postings:

> It is the chance to be someone else and experience a day or two away from reality.

> The atmosphere is one of fun and enchantment. It's a place to forget your troubles and escape for a day.
>
> I enjoy being able to participate in an earlier time when life seems so easy.
>
> It's a bit like stepping into a fantasy novel for a day.

Overall, respondents describe escape to the fantasy world of Ren Fest as temporary. In his book *Escapism*, Yi-Fu Tuan argues that escape finds expression across cultures, and that 'there is nothing wrong with escape as such [. . .] so long as it remains a passing mood, a brief mental experiment with possibility' (1998: *xvi*). 'Fantasy that is shut off too long from external reality,' intones Tuan, 'risks degenerating into a self-deluding hell' (ibid.). This begs the question as to a presumed tidy distinction between fantasy and reality, a binary imploded in Baudrillard's *Simulacra and Simulation*: 'Disneyland [Ren Fest] is presented as imaginary to make us believe the rest is real' (1994: 12). Is Phoenix not a spectacular, hyperreal desert metropolis? Consider the following scenario. At the end of a long Ren Fest day, exhausted revellers mount their SUVs and gallop home to gated, amenity-saturated, master-planned sanctuaries perched astride mountain preserves in a sizzling desert metropolis of 3.8 million consuming souls. 'In an extreme environment where plants use body armor and chemical warfare to survive aridity and scorching temperatures, Phoenix is an impossible city wild with possibility' (Kitson 2007: n.p.),[1] a spectacular place, a phantasm conjured from the vapors of capitalist will, political acumen and engineering marvel. Spectacle trumps spectacle.

Movement II: The Wink

Renaissance Festival as commodified spectacle displays similarities with festival marketplaces and theme parks in America (Goss 1999; Klugman et al. 1995), yet the ambience and vibe feels different.

Happenings and events such as Ren Fest wink to the past, carrying vestiges of premodern carnivals and festivals that served as sites of celebration and transgression. In his iconic work *Rabelais and His World* (1984), Mikhail Bakhtin elaborates the history of the 'second world' of folk culture in the Middle Ages and the Renaissance that existed outside, yet parallel with, officialdom. The drudgery of daily life in premodern European societies, rigidly hierarchical and religious, was punctuated by a calendar of carnivals and celebrations taking place several times a year. These ritualized inversions of the social order celebrated a second world in which all classes participated and laughter prevailed. Carnival provided a place and time for folly and laughter, for the mocking of established authority, for curses to be uttered, for comic references to the 'lower stratum' of the body, which conveyed the leitmotif of regeneration and renewal (Bakhtin 1984).

Carnivals and feasts in the Middle Ages and Renaissance have been interpreted by some as events that served to maintain authority and everyday life; as a safety valve or release of pent-up energies, anxieties and frustrations (Cresswell 1996; Jackson 1989: 80). One example, cited by Bakhtin, is an apology for 'feasts of fools', expressed in a 1444 circular of the Paris School of Theology:

> Foolishness which is our second nature and seems to be inherent in man might freely spend itself at least once a year. Wine barrels burst if from time to time we do not open them and let in some air. All of us men are barrels poorly put together, which would burst from the wine of wisdom, if this wine remains in a state of constant fermentation of piousness and fear of God. We must give it air in order to not let it spoil. This is why we permit folly on certain days so that we may later return with greater zeal to the service of God (quoted in Bakhtin 1984: 75).

Feasts, festivals and mockery of rituals were bound by temporal limits, with life returning to 'normal' once the festive period was over. Tim Cresswell (1996) argues that the containment interpretation is oversimplified, as carnival merriment sometimes engendered unpredictably, riots and upheaval, such as during the French Revolution. Cresswell discusses this debate and concludes sensibly that it is not possible to generalize the effects of carnival as either conservative or revolutionary; it is necessary to examine 'specific histories and instances of carnivals in the places they occur' (ibid.: 130).

As European societies modernized ritual calendars of feasts—many religious and connected with seasonal cycles—gave way to a more regimented industrial work schedule. As a result, festivals were reduced in number and spatially constricted. The bourgeoisie and emerging middle class urbanized and distanced themselves from the 'lower' culture practised by rural peasants. The occurrence of festivity became increasingly circumscribed, for such celebrations 'encoded all that which the proper bourgeois must strive *not to be* in order to preserve a stable and "correct" sense of self' (Stallybrass and White 1999: 387). In England, fairs 'had once taken over the whole of the town', but during the seventeenth and eighteenth centuries they were banished from wealthier neighbourhoods (ibid.). By the end of the nineteenth century, festivals had been driven away from the city to the outskirts, such that London found itself surrounded by country fairs, and many festivities and holiday celebrations were moved into the private arena of the home (ibid.; Bakhtin 1984).

Roger Caillois, writing in 1940, articulates critical aspects of festival in terms of expenditure, the sacred and societal regeneration, and ends the essay by arguing that in modern societies vacation is the vapid successor of festival:

> The values are completely reversed because in one instance each one goes off on his own [vacation], and in

> the other [festival] everyone comes together in the same place. Vacation (its name alone is indicative), seems to be an empty space . . . incapable of *overjoying* an individual [. . .]. The happiness it brings is primarily a result of a distraction and distancing from worries [. . .]. Rather than communication with the group in a moment of exuberance and jubilation, it is further isolation. Consequently vacation, unlike festival, constitutes not the flood stage of collective existence, but rather its low-water mark. From this point of view vacations are characteristic of an extremely dissipated society in which no mediation remains between the passions of an individual and the State apparatus. . . . Is a society with no festivals not a society condemned to death? (1988: 302)

In *The Poetics and Politics of Transgression* (1986), Peter Stallybrass and Allon White present a riveting discussion of the repression and displacement of carnival with the rise of bourgeois society. They argue that despite being suppressed culturally and confined spatially, 'carnival did not simply disappear' (1986: 178). Through processes of fragmentation, marginalization, sublimation and repression, carnival has been displaced and transformed, erupting in myriad forms in modern societies. Elements of the carnivalesque can be found everywhere in the 'aesthetics of modernism', in Freud's studies of hysteria, in art, literature, theatre and popular culture (ibid.: 177). Stallybrass and White conclude:

> The bourgeoisie [. . .] is perpetually rediscovering the carnivalesque as a radical source of transcendence. Indeed that act of rediscovery itself, in which the middle classes excitedly discover their own pleasures and desires under the sign of the Other, in the realm of the Other, is constitutive of the very formation of middleclass identity. [. . .] As we have seen, the carnivalesque was marked out as an

> intensely powerful semiotic realm precisely because bourgeois culture constructed its self-identity by rejecting it. The 'poetics' of transgression reveals the disgust, fear and desire which inform the dramatic self-representation of that culture through the 'scene of its low Other' (ibid.: 201–2).

The Arizona Renaissance Festival is an example of the carnivalesque in contemporary society, restrained and sanitized, dampened by conventions of acceptable public behaviour. Within these bounds, it is a place where the 'out of place' (Cresswell 1996; Goldstein 2003) is playfully encouraged. A central part of the festival experience for enthusiasts is the opportunity to dress in period 'garb' and play 'make believe'. Festival cast members adopt a persona, conferring upon themselves an appropriate name, title, lifespan and, of course, costume. Renaissance festivals have bred a subculture in the US, complete with a lexicon, a bimonthly magazine *Renaissance* and faire-centred websites and discussion boards. A sizable portion of the entertainers and cast members of the Arizona Festival are 'rennies'—people who enjoy the 'unorthodox' lifestyle of travelling faire-to-faire throughout the year. In addition, craftspeople practising the medieval system of apprenticeship follow faires, peddling their wares. This transitiveness draws a notable New Age element to the Ren Fest, described humorously by one faire performer as 'people who are never completely out of costume' (Zilch the Storyteller, personal interview, 2007).

Some faire patrons who are neither rennies nor official cast members come to the festival dressed in period attire. These folk, termed 'playtrons' in Ren Fest parlance, point to the festival as a welcoming stage for acting out fantasies, whether playing a lady, lord, knight, jester, peasant, pirate, bar wench or dungeon master. Flocks of faire attendees dressed in everyday street clothes are referred to as 'mundanes' in Ren Fest lexicon. It can be difficult to distinguish between playtrons and official cast members—part of the participatory charm of Ren Fest—as cast members and playtrons wander about the Festival grounds delivering greetings, posing for pictures, offering quips and barbs, singing and revelling and acting out impromptu comic performances (See Figure 4.5.).

FIGURE 4.5. **Mundane approaches two Rennies and a Playtron, Arizona Renaissance Festival, 2008.**
Photograph courtesy of the authors.

One may discern in contemporary Renaissance festivals tamed remnants of social inversion and transgression that characterized carnivals of old (Stallybrass and White 1986; Shields 1991). Coming to such judgement about commodified and sanitized spectacles such as Ren Fest may itself be farcical and therefore—ironically—in keeping with the carnival spirit. To jest, treatment of contemporary festival as farcical parody of carnival smacks of paltry pleasures in postmodern decoding. Surely, you (dear reader) know the (knowing) wink—'the joy and the bursting forth of consumption, and the mocking of it at the same time' (Nancy 1987: 727).

Movement III: The Catapult

Apart from any discernment or deconstruction we (observing participants) may muster, our viscera certainly registered *their* 'story' of Ren Fest, which is *the* story of festival: *laughter*. Through an eruption of laughter, we are catapulted, flung through the air like rag dolls, landing in a heap. THUD. Returning to our senses (where did we go?), what can we make of laughter—this elusive, jumbled emote? Or more to the point, what does *it* make of us? We find ourselves launched into a terrain of bewildering affective contours that sculpt being, belonging and becomings.

To begin, we are intrigued by Bakhtin's argument that we moderns can scarcely grasp the communal quality of laughter (1984). Carnival laughter in premodern times, writes Bakhtin, was the laughter of all the people, not individual reactions to antics and comic events. Laughter was simultaneously triumphant and mocking, a temporary suspension of hierarchic distinctions, norms and prohibitions. In modern times, the bourgeois ego reigns, such that parody and satire are now directed at individuals, carrying an air of superiority whereby the satirist places him or herself above the 'object' of mockery (Bakhtin 1984; Stallybrass and White 1986). Language and gesticulations in reference to the body and bodily life, for example, are now individualized and negative rather than inhabiting the bawdy, grotesque realism of the premodern in which laughter is linked with the lower bodily stratum of regeneration and renewal: earth, birth, growth and flesh (Bakhtin 1984).

Bakhtin paints an idyllic portrait of premodern carnival laughter and seemingly downplays the potency and communal qualities of laughter in modern times, themes that we examine below. We must say at the outset that in championing laughter, Bakhtin is exceptional. The history of Western philosophy and thought is marked by a diminution, if not repression and dismissal, of laughter. On this score, Samuel Weber cites Socrates' mistrust of laughter in

FIGURE 4.6. **Jester engaging in playful antics, Arizona Renaissance Festival, 2008.**
Photograph courtesy of the authors.

Book III of Plato's *Republic*. Laughter is frowned upon as frivolous. Lacking in high-minded seriousness, 'laughter, like tears, is a "waste of wisdom", an emission' (1987: 693). Beyond frivolity and wasted emission, laughter is problematic because it is a rupture and, hence, potentially uncontrollable and threatening to the state, as expressed by Socrates: 'Again, [our young men] must not be prone to laughter [*philogelos*]. For ordinarily when one abandons himself to violent laughter his condition provokes a violent reaction' (ibid.: 692). For Socrates, laughter is not a reasoned act of the will; it is self-abandonment that might overpower and be directed against others (ibid.: 693). Such unease speaks to suspicions of laughter as mischievous or disruptive of rules and decorum—a quality identified in the accusatory question: What are you laughing *at*? Mischievous laughter is often exploited to great effect, including by the aptly named Ren Fest entertainer Danny Lord of Mischief. Beyond 'harmless' entertainment (can entertainment be harmless?), there are apprehensions about laughter as contagious dis-ease, swirling energies that may coalesce, unpredictably, and spiral out of control.

That laughter eludes studied reflection and reason is brought to the fore in comments made by Georges Bataille about the philosopher Henri Bergson, who published *Le Rire* (*Laughter*) in 1900. Abhorrent to Bataille are normative dimensions implicit in Bergson's 'functional' view of laughter as a societal corrective aimed to rectify maladapted individuals—laughter in the service of reinforcing bourgeois life (Zwart 1996: 60). Borch-Jacobsen draws on Bataille's cutting remarks about Bergson in relaying that one cannot 'philosophize' laughter:

> This prudent little man [Bergson], this *philosopher*—this little man who spoke of the 'little problem,' the 'little mystery' of laughter. How would he have seen in it the final enigma of being? A prudent man (as have been all philosophers since Aristotle), he persisted in making of it the *object* of his reflection, instead of letting himself be overcome by laughter. [. . .] Too wise, the philosopher does not laugh, not even—and especially not—when he theorizes about laughter, and thus he cannot sense all of its gravity, all of its tragedy. For in this way he separates himself from laughter (represents it, as a spectacle), never undergoing it after the fashion of this 'experience' which Bataille termed 'interior'—interior because non-objective, and non-objective because [. . .] communicative (1987: 741–2).

Here we arrive at the confluence of two coursing streams, the communicative quality of laughter and its nonrepresentational register. Laughter is spontaneous, bursting forth such that we come to find ourselves already engulfed in laughter. Bataille expresses it thus: 'Seeing laughter, hearing laughter, I *participate from within* the emotion of the [other] one who laughs. It is this emotion experienced from within which, communicating itself to me, laughs within me' (quoted in ibid.: 742; emphasis original). In a similar vein, Jean-Luc Nancy writes of laughter as coming and presence, a decidedly anti-representational posture: 'Laughter bursts out without presenting or representing its reasons or its meaning. [. . .] Laughter comes, and it is laughing (joy, pleasure, and mockery, all at the same time) about this very coming, which comes out of nowhere and does not go anywhere. Laughter is presence enjoying "being" (or coming as) presence' (1987: 730).

The issue of representation is, again, central in a Freudian view. Laughter, according to Freud, is the free discharge of psychic energy relating to *cathexis,* the attachment of psychic energy to one or more representations—attachment that entails an inhibitory force necessary in stabilizing and anchoring meaning (Weber 1987). Laughter, then, is the temporary lifting of this inhibitory force, a suspension of *cathexis* itself (representation), *experienced* as an explosive movement that overwhelms. This is why true laughter cannot be sustained. No sooner do we come to realize that we are laughing than it passes (ibid.). We come to our senses; the weight of reality returns. François Roustang tells us that laughter is a detachment, if only briefly, from the 'very substance of humanity, from suffering: not from suffering as a fleeting feeling, but from the suffering which comes with the weight of destiny' (1987: 710). In lyrical prose, he elaborates laughter as rupture: 'It is this suffering, thicker than night, denser than iron, deafer than stone, truer than necessity, which laughter must rupture. Laughter is the smallest conceivable unit of detachment, of difference, of removal; it is the quantum unit of distance' (ibid.: 711).

Rupture is taken to the limits of being by Bataille, the 'impossible' thinker who ascends the vertiginous summit and, in a burst of trembling laughter, collapses the pyramid, falling into the abyss of nothingness. Borch-Jacobsen's essay on Bataille's ascent and tumble, 'The Laughter of Being' (1987), is a paroxysm that shakes the reader. Perhaps more than any other writer, Bataille expresses the ecstatic and communicative qualities of laughter. Called the 'emotive intellectual' (Besnier 1995), Bataille writes with a passion that is 'furiously Nietzschean' (Lotringer 1992). He believed that modern subjectivity and rationality cover over, and mask, deep experiences of existence, 'vitalist' spiritual and sexual energies (Botting and Wilson 1997, 1998). That he draws on laughter as 'excess' is in keeping with his conviction that the overabundance of life cannot be explained or accounted for in systems of representation and meaning (Rose 2002; Bataille 1985). In Bataille's atheology, the sovereign and the sacred do not reside in God; rather, 'man is divine in the experience of his limits' (Borch-Jacobsen 1987: 751). What is divine is the fall of man, not exalted superiority. When we see someone stumble, when we witness foibles, we laugh not only *at* the other, but more profoundly *with* the other. We laugh at ourselves and, in so doing, move beyond ourselves, a suspended moment 'in which we are at once ourselves and the other' (ibid.: 758). It is this (re)uniting experience that charges Nietzsche's startling aphorism cited by Bataille: 'To see tragic figures founder and to be able to laugh at the spectacle, despite the profound understanding, the emotion and the sympathy that one feels, that is divine' (quoted in ibid.: 751).

At Ren Fest, crowds cheer and cajole combatant knights in the spectacle, 'A Joust to the Death'; at a wake, mourners commemorate the beloved who has fallen and comfort the living through a mixture of tears and laughter. It is in the finitude of being, of death, that laughter registers the ultimate limit. Borch-Jacobsen's essay on Bataille and laughter crescendos in a breathtaking finale:

> Being (that is to say death) is given to us, and it is given to us in the laughter that seizes us before the fall or the death of our fellow-man. [. . .] We do not laugh, in other words, because we are not dead. We laugh, very much to the contrary, because we are dead, because we are, laughing, ourselves the dead man—namely no one who constitutes an *ipse*, a 'oneself'. Admittedly, it is the other who falls, who dies, and not ourselves. But this other, precisely, does not die *himself*, of his *own* death, and that is what enraptures us, beyond all measure and all limit. Contaminated by what he is not, communicating ecstatically with the 'beyond of all beings', the dead man communicates to us communication, 'being in relation' [. . .]. Foundering beyond himself, the dead man drags us with him into a vertigo where we *are* finally—*other*: being and at the same time not being, laughing and at the same time being dead, laughing at already being dead. Laughing at being. [. . .] Being was thus NOWHERE. It was neither in me nor in the other. It was—'was', for already it is no more—in our brief passage one into the other (ibid.: 759).

In the 'fusion of laughter,' writes Bataille, 'life slips from one into the other, in a magical sensation of subversion' (quoted in ibid.: 759). This is a stirring expression of relational being qua becoming, calling to mind Jean-Luc Nancy's *Being Singular Plural*: 'Being cannot be anything but being-with-another, circulating in the *with* and as the *with* of this singularly plural coexistence' (2000: 3).

Coda: Moments of Possibility

The Bataille-induced whirling of our heads subsides, and we return to (re)consider festival laughter. For a long time now, something has disturbed us, an ill-defined unease. Even as we move merrily with the festive throng, are we not *all* onlookers, members of the lonely crowd? Might this be the source of unease? Stallybrass and White write:

> There is no more easily recognizable scene of bourgeois pathos than the lonely crowd in which individual identity is achieved *over against* all the others, through the sad realization of not-belonging. That moment, in which the subject is made the outsider to the crowd, an onlooker, compensating for exclusion through the deployment of the discriminating gaze, is at the very heart of bourgeois sensibility (1986: 187).

In *The Society of the Spectacle* (1967), Guy Debord asserts: 'The reigning economic system [. . .] strives to reinforce the isolation of "the lonely crowd"' (1994[1967]: 22), and that 'society eliminates geographical distance only to reap distance internally in the form of spectacular separation' (ibid.: 120). In this vein, Ren Fest is a spectacle that David Harvey would call a 'degenerate utopia', for like Disneyland it 'perpetuates the fetish of commodity culture', offering 'no critique of the existing state of affairs on the outside' (2000: 167, citing Marin 1984). Surely, the ripple of unease we sense in laughter at Ren Fest is an expression of bourgeois sensibilities: alienation and spectacular separation in commodity culture.

Yet, there is some *thing* more at play in the throes of laughter: in an exhilarating rush, the wild laughter of Bataille smashes bourgeois sensibilities, the authority of high-minded seriousness; it moves beyond oppositional binaries and eclipses the sort of societal critiques offered by Debord and Harvey. Bataille's wild laughter—exuberant, laced with ambivalence, saturated with absurdity and tragedy—communicates that, paradoxically, we beings called human are united in 'senseless' detachment, and sovereign in the wilful affirmation of nothing. This is the disturbance that reverberates in laughter. Laughter is disorienting, calling to mind Brian Massumi's autonomy of affect; excess that escapes capture in systems of representation and meaning (2002). Moments when we are 'beside ourselves' are moments of the unexpected, moments of vitality, moments of difference, moments of possibility.

We see affinity between our work accentuating ecstatic and communicative qualities in laughter, inspired by Bataille and Borch-Jacobsen, and Jill Dolan's utopian moments in theatrical performance. Dolan painstakingly distances her utopian performatives from utopia as a vision entailing a fixed image, structure or spatial form, because the latter, ultimately, proves rigidifying and stultifying (Dolan 2005; Harvey 2000; Marin 1984). Dolan refers to fleeting moments of affect and emotion that arise spontaneously in performance, uniting performers and audience in communitas, lifting us to another place, offering 'intimations of a better world' (2005: 2). She writes eloquently about the fragility of utopian moments in performance, arguing that the 'intensity of *feeling* is politics enough'; that effectiveness of utopian performatives cannot be gauged like a 'piece of legislation, or a demonstration, or a political campaign' (ibid.: 20). It is her belief that 'the experience of performance, and the intellectual, spiritual, and affective traces it leaves behind, can provide new frames of reference for how we see a better future extending out from our more ordinary lives' (ibid.). 'The politics lie,' says Dolan, 'in the desire to feel the potential elsewhere' (ibid.).

Can we say the same of festival laughter? Are there communal registers and sensibilities in festival laughter that linger beyond the commodity spectacle of the fairgrounds? What of laughter within the contours of everyday life? Affect and emotional geographies are receiving much attention (e.g. Anderson and Smith 2001; McCormack 2003, 2010; Thrift 2004, 2008; Anderson 2009; Anderson and Harrison 2010; Pile 2010; Woodward and Lea 2010), yet laughter has received scant treatment within this rich and expanding literature.[2] Laughter is ripe for exploring emotional topographies—laughter reverberating through the nooks and crannies of daily living, registering tonalities of joy, delight, surprise, anxiety, fear, frustration, suffering, mockery, madness, helplessness and hope.

Notes

1 This quotation is from an unpublished essay by Jennifer Kitson, a doctoral student in the School of Geographical Sciences and Urban Planning at Arizona State University. Thanks to Jennifer for permission to quote.

2 An exception is Hannah Macpherson's article (2008) on the workings of humour and laughter among walkers who are visually impaired.

Works Cited

ANDERSON, Ben. 2009. 'Affective Atmospheres'. *Emotion, Space and Society* 2: 77–81.

——, and Paul Harrison (eds). 2010. *Taking-Place: Non-representational Theories and Geography*. Surrey: Ashgate.

ANDERSON, Kay, and Susan Smith. 2001. 'Editorial: Emotional Geographies'. *Transactions of the Institute of British Geographers* 26(1): 7–10.

ARIZONA RENAISSANCE FESTIVAL. 2011. Official website. Available at: www.royalfaires.com/arizona (last accessed on 11 February 2011).

BAKHTIN, Mikhail. 1984. *Rabelais and His World* (Hélène Iswolsky trans.). Bloomington: Indiana University Press.

BATAILLE, Georges. 1985. *Visions of Excess: Selected Writings, 1927–1939* (Allan Stoekl trans.). Minneapolis: University of Minnesota Press.

——. 1992. *On Nietzsche* (Bruce Boone trans.). New York: Paragon House.

BAUDRILLARD, Jean. 1981. *For a Critique of the Political Economy of the Sign* (Charles Levin trans.). St. Louis, MO: Telos.

——. 1994. *Simulacra and Simulation* (S. Faria Glaser trans.). Ann Arbor: University of Michigan Press.

BERGSON, Henri. 1981. *Le Rire: Essai sur la Signification du Comique*. Paris: Presses Universitaires de France.

BESNIER, Jean-Michel. 1995. 'Bataille: The Emotive Intellectual' in Carolyn Bailey Gill (ed.), *Bataille: Writing the Sacred*. London: Routledge, pp. 13–26.

BOORSTIN, Daniel. 1992. *The Creators: A History of Heroes and the Imagination*. New York: Random House.

BORCH-JACOBSEN, Mikkel. 1987. 'The Laughter of Being'. *Modern Language Notes* 102(4): 737–60.

BOTTING, Fred, and Scott Wilson (eds). 1997. *The Bataille Reader*. Oxford: Blackwell.

——. 1998. *Bataille: A Critical Reader*. Oxford: Blackwell.

BRUNS, John. 2000. 'Laughter in the Aisles: Affect and Power in Contemporary Theorietical and Cultural Discourse'. *Studies in American Humor* 3(7): 5–23.

CAILLOIS, Roger. 1961. *Man, Play and Game* (Meyer Barash trans.). New York: Free Press of Glencoe.

——. 1988[1940]. 'Festival' in Denis Hollier (ed.), *The College of Sociology, 1937–1939* (Betsy Wing trans.). Minneapolis: University of Minnesota Press.

CRESSWELL, Tim. 1996. *In Place/Out of Place: Geography, Ideology, and Transgression*. Minneapolis: University of Minnesota Press.

DAVIS, M. 1998. 'Renaissance Festival Is a Blast from the Past'. *Arizona Republic*, 25 February, Central Phoenix Community Section, p. 2.

DEBORD, Guy. 1994[1967]. *The Society of the Spectacle* (Donald Nicholson-Smith trans.). New York: Zone Books.

DELEUZE, Gilles, and Félix Guattari. 1983. *Anti-Oedipus: Capitalism and Schizophrenia* (Robert Hurley, Mark Seem and Helen R. Lane trans). Minneapolis: University of Minnesota Press.

DOLAN, Jill. 2005. *Utopia in Performance: Finding Hope at the Theater*. Ann Arbor: University of Michigan Press.

ECO, Umberto. 1986. *Travels in Hyperreality*. San Diego: Harcourt Brace Jovanovich.

GILL, Caroline Bailey (ed.). 1995. *Bataille: Writing the Sacred*. London: Routledge.

GOLDSTEIN, Donna M. 2003. *Laughter Out of Place: Race, Class Violence, and Sexuality in a Rio Shantytown*. Berkeley: University of California Press.

GOSS, Jon. 1999. 'Once-Upon-a-Time in the Commodity World: An Unofficial Guide to Mall of America'. *Annals of the Association of American Geographers* 89(1): 45–75.

GRENDLER, Paul F. 2006. *The European Renaissance in American Life*. Westport, CT: Praeger.

HARVEY, David. 2000. *Spaces of Hope*. Berkeley: University of California Press.

HEART OF THE FOREST RENAISSANCE FAIRES. 2007. 'Origins of the Faire'. Available at: http://goo.gl/sD29Do (last accessed 13 March 2007).

HOLLIER, Denis. 1989. *Against Architecture: The Writings of Georges Bataille*. Cambridge, MA: MIT Press.

JACKSON, Peter. 1989. *Maps of Meaning: An Introduction to Cultural Geography*. London: Unwin Hyman.

KITSON, Jennifer. 2007. 'Reconciling the Scene and Seen in Phoenix'. Unpublished essay.

KLUGMAN, Karen, Jane Kuenz, Shelton Waldrep and Susan Willis. 1995. *Inside the Mouse: Work and Play at Disney World*. Durham, NC: Duke University Press.

LACAN, Jacques. 1977. *Écrits: A Selection* (Alan Sheridan trans.). New York: W. W. Norton.

LORD MAYOR, THE. 2007. Interview with authors. Arizona Renaissance Festival, 19 March.

LOTRINGER, Sylvère. 1992. 'Furiously Nietzschean', introduction to Georges Bataille, *On Nietzsche*. New York: Paragon House., pp. *vii–xvi*.

LOWENTHAL, David. 1975. 'Past Time, Present Place: Landscape and Memory'. *Geographical Review* 65(1): 1–36.

MACPHERSON, Hannah. 2008. '"I Don't Know Why They Call It the Lake District!": The Workings of Humour and Laughter in Research with Members of Visually Impaired Walking Groups'. *Environment and Planning D: Society and Space* 26: 1080–95.

MARIN, Louis. 1984. *Utopics: Spatial Play* (Robert A. Vollrath trans.). Atlantic Highlands, NJ: Humanities Press.

MASSUMI, Brian. 2002. *Parables for the Virtual: Movement, Affect, Sensation*. Durham, NC: Duke University Press.

MCCORMACK, Derek P. 2003. 'An Event of Geographical Ethics in Spaces of Affect'. *Transactions of the Institute of British Geographers* 28(4): 488–507.

——. 2010. 'Remotely Sensing Affective Afterlives: The Spectral Geographies of Material Remains'. *Annals of the Association of American Geographers* 100(3): 640–54.

MID-AMERICA FESTIVALS CORPORATION. 2007. 'The Renaissance Festival'. Available at: www.renaissancefest.com (last accessed 20 March 2007).

MYERS, Patricia. 1996. 'Festival Bids All Welcome: Men, Maidens, Seek Merriment'. *Arizona Republic*, 9 February, Central Phoenix Community Section, p. 5.

NANCY, Jean-Luc. 1987. 'Wild Laughter in the Throat of Death'. *Modern Language* Notes 102(4): 719–36.

——. 2000. *Being Singular Plural* (Robert D. Richardson and Anne E. O'Byrne trans). Stanford, CA: Stanford University Press.

NOYS, Benjamin. 2000. *Georges Bataille: A Critical Introduction*. London: Pluto Press.

PILE, Steve. 2010. 'Emotions and Affect in Recent Human Geography'. *Transactions of the Institute of British Geographers* 35(1): 5–20.

RENAISSANCE ENTERTAINMENT CORPORATION. 2007. Official website. Available at: www.renfair.com (last accessed on 20 March 2007).

RINGEL, Faye. 2002. 'Building the Gothic Image in America: Changing Icons, Changing Times'. *Gothic Studies* 4(2): 145–54.

ROSE, Mitch. 2002. 'Landscape and Labyrinths'. *Geoforum* 33(4): 455–67.

ROUSTANG, François. 1987. 'How Do You Make a Paranoiac Laugh?' *Modern Language* Notes 102(4): 707–18.

SHIELDS, Rob. 1991. *Places on the Margin: Alternative Geographies of Modernity*. London: Routledge.

SIEGEL, Jeffrey. 2007. Interview with authors, Arizona Renaissance Festival, 11 March.

STALLYBRASS, Peter, and Allon White. 1986. *The Politics and Poetics of Transgression*. London: Methuen.

——. 1999. 'Bourgeois Hysteria and the Carnivalesque' in Simon During (ed.), *The Cultural Studies Reader*. London: Routledge, pp. 382–9.

STEWART, Susan. 1993. *On Longing: Narratives of the Miniature, the Gigantic, the Souvenir, the Collection*. Durham, NC: Duke University Press.

THRIFT, Nigel. 2004. 'Intensities of Feeling: Towards a Spatial Politics of Affect'. *Geografiska Annaler* 86B: 57–78.

——. 2008. *Non-representational Theory: Space/Politics/Affect*. London: Routledge.

TUAN, Yi-Fu. 1998. *Escapism*. Baltimore, MD: Johns Hopkins University Press.

WEBER, Samuel. 1987. 'Laughing in the Meanwhile'. *Modern Language Notes* 102(4): 691–706.

WOODWARD, Keith, and Jennifer Lea. 2010. 'Geographies of Affect' in Susan J. Smith, Rachel Pain, Sally A. Marston and John Paul Jones III (eds), *The Sage Handbook of Social Geographies*. Oxford: Blackwell, pp. 154–75.

ZILCH THE STORYTELLER. 2007. Interview with authors. Arizona Renaissance Festival, 19 March.

ZWART, Hub. 1996. *Ethical Consensus and the Truth of Laughter*. Kampen, Netherlands: Kok Pharos.

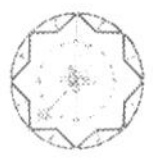

Chapter 5

THE WENCHES OF THE PHILADELPHIA MUMMERS PARADE

A Performance Genealogy

Christian DuComb

In December 1963, under pressure from civil rights activists, the city of Philadelphia banned blackface make-up from the Mummers Parade, an annual New Year's Day celebration with roots dating to the nineteenth century. To protest the ban, a group of white mummers staged a sit-in that briefly halted the 1964 parade. As mummers historian Charles E. Welch recalls it:

> Members of the H. Philip Hammond Comic Club sat down in the middle of the street, some shouting, 'Negroes sat down in City Hall, we'll sit down here.' A new chant started: 'One, two, three, four, we hate Cecil Moore' (local leader of the NAACP). The police quickly moved in and forced the mummers to rise. The entire incident lasted about twenty minutes, after which the paraders again started up the Street (1991: 154).

The appropriation of the sit-in, a tactic of the civil rights movement, to defend the practice of racial impersonation is among the more ironic examples of the interracial history of the Mummers Parade. The performance genealogy of the mummers wench, one of the most enduringly popular figures in the parade, captures much of this interracial history. Philadelphia's African American brass-band tradition, the nineteenth-century minstrel show, and the cakewalk—an antebellum slave dance popularized in the cities of the Atlantic rim at the turn of the twentieth century—all remain audible and visible in the performance practices of the contemporary mummers wench.[1]

Frank Dougherty and Ron Goldwyn, who spent decades reporting on the Mummers Parade for the *Philadelphia Daily News*, describe the mummer wench as 'the most traditional, outrageous, and politically incorrect of all Mummers. Basically, it's a guy in a dress. The hairier the legs, the longer the braids, the colder the beer, the better' (1994: M8). The persistence of racial and gender impersonation among the wenches of the Philadelphia Mummers Parade suggests a genealogical connection between the mummers wench and the 'wench act' of the early 1840s: a burlesque form of gender impersonation performed onstage by white men in blackface, often in the context of the antebellum minstrel show. A staple of mid-nineteenth-century popular culture, the minstrel show of the 1840s and 50s featured a group of musicians arranged in a semicircle, with an interlocutor in the middle and a blackface comedian on each end. The banter between the pompous interlocutor (who did not wear blackface) and the two 'endmen' loosely structured a full evening of performances, which included song-and-dance numbers, parodic stump speeches, novelty acts and short skits, usually set on southern plantations. Although many mid-century minstrel troupes incorporated blackface gender impersonation into their routines, the wench act first became popular in 1842, before the conventional format of the antebellum minstrel show had come into its own. Thus, the wench act stands at a threshold between the short blackface scenes and sketches of early-nineteenth-century popular theatre and the emergence of the minstrel show as a full-fledged theatrical genre.

The genealogy of the mummers wench encompasses not only the wench act but also two other, equally complex performance traditions: the cakewalk, a dance absorbed into blackface minstrelsy, African American theatre, and the 'strut' of the mummers wench; and Philadelphia's African American brass bands, which have played music for white men on parade since the early nineteenth century. These three genealogical strands came together in the performances of the early-twentieth-century mummers wench and then frayed when confronted with the 1960s civil rights campaign to rid the Mummers Parade of blackface make-up—a campaign that brought important changes, though hardly an end, to wench performances of racial and gender impersonation.

Until 1964, wenches in the Mummers Parade usually marched in blackface, recalling the frequent concurrence of blackface make-up and male-to-female transvestism in rowdy Christmas celebrations in nineteenth-century Philadelphia. As Susan G. Davis has shown, disorderly bands of young, working-class white men roamed the streets of the city on Christmas Eve from the 1830s to the 1880s, intimidating 'respectable Philadelphians' and mocking women, black people and ethnic minorities (1982: 185). The formation of a central police force in 1854 gradually imposed 'organized crowd control' on holiday revellers and 'shift[ed] the theatre of disorder from holy Christmas Eve to secular New Year's Eve and eventually to New Year's Day' (ibid.: 196). In 1901, the city consolidated its jurisdiction over holiday street festivities by sponsoring the first annual Mummers Parade, a publicly sanctioned event terminating at City Hall after a procession up Broad Street, the major thoroughfare connecting the working-class neighbourhoods of South Philadelphia to the city centre. One newspaper reported that 'three thousand men and boys in outlandish garb frolicked, cavorted, grimaced, and whooped' in the first Mummers Parade 'while the Mayor and members of Councils, Judges, and other officials, State and municipal, looked on'. Clearly, 'the city had put its official seal upon mummery', and city government has attempted to regulate the parade ever since (quoted in Douglas 1937: 8).

Although both participation and attendance at the Mummers Parade have declined in recent years, roughly 10,000 marchers and 50,000 to 100,000 spectators still crowd the 2.5-mile parade route each New Year's Day, and hundreds of thousands of viewers in metropolitan Philadelphia watch the parade on local television. Most marchers participate in the parade through licensed mummers clubs, which compete in one of four categories: the comic division, which emphasizes satire and clowning; the string band division, which features live music by large ensembles of banjoes and brass; the fancy division, which prizes elaborate costume design; or the fancy brigade division, which focuses on Broadway-style staging and choreography.[2] Most mummers clubs are subdivided into smaller groups, and each group's performance is professionally judged, contributing to the overall score of its parent club. Until the financial crisis of 2008, the city of Philadelphia offered over $300,000 in cash prizes to be divided among all but the lowest-scoring groups in the parade. According to Goldwyn, wenches participated in the Mummers Parade for much of the twentieth century through a tense but mutually beneficial arrangement with the comic clubs:

> For decades and decades, people [who performed as wenches] would do it on their own. They bought badges from comic clubs, who would put them up for sale. A lot of the comic club officials didn't like wenches; they felt the wenches gave them a bad name. But [some officials] would sell or hand out badges [. . .] so that the wenches could march (Goldwyn 2010).

By the 1990s, the wenches had organized a few large brigades of their own, which now compete in the Mummers Parade independent of the comic clubs.[3]

Since the 1964 sit-in on Broad Street, both the comic clubs and the wench brigades have occasionally challenged the city's authority over the Mummers Parade—most notably in 1995, when the 700 wenches of the James 'Froggy' Carr brigade sat down in the middle of the parade route to protest the arrest of their captain and the confiscation of their beer. More often, however, the comics and wenches wait until their after-hours party on Second Street (or 'Two Street') to flout city-imposed rules. In 1964, some mummers donned blackface make-up on Two Street after the official parade had ended, an act of defiance foreshadowed by a large poster of a blackface minstrel displayed on Broad Street earlier in the day. The caption: 'Gone Yes, Forgotten Never' (Welch 1991: 154)—a testament to the indelible memory of blackface performance that continues to haunt the Philadelphia Mummers Parade.

'Lucy Long' and *Tom and Jerry*

> Given that North American blackface musical performance goes back at least to 1815, probably in Albany first, why is the minstrel show said to begin in 1843 in New York City? Given that the minstrel show has seeped well beyond its masked variants into vaudeville, thence into sitcoms; into jazz and rhythm 'n' blues quartets, thence into rock 'n' roll and hip hop dance; into the musical and the novel, thence into radio and film; into the Grand Old Opry, thence into every roadhouse and the cab of every longhaul truck beyond the Appalachians—why, then, is the minstrel show said to be over? (Lhamon 1998: 56)

On 15 June 1842, six months before the 'first' minstrel show at the Chatham Theatre in New York City, five blackface performers appeared in an *entr'acte* entertainment at Philadelphia's Walnut Street Theatre. Billed as a performance of 'Negro Oddities, by Five of the Best Niggers in the World', the programme featured 'Jim

Sanford, Master Diamond, Ole Bull Myers, Pickanniny Coleman, and Master Chestnut, in a grand trial dance: "Lucy Long" by Jim Sanford; "Piney Woods Jig," by Master Diamond' (in Dumont 1914: ii). This performance lacked the full-evening format that probably originated with the Virginia Minstrels at the Chatham Theatre in January or February 1843, but already in the summer of 1842 it signalled a trend towards larger blackface troupes performing multipart programs—a structural transformation in North American blackface performance that facilitated the emergence of the minstrel show.[4]

This structural transformation coincided with the rise of wench songs like 'Lucy Long', which Robert B. Winans has called 'unquestionably *the* most popular song of the first minstrel decade' (1984: 150). According to S. Foster Damon, 'Lucy Long' circulated in numerous versions copyrighted 1842 or 1843, 'all popular and many of them claiming to be the original' (1936: n.p.). Jim Sanford and Ole Bull Myers—who later became principals in the Virginia Serenaders, Philadelphia's most popular early minstrel troupe—both appeared at the Walnut Street Theatre on 15 June 1842, which suggests that the 'Negro Oddities' act probably featured the Virginia Serenaders' version of 'Lucy Long':

Oh, I jist come out afore you,
To sing a little song,
I plays it on de banjo,
And dey calls it Lucy Long.
Oh, take your time Miss Lucy,
Take your time Miss Lucy Long.

Miss Lucy she is handsome,
Miss Lucy she is tall,
And de way she spreads her ancles,
Is death to de niggers all.
Oh, take your, &c.

Oh, Miss Lucy's teeth is grinning,
Just like an ear ob corn,
And her eyes dey look so winning,
I wish I ne'er was born.
Oh, take your, &c.

[. . .]

If I had a scolding wife,
I'd lick her sure as I'm born;
I'd take her down to New Orleans,
And trade her off for corn.
Oh, take your time, &c.
(Virginia Serenaders 1843: 30–1)

FIGURE 5.1. **'The Dancing Lucy Long'.**
White's New Illustrated Melodeon Song Book, 1848. Courtesy of Brown University Library.

In *Love and Theft*, his influential study of blackface minstrelsy, Eric Lott argues that 'the "wench" [. . .] usually did not sing the songs she starred in' (1993: 160). Rather, she became the 'theatrical object of the song, exhibiting [her]self in time with the grotesque descriptions' in the lyrics, sung by an onstage accompanist while the wench performer danced (ibid.). Lott reads the 'popular misogyny' of antebellum wench songs like 'Lucy Long' against a background of changing gender roles among the urban working class in the northern US (ibid.). As Christine Stansell has shown, 'hard times and the irregularity of employment made many husbands poor providers and weakened their control of their families, [while] at the same time, female wage work, however lowly, provided many women some means of support apart from men' (1987: 81). Lott relates this theatre of gender relations outside the playhouse to what he calls the 'social unconscious' of the wench act, which converted the gender anxiety of its white, working-class, male audience into a source of 'comic pleasure' (1993: 161). This psychoanalytic interpretation ultimately locates the blatant sexism of the wench act within the larger symbolic economy of 'white male desire for black men', which Lott believes is 'everywhere to be found' in the minstrel show (ibid.: 163). For the spectator, this volatile combination of gender anxiety and interracial desire led to an 'unsteady oscillation in "wench" acts between a recoil from women into cross-dressing misogyny and a doubling-back from the homoeroticism that this inevitably also suggested, with the misogyny serving as a convenient cover story for or defense against the homoerotic desires' (ibid.: 164). Bruce McConachie disputes this conclusion, arguing that it is 'very difficult to believe that actor-dancers playing minstrel wenches would try to induce erotic desire in their spectators' (2006: 64).[5] McConachie's 'cognitive simulation' of wench-act spectatorship—putting himself 'in the shoes of an antebellum spectator at a minstrel show in order to imagine what would interest me if I were seeking to enjoy a wench act' (ibid.: 63)—allows him to recover the humour of these performances with remarkable specificity.

In the wench act, McConachie argues, 'the fun occurred in the contrast between the pose of frail femininity adopted by the wench and the reality of male muscle underneath' (ibid.: 65)—a contrast suggested in the Virginia Serenaders' version of 'Lucy Long'. In verse two, for example, the words 'handsome' and 'tall' hint at Miss Lucy's masculinity, a subtlety punctured when she 'spreads her ancles' and brings 'death to niggers all'—presumably by revealing masculine undergarments beneath her frilly dress. The analogy of Miss Lucy's teeth to an ear of corn in verse three lends her a grotesque aspect, and the last verse recycles this corn imagery when a 'scolding wife'—perhaps Miss Lucy, perhaps another woman—is traded off for corn. The final lines of the song laminate a misogynistic fantasy of conjugal control—connected, no doubt, to the anxieties of working-class, male audiences about changing gender roles in society at large—to the sale of flesh. And given that the antebellum wench dancer usually impersonated a black woman, trading 'her' off for corn cruelly exploits the flesh trades of slavery and prostitution as fodder for the audience's fun.

Later minstrel-show female impersonators such as Frances Leon departed from the burlesque style of the wench act, abandoning blackface make-up and achieving verisimilitude in their performances of gendered drag. 'Some of the men who undertake this business are marvelously well-fitted by nature for it,' wrote Olive Logan in 1879, 'having well-defined soprano voices, plump shoulders, beardless faces, and tiny hands and feet. Many dress most elegantly as women' (1879: 698). However, Logan also noted that the wench, or 'funny old gal', remained a part of the post-bellum minstrel show, appearing in the 'walk-around' finale: 'Clad in some tawdry old gown of loud, crude colors, whose shortness and scantness display long frilled "panties" and No. 13 valise shoes [. . .] the funny old gal is very often a gymnast of no mean amount of muscle, as her saltatory exercises in the break-down prove' (ibid.). These 'saltatory exercises' included the cakewalk, appropriated into the minstrel-show walk-around in the late nineteenth century. Dance historian Lynne Fauley Emery describes the cakewalk as 'originally a kind of shuffling movement, which evolved into a smooth, walking step with the body help erect [. . . Later, a] backward sway was added, and as the dance became more of a satire on the dances of the white plantation owners, the movement became a prancing strut' (1988: 208).

I view the cakewalk as the template for the signature 'strut' of the mummers wench: a high, walking step with a backward sway, danced by the contemporary wench with his knees bent, one hand on his waist or the hem of his dress, and the other hand gleefully swinging a parasol through the air. Dougherty and Goldwyn note that 'the high-stepping gyrations of the [wench's] strut are ideal for revealing the matching satin bloomers that each wench wears beneath his skirts' (1994: M8). According to dress historian Gayle V. Fischer, the term 'bloomers' first appeared in newspaper satires of the thin, loose-fitting trousers popular among advocates of women's dress reform in the early 1850s. Named for women's rights activist Amelia Jenks Bloomer, the 'bloomer costume' featured pantaloons elasticized at the ankles and worn under a knee-length skirt. Although 'dress reformers [. . .] stressed that there was nothing inherently male about trousers', critics—including some feminists—condemned bloomers as 'a travesty of male attire' (Fischer 2001: 83). The mummers wench strutting in feminine dress while displaying hairy legs and satin bloomers recalls the blackface wench act of the pre-bloomer era, which contrasted women's costumes with masculine undergarments and 'saltatory' choreography. Although Dale Cockrell suggests that the lyrics to early versions of 'Lucy Long' contained 'no hint of anything fraught with political or social concerns' (1997: 147), later iterations of the blackface wench act often used the satire of women's dress reform to explicitly political ends. One New Orleans minstrel show programme, for example, advertises Lucy Long appearing 'à la bloomer', suggesting the appropriation of the bloomer costume into minstrelsy's persistent assault on women's rights (New Orleans Minstrel Show Program n.d.).

As Marjorie Garber has shown, the minstrel show frequently lampooned 'bloomers in particular, and women's desire to wear pants in general' (1992: 277). When I first began to study the historical relationship between the minstrel show and the Mummers Parade, the retention of bloomers as a costume piece by the mummers wench struck me as an obvious remnant of minstrel-show sexism, amplified by the ongoing exclusion of women from the wench brigades.[6] But on New Year's Day 2010, I saw a street-side performance that challenged my impulse to connect the minstrel wench and the mummers wench. About a mile south of City Hall, an older woman stood watching the parade and enthusiastically waving a large, hand-lettered sign. 'Real Men Wear Bloomers,' it said. The irony staggered me. In the nineteenth-century women's movement, women wore bloomers to assert their right to dress in practical, 'masculine' garb, thereby transgressing gender norms. In the nineteenth-century minstrel show, male wenches wore bloomers to mock women's political aspirations, crossing the gender barrier in order to consolidate it. In the twenty-first century, could it be that bloomers in the Mummers Parade have come to embody masculinity *tout court* rather than a series of inversions in which men imitate women imitating men? Could this be so, even though the mummers wench wears a feminine dress over his bloomers? Is the minstrel-show wench act even a valid historical referent for understanding the contemporary mummers wench?

FIGURE 5.2. **A wench strutting in the 1987 Mummers Parade.**
Photograph by Vicki Valerio. Courtesy of the *Philadelphia Inquirer*.

These questions, from field notes composed after a long day at the Mummers Parade, assume that the past vanishes from a performance as soon as the actors and the audience forget that performance's history. But as Mikhail Bakhtin points out, carnivalesque celebrations like the Mummers Parade have often served as 'a reservoir into which obsolete genres [are] emptied' (1965: 218). Viewed historically, the dance steps and costume pieces of the mummers wench overflow with remnants of the 'obsolete genre' of the nineteenth-century wench act—despite what contemporary wenches and their fans may say. The slogan 'Real Men Wear Bloomers' works to untether the mummers wench from the minstrel wench, and most of the mummers I have interviewed offer ahistorical explanations of the appeal of performing as a wench in today's parade. In the words of Rich Porco, president of the Murray Comic Club, 'Going in the parade in a wench suit is cheap and easy, and it's a fun thing to do' (2010). Ed Smith, captain of the O'Malley Wench Brigade, explains that he left a fancy brigade in 1988 to help start O'Malley because 'marching with the fancies takes a lot of time and a lot of money. I decided to go with the [wenches] because it was easier. [. . .] You don't have to have talent to be a part of the wenches. All you have to be able to do is swing an umbrella in the air, and everybody's got enough talent for that' (2010).

Porco and Smith are correct that the wench brigades offer the least demanding avenue for participation in the contemporary Mummers Parade. Most clubs in the four official Mummers divisions spend significant time and money designing and building their costumes and rehearsing their music and choreography. Although wench brigades choose a different theme for each year's parade, most wenches wear identical costumes; for the casual spectator, only the colour of the dress, bloomers and parasol distinguishes one wench brigade from another. In addition, most wench brigades (including O'Malley) hire African American brass bands to march with them rather than play or record their own music, and the wenches spend little or no time rehearsing their choreography before New Year's Day. The minimal commitment and preparation required to parade as a wench helps explain why the wench brigades are among the only mummers groups *adding* rather than *losing* members. In 2010, roughly 2,000 wenches in seven brigades marched up Broad Street; 'for comparison, the string bands [had] about 1,100 costumed marchers' (Goldwyn 2010).[7] But accepting low-hassle fun as a sufficient explanation of the wench brigades' explosive growth skirts the question of *why* so many straight, white men enjoy strutting in the Mummers Parade in costumes borrowed from the antebellum wench act.

Although the vast majority of mummers now obey the 1964 ban on blackface make-up, the anachronistic style of the mummers wench registers an affective affiliation with the cross-dressed, blackface performers who walked the streets and stages of nineteenth-century Philadelphia. As such, the performance practices of the contemporary mummers wench tap into what W. T. Lhamon has called 'the blackface lore cycle' (1998: 56–115), a repertoire of expressive gestures that crystallized in minstrel and proto-minstrel performances in the early nineteenth century. Through the lore cycle, blackface shifts and recurs across historical contexts, accreting new meanings without necessarily shedding old ones. Lhamon's suggestive list of examples (quoted at the beginning of this section) shows blackface on the move, seeping 'well beyond its masked variants' into US, Atlantic and global popular culture—both past and present. The minstrel show is not over, and the mummers wench continues to evoke both 'Lucy Long' and the mid-nineteenth-century emergence of blackface minstrelsy as an autonomous theatrical genre.

The performance of 'Lucy Long' in the 'Negro Oddities' act not only pre-enacts aspects of the minstrel show and the Mummers Parade; it also reenacts the blackface dance scene in W. T. Moncrieff's play *Tom and Jerry; or, Life in London*, a staple of US playhouses in the 1820s and 30s. *Tom and Jerry*, a plotless romp by three young men of leisure through the slums of London, immediately followed the 'Negro Oddities' act on the 15 June 1842

FIGURE 5.3. **'Lowest Life in London' by I. R. and George Cruikshank.** From Pierce Egan's novel *Life in London* (1821). Courtesy of The Winterthur Library, Printed Book and Periodical Collection.

programme at the Walnut Street Theatre. Moncrieff based his play on Pierce Egan's enormously popular novel *Life in London,* with illustrations by the celebrated caricaturists I. R. and George Cruikshank. A programme for the Philadelphia premiere of *Tom and Jerry* in April 1823 advertised 'scenery and dresses [. . .] copied from the plates' of Egan's novel (quoted in Durang 1854: 25), one of which shows Tom, Jerry and Logic—Egan's three principal characters—visiting an East London club called All Max. In Egan's novel, Tom,

Jerry and Logic immerse themselves in the revelry at the club, where 'Lascars, blacks, jack tars, coal-heavers, dustmen, women of colour, old and young, and a sprinkling of the remnants of once fine girls, &c. [are] all *jigging* together' (Egan 1821: 286). But in Moncrieff's dramatic adaptation, the three gentlemen visitors to All Max remain aloof from the action, choosing to watch a 'comic *pas de deux*' by 'Dusty Bob and African Sal' rather than joining in the dance themselves (Moncrieff n.d.: 62).

In his book *Rogue Performances*, Peter P. Reed argues that white men in blackface usually played the roles of Dusty Bob and African Sal in early US productions of *Tom and Jerry*, presaging the wench acts of the 1840s.[8] As such, the juxtaposition of *Tom and Jerry* and 'Lucy Long' on a June 1842 evening at the Walnut Street Theatre suggests a threshold in cross-dressed, blackface performance between Moncrieff's play—a waning theatrical fad of the previous two decades—and the wench act, a popular form of blackface gender impersonation that would soon emerge as a staple of the antebellum minstrel show. Unlike the wenches of the 1840s, who most often danced solo, *Tom and Jerry*'s Dusty Bob and African Sal performed as a couple—a detail underscored by Moncrieff's stage directions, which call for Bob and Sal's 'black Child' to '[squall] violently [. . .] thinking there is something the matter with its mother' as Sal, 'in the fullness of her spirits, keeps twirling about' (ibid.). This primal scene unfolds as a command performance for the three white gentlemen onstage, witnessed on 15 June 1842 by the predominantly male and working-class audience at the Walnut Street Theatre.[9]

Reed argues that Bob and Sal's *pas de deux* 'imagines blackface dance as constructed and patronized, conjured into being by upper-class observers' (2009: 131). Although this analysis illuminates the racial and class dynamics of the scene, it overlooks the importance of gender and sexuality in a performance where two white men in blackface—one of them dressed as a woman—dance hysterically before the gaze of a terrified child. If white male desire for black men permeates the minstrel show, as Lott contends, then US productions of *Tom and Jerry* should be read as a genealogical tributary of this cross-racial homoeroticism. Just before Bob and Sal begin dancing, Logic—a member of the onstage, upper-class audience for their performance—'gives [the] Fiddler gin and snuff, and begrimes his face' (Moncrieff n.d.: 62), staging rituals of intoxication and blackening to license the gender-bending and homoerotic scene ahead.

Flash forward to the Mummers Parade, which refracts the racial, gendered, sexual and class dynamics enmeshed in the performance and attendant spectatorship of Bob and Sal's comic dance scene in *Tom and Jerry*. 'Decades ago,' write Dougherty and Goldwyn, '[mummers] wenches marched with dudes, tuxedoed figures who carried a cane. Both wore blackface, until it was banned following civil rights protests in 1964. At that point, dudes went extinct' (1994: M8), and the strutting of the mummers wench transformed from a couples dance à la *Tom and Jerry* to a solo dance à la 'Lucy Long'. This transformation shifted mummers wench performances away from the explicit homoeroticism of wench-dude partnering and towards the homosocial dynamic of the contemporary wench brigades, in which large groups of cross-dressed white men dance together—a transformation that resulted at least in part from the city-imposed ban on blackface in the Mummers Parade. The fierce attachment of some wenches and comics to blackface make-up may have as much to do with the homoerotic license it provides as with its racializing and racist implications, but the spectatorship practices surrounding the Mummers Parade have remained largely unchanged by the 1964 blackface ban. To this day, a predominantly white, working-class crowd gathers to watch the mummers strut up Broad Street in South Philadelphia; and an elite panel of judges made up of 'deans of musical colleges, people with doctorates in their fields, artists, writers [and] TV producers' awards prizes for the best performances at City Hall (Goldwyn 1988: M2). Although contemporary judges enforce the 1964 blackface ban by disqualifying any group that appears in blackface, other forms of racial and ethnic impersonation in the parade continue to flourish unchecked, as I discuss below. And thus, a small, privileged group of spectators authorizes performances of racial and gender impersonation to be enjoyed by the working-class crowd, a pattern of spectatorship homologous to that found in early nineteenth-century stagings of *Tom and Jerry* on this side of the Atlantic.

White Strutting and African American Brass Bands

> There are but two couples, and as the cake is now in evidence, the walkers promptly get down to business. One pair holds the floor at a time, and the men's manners are in strong contrast. One chap is clownish, though his grotesque paces are elaborate, practiced, and exactly timed, while the other is all airiness [. . .]. Away upstage he and his partner meet and curtsy, she with utmost grace, he with exaggerated courtliness. Then down they trip, his elbows squared, his hat held upright by the brim, and with a mincing gait that would be ridiculous were it not absolute in its harmony with the general scheme of airiness [. . .]. The other chap's rig is rusty, and his joints work jerkily, but he has his own ideas about high stepping, and carries them out in a walk that begins like his companion's but that ends at the other side of the stage. Then the first fellow takes both women, one on each arm, and leaving the other man grimacing vengefully, starts on a second tour of grace (quoted in Sampson 1980: 78–9).

This passage from the 3 March 1897 issue of the *Indianapolis Freeman*, the first illustrated black newspaper in the US, reviews Bert Williams and George Walker's cakewalk act, which they performed with their female dance partners to great acclaim. After meeting in San Francisco in the early 1890s, Williams (the 'clownish' chap) and Walker ('all airiness') found success with their cakewalk act in New York City in 1895, billing themselves as 'Two Real Coons'—a sly dig at white minstrels in blackface, whose performances still drew large though dwindling crowds in the late nineteenth century. In March 1897, the same month as the *Indianapolis Freeman* review, a Philadelphia correspondent for the *New York Dramatic Mirror* called Williams and Walker 'the greatest negro comedy act ever witnessed in this city, their cakewalk act creating a genuine sensation' (1897).

The cakewalk was hardly new to Philadelphia, which had hosted one of the earliest cakewalking exhibitions in the North at the 1876 Centennial of American Independence celebration. In his 1899 study *The Philadelphia Negro*, W. E. B. DuBois identified 'gambling, excursions, balls and cake-walks' as the 'chief amusements' of poor black Philadelphians (1996[1899]: 319). As the cakewalking craze of the 1890s unfolded, working-class whites in the emerging mummers stronghold of South Philadelphia got in on the act. In imitation of their African American neighbours, white women in South Philadelphia began offering cakes as prizes at street-performance competitions among predominantly white, male mummers clubs, many of which hosted 'cake-cutting balls' to raise money for their New Year's Day processions (Welch 1991: 37). In 1905, several mummers clubs began dancing their cakewalk-inspired strut to the tune of black minstrel composer James Bland's 1879 spiritual 'Oh Dem Golden Slippers', a song that remains integral to the contemporary Mummers Parade.[10]

In his biography of Bert Williams, Louis Chude-Sokei has recovered the subversion of racial stereotypes in Williams and

Walker's stage performances. Like many black entertainers at the turn of the century, Williams frequently performed in blackface, and Chude-Sokei contends that Williams' blackface make-up 'signified' on the conventions of the white minstrel show 'by ironizing and reclaiming the previously white artifice [. . .] of the "darky" or the "coon"' (2006: 20). In *The Signifying Monkey*, his landmark theory of African American literary criticism, Henry Louis Gates argues that, 'Signifyin(g) in jazz performances and in the play of black language games is a mode of formal revision [. . . that], most crucially, turns on repetition of formal structures and their differences' (1988: 52). Judged against this definition, James Bland's sentimental, lightly syncopated songs do not signify. Robert C. Toll has shown that most of Bland's 700 compositions remained firmly confined by minstrelsy stereotypes, as the lyrics to the second verse of 'Oh Dem Golden Slippers' amply demonstrate:

> Oh, my ole banjo hangs on de wall,
> Kase it aint been tuned since way last fall,
> But de darks all say we will hab a good time,
> When we ride up in de chariot in de morn;
> Dar's ole Brudder Ben and Sister Luce,
> Dey will telegraph de news to Uncle Bacco Juice,
> What a great camp-meetin' der will be dat day,
> When we ride up in de chariot in de morn.
>
> (Bland 1879: 3–4)

I view the mummers' adaptation of the cakewalk to the tune of 'Oh Dem Golden Slippers' as a symptom of nostalgia for the racial caricatures of the minstrel show, despite the interracial appropriation by white street performers of an African American composer's song.

'Oh Dem Golden Slippers' still reigns as the anthem of the Mummers Parade, played on New Year's Day by African American brass bands, most of which march as paid accompanists for mummers wench brigades rather than as independent, competing organizations. African American brass bands have a long history in Philadelphia, first emerging in significant numbers in the early nineteenth century. In 1780, Pennsylvania became the first state to enact legislation gradually abolishing slavery, and within a generation, Philadelphia had grown into 'the largest and most important center of free black life in the United States' (Nash 1988: 2). Despite the mounting hostility of white Philadelphians towards their black neighbours from the 1820s to the Civil War, Philadelphia remained—and remains—a major cultural and population centre for African Americans. At the beginning of the nineteenth century, the city was home to a vibrant community of black artists and musicians, including Francis Johnson—a bandleader, a master performer on the bugle and French horn, and the most important African American composer of his era. Johnson catapulted to fame soon after the War of 1812, composing and playing music for elite white militia regiments and society soirees. In 1819, Philadelphia businessman and politician Robert Waln identified Johnson as 'leader of the band at all balls, public and private; sole director of all serenades, acceptable and not acceptable; inventor-general of cotillions; to which add, a remarkable taste in distorting a sentimental, simple and beautiful song, into a reel, jig, or country-dance' (1819: 155). Johnson wrote and played music in a variety of styles, including military marches and minstrel songs; but as Waln suggests, it was his dance music that made him a celebrity.

John F. Szwed and Morton Marks have argued that European dance forms like the cotillion and the quadrille were 'flexible and open to transformation and improvisation' in nineteenth-century African American musical performance, and they believe that Johnson's dance band played music akin to what later listeners would recognize as ragtime or jazz (1988: 32). Musicologist Eileen Southern makes a similar argument, suggesting that Johnson infused his performances 'with rhythmic complexities such as are found in black folk music or twentieth-century jazz' to make his cotillions and quadrilles infectiously danceable (1983: 113). Southern also shows that African American musicians in Philadelphia continued to cultivate Johnson's legacy after his death in 1844. Thus, it is likely that African American brass bands hired to play for white mummers in the early twentieth century distorted and transformed the songs in their repertoire—including 'Oh Dem Golden Slippers'—as a way of signifying on the mummers' minstrel-show nostalgia.

That said, the dizzying performance genealogy of the cakewalk complicates the relationship between white strutting and African American brass band music in both historical and contemporary wench performances of 'Oh Dem Golden Slippers'. As the cakewalk migrated from southern plantations to the urban streets and stages of the Atlantic rim, its racial, gendered, sexual and class implications were constantly in flux. Will Marion Cook's 1898 musical *Clorindy, the Origin of the Cakewalk*—which he wrote for Williams and Walker, though they were unable to perform in the show's Broadway run—'creat[ed] a story of how the cakewalk came about in Louisiana in the early Eighteen Eighties' (Cook 1983[1947]: 228). An 1897 article in the *New Orleans Times–Democrat* also traced the origin of the cakewalk to Louisiana, where African Americans in the antebellum period used the dance to circumvent the prohibition on slave marriage 'by allowing a man [. . .] to show his preference for a woman and thus to publicly claim her as wife' (quoted in Hill and Hatch 2003: 152). Folklorist Roger D. Abrahams points out that the organization of slave dances into male–female couples was 'far from the norm' (1992: 100), and many African American performers—unlike their white minstrel counterparts—retained the heterosexual partnering of the plantation cakewalk when they put the dance onstage later in the nineteenth century. African American showman Tom Fletcher recalls that *The Creole*

Show, with an all-black cast and a white producer, included women in the cakewalk finale as early as 1890; 'from then on,' he writes, 'nearly every colored show, minstrels and all, put women in the cast' (1984[1954]: 103). Some 'colored shows' like the 1892 hit *South Before the War* even capitalized on the vogue for amateur cakewalking contests, directly involving their interracial audiences in cakewalk competitions.

In their exhaustive history of jazz dance, Marshall Stearns and Jean Stearns quote the recollections of a former slave and cakewalking champion regarding the plantation cakewalk:

> Us slaves watched white folks' parties [. . .] where the guests danced a minuet and then paraded in a grand march, with the ladies and gentlemen going different ways and then meeting again, arm in arm, and marching down the center together. Then we'd do it, too, *but we used to mock 'em*, every step. Sometimes the white folks noticed it, but they seemed to like it; I guess they thought we couldn't dance any better (1968: 22).

Clearly, some plantation cakewalkers revelled in signifying on the dances of their masters, and as Stearns and Stearns point out, there was little the 'white folks' could do about it: 'Any reprimand would be an admission that they saw themselves in the dance, and they would be the only ones—apparently—to whom such a notion had occurred' (ibid.: 22–3). A courtship dance in which slaves parodied their masters; parodied in turn by white minstrels in blackface; copied and adapted from plantation life and the white minstrel show by African American theatre; and staged in a variety of interracial contexts as a public competition, the cakewalk is, in David Krasner's view, a 'hall of mirrors' (1997: 81).

Mimetic vertigo overwhelms me as I look down cakewalking's mirrored hallway to try to see who contemporary mummers wenches are imitating.[11] But the reflections dancing in the mirror—white planters, black slaves, minstrel-show wenches, African American theatre artists—disclose no original at the end of the hall. Viewed genealogically, there *is* no original, since 'genealogists resist histories that attribute purity of origin to any performance'. Instead, argues Joseph Roach, 'they have to take into account the give and take of joint transmissions, posted in the past, arriving in the present, delivered by living messengers, speaking in tongues'—or dancing in movements—'not entirely their own' (1996: 286). Today's mummers wenches are the living messengers of both the antebellum wench act and the turn-of-the-century cakewalk, strutting to the music of African American brass bands, produced by and producing an interracial performance genealogy with no single origin and no single end.

African American Mummers and the Blackface Controversy

> Of all the stereotypes that have dogged the Mummers over the years, 'white guys only' is the most persistent. Mummers have always argued vehemently, but unsuccessfully, against this label, and their arguments are valid [. . .]. News clippings document that 'all-Negro' units competed throughout the first quarter-century of the Broad Street Parade, and it is likely that they were part of the free-for-all neighborhood parades prior to that time (Masters 2007: 70).

On New Year's Day 1901, three African American groups—the Ivy Leaf Club, the Blue Ribbon Club and the Homebreakers String Band—competed for prizes in Philadelphia's first city-sponsored Mummers Parade. Regular African American participation in the parade continued through 1929, when the Octavius V. Catto String Band, named for a martyred nineteenth-century civil rights leader, made its final appearance. Sociologist Patricia Anne Masters attributes the withdrawal of independent African American clubs from the 1930 Mummers Parade to the Depression, which hit Philadelphia's black community especially hard. Welch makes a similar argument, though he also acknowledges that the Catto String Band's undeserved last-place finish in 1929 probably discouraged African American groups from competing for city prize money in the parade the next year. Nonetheless, African American brass bands continued to march throughout the 1930s as paid accompanists for white mummers groups, a practice that remains common today. Although economic hardship helps explain the changing nature of African American participation in the parade, objections to the prolific use of blackface by white mummers also may have contributed to the withdrawal of the Catto Band and other African American groups from competition. As mummers documentarian E. A. Kennedy has argued, 'Since the 1930s, the African-American community [in Philadelphia] has taken justified offense over the Mummers' historic use of the blackface minstrel as a theme for disguise' (2007: 10).

This justified offence erupted into full-blown conflict in December 1963, when Cecil B. Moore, head of the Philadelphia chapter of the NAACP, and Louis Smith of the Congress of Racial Equality (CORE) successfully pressured parade director Elias Myers, a city official, to ban blackface from the Mummers Parade. This decision prompted 200 outraged mummers—in blackface—to picket Myers's home, leading to a compromise that pleased neither side: blackface make-up would be allowed in the parade 'if it was used to create a character, but not if it was to be used to ridicule any ethnic group' (quoted in ibid.: 75). Civil rights activists were dissatisfied with Myers's equivocation, and NAACP attorney Charles Bowser petitioned the Philadelphia Court of Common Pleas to uphold the blackface ban: 'We feel that the city should not take part in a parade where Negroes are depicted in an unfavorable light, provoking, taunting, humiliating and embarrassing to them. We are taxpayers and we do not think our money should be used to support it' (quoted in Welch 1991: 153). Under Moore's leadership, the Philadelphia chapter of the NAACP combined its traditional tactics of legal action and economic pressure with public protests and threats to demonstrate, and the controversy over blackface in the Mummers Parade was no exception. The escalating militancy of Philadelphia's NAACP chapter led to a rapid growth in membership, from 6,000 before Moore's election in 1962 to a peak of more than 20,000 by the end of 1963. As such, the NAACP's collaboration with CORE to fight blackface in the Mummers Parade marked a high point of organizational cooperation and community involvement in the civil rights movement in Philadelphia.

A snowstorm on New Year's Day 1964 forced a delay in the Mummers Parade until 4 January, and one day beforehand, the Philadelphia Court of Common Pleas issued a preliminary injunction banning blackface on Broad Street—though not on Second Street—and prohibiting the NAACP and CORE from picketing the parade. Despite the ruling, one white mummer recalls that a group of Moore's supporters tried to stop the comic clubs from marching:

> There was a lot of bad feelings on both sides. And this Cecil Moore brought down all these people from North Philadelphia from the black community, and they tried to stop the Mummers; it was a mistake on their part because when [the Mummers are] all together, they're not easily dissuaded. There was a big fight and a lot of black people got hurt very bad (quoted in Masters 2007: 81–2).

If the anti-blackface campaign led to this tragic but predictable incident of interracial violence, it also functioned less predictably to aggravate political fissures within Philadelphia's African American community. On 31 December 1963, the *Philadelphia Tribune* (the city's principal African American newspaper) reported that '400 Negro ministers went into their pulpits [. . .] and urged members not to watch the [mummers] parade either on television or in person' (Perry 1963: 1, 4). But as the *Tribune* revealed four days later, 'At least five and possibly more Negro marching bands will participate in the Mummers Parade [. . .] despite the controversy which has arisen over blackface' (Peters 1964: 1). According to Masters, an African American bandleader was thrown down a subway stairwell by civil rights activists for refusing to boycott the Mummers, prompting one comic club president to ask his club's black accompanists 'if they wanted to be released from their obligation to parade'—to which they replied, 'definitely not' (quoted in Masters 2007: 84). In an interview in the *Tribune*, George E. Hawkins—a prominent African American brass player who marched with the Catto String Band in the 1920s—defended black musicians who, like himself, chose to participate in the 1964 Mummers Parade. The danger faced by Hawkins and his compatriots suggests that support for white mummers, as well as economic considerations, spurred some African American musicians to defy the boycott, inspiring a show of interracial solidarity that coalesced in *opposition* to a just and powerful civil rights campaign.

The following year, Philadelphia's civil rights movement succeeded in greatly reducing the visibility of blackface make-up in the Mummers Parade. At the behest of Mayor James Tate, the police enforced the 1963 ban on blackface, ejecting 25 mummers from the parade route for wearing burnt cork. Even the Hammond Comic Club largely acquiesced to the blackface ban in 1965, with only four of its members marching in blackface. But to some extent, this show of compliance with the blackface ban has deflected attention from the persistence and development of other forms of racial and ethnic impersonation in the Mummers Parade in the years since 1964. In a controversial performance in 2009, the B. Love Strutters Comic Brigade paraded up Broad Street with a skit entitled 'Aliens of an Illegal Kind', in which a group of white

Mummers impersonated immigrants clashing with the border patrol. An editorial in the *Philadelphia Daily News* chastised the performance for its 'blatant racism', correctly pointing out that 'Arabs had long beards and turbans, Mexicans wore sombreros, and Asian women were depicted as geishas' (*Philadelphia Daily News* 2009). The B. Love Strutters finished in 11th place out of 17 in the judges' scoring of the comic brigades, and none of the other 2009 Mummers Parade skits involving racial and ethnic impersonation garnered negative media coverage or sparked public debate.

Despite the xenophobia evident in 'Aliens of an Illegal Kind', the Mummers Parade has grown considerably more diverse and inclusive in recent decades. Beginning in the 1970s, most clubs in all four divisions of the Mummers Parade opened their membership to women, though the wench brigades have remained almost exclusively male. In 1984, the newly formed Goodtimers Comic Club—with an African American president and a largely minority membership—began competing in the Mummers Parade, and the Goodtimers have remained an integral part of the comic division for over 25 years. In 1992, a group of Cambodian American artists and students teamed up with the Golden Sunrise Fancy Club to stage a Khmer dance drama in the Mummers Parade, and new nontraditional mummers groups have sprouted up almost every year since.

I joined one such group in 2009: the Vaudevillains, a comic brigade established in 2007 as part of the Murray Comic Club. Sonja Trauss, a co-founder of the Vaudevillains, describes the group as 'anti-capitalist' (2010), and the Vaudevillains' parade performances have confronted global warming, nuclear proliferation and the industrialized food system in the US. In theoretical terms, the Vaudevillains aspire to stage what Jill Dolan has called *utopian performatives*, 'small but profound moments in which performance [. . . makes] palpable an affective vision of how the world might be better' (2005: 5–6). Of course, any one affective vision of a better world might appear dystopic from elsewhere on the political spectrum, and multiple, conflicting visions of utopia compete for the audience's allegiance in the contemporary Mummers Parade. The Murray Comic Club, the Vaudevillains' parent organization, sponsors over a dozen comic brigades—including both the Vaudevillains and the B. Love Strutters, the group that performed 'Aliens of an Illegal Kind' in 2009. According to club president Porco, 'we're not a politically motivated organization' (2010). Porco competes to win, and the broad range of groups that perform under the Murray Club banner have earned 18 consecutive victories for Murray as the best overall club in the comic division of the Mummers Parade.

While documenting the 2006 parade, Kennedy snapped a photograph of a mummer named Tom Spiroploulos wearing a rainbow-coloured wig, blackface make-up, a wench dress and a Murray Club badge.[12] Spiroploulos, who was carried up Broad Street as an infant in the Mummers Parade on 4 January 1964, told Kennedy that he 'don't mean nothing' by blacking up: 'I'm not trying to put nobody down. It's just tradition. It's the way my father paraded' (quoted in Kennedy 2007: 24). Spiroploulos' remarks may strain belief, but they also point to the changing implications of blackface make-up for the mummers in the years since the 1964 blackface controversy. David R. Roediger has argued that blackface performance on both stages and streets helped to define the emergent category of whiteness for working-class, immigrant men in the nineteenth-century US; but for Spiroploulos and the few other recalcitrant mummers who still black up today, blackface serves an additional purpose. Masters has argued that, by the 1960s, blackface as a mummers 'tradition' had come to imply 'a symbolic link to grandfathers and fathers' (ibid.: 86), a point Spiroploulos echoes in defence of his blackface make-up. By claiming blackface as a

FIGURE 5.4. **Tom Spiroploulos performing in blackface in the 2006 Philadelphia Mummers Parade.**
Photograph by E. A. Kennedy. Courtesy of The Image Works.

patriarchal inheritance, Spiroploulos identifies with an earlier generation of mummers as a tactic to mitigate the racist sting of the blackface mask. Such a tactic is insensitive at best; but it also discloses an ambivalent fantasy, at once nostalgic for a time of white, male dominance and loaded with interracial desire.

From an antiracist perspective, a lone wench in blackface in the contemporary Mummers Parade embodies a dystopic politics of white, male privilege, naturalized as a mummers 'tradition'. But among the wench brigades—most of which eschew blackface—

the communal spirit in evidence on New Year's Day suggests a utopian performative. The genealogy of the wench brigades carries generations of displacements and compromises in its train: the grudging acceptance of the blackface ban, the disappearance of dudes, and the vertiginous history of parodic mimesis embodied in the dancing and music of the mummers strut. This performance genealogy does not absolve the wench brigades of their racist and sexist tendencies, past or present; but it reveals an ongoing, cross-racial engagement that keeps white wenches and African American brass bands parading together. This may not be utopia, but the rush of a wench brigade strutting in front of City Hall sends both the performers and the audience into a joyful abandon where boundaries between people blur and anything feels possible. This is the promise of carnival in the classic, Bakhtinian sense, where dance, music, laughter, crowds, intoxication and disguise somehow coalesce into a fleeting illusion of universal harmony. But to spurn cross-racial engagement by wearing blackface in the midst of this revelry is to reinstate the unequal power relations that carnival, at its best, always gestures beyond.

The presence of occasional blackface wenches like Spirploulos in the Murray Comic Club made me hesitant to join the Vaudevillains, given the brigade's association with Murray. But as one member of the Vaudevillains explained to me:

> What we [are] doing, if I may dare say, is making history [. . . ;] tackling weird and interesting issues [in the Mummers Parade] while integrating [. . .] the festive debauchery that is Philadelphia's New Year's Day. There are a lot of things deeply rooted and historically unjust about the Mummers Parade, but I am proud of this brigade's contradictions and its approach to infiltrating, invigorating and intervening into [the parade's] cultural conventions (Smirnov 2010).

Indeed, the best way to intervene in the Mummers Parade, to enact a utopian performative, is to join the festivity: to broaden the diversity of participation, like the Goodtimers Club and the Cambodian American Mummers group; to claim 'the tiniest bully pulpit for anti-capitalist politics', like the Vaudevillains (Trauss 2010); and to counter dystopic performances of racial and gender impersonation—like those of the blackface mummers wench—which attempt to justify their presence by denying their past.

Notes

1 A dissertation fellowship from Brown University and short-term research fellowships at the Library Company of Philadelphia / Historical Society of Pennsylvania and the Winterthur Museum and Library made it possible for me to research and write this article. I thank Rebecca Schneider, John Emigh, Heather Nathans, Patricia Ybarra, the editors of this volume and the members of the Popular Fiesta and Carnival Working Group for their feedback on earlier drafts of my work on the mummer wench. Thanks also to the many librarians who assisted me with the research for this project, and to the Vaudevillians and the Murray Comic Club for welcoming me into the world of the Mummers Parade.

2 The fancy brigades perform indoors at the Pennsylvania Convention Center as well as on Broad Street with the other three mummers divisions.

3 Rich Porco, president of the Murray Comic Club, gives the following description of the current relationship between the wench brigades, the comic clubs and the city of Philadelphia: '[Until] the 2008 parade [. . .] the wenches still had to march with a mother [comic] club, and the city didn't want to make the wenches into their own division. So I [. . .] proposed creating a separate association [for the wenches] —not a separate division, but a separate association, a recognized association. And the message was, "If you want to be recognized, you've got to be responsible."' The wench brigade captains and Leo Dignam, the city-appointed director of the Mummers Parade, agreed to Porco's proposal (Porco 2010).

4 Most historians of blackface minstrelsy argue that the Virginia Minstrels—Billy Whitlock, Frank Pelham, Dan Emmett and Frank Brower—performed North America's 'first' minstrel show at the Chatham Theatre in New York City in January or February 1843. W. T. Lhamon disputes this claim, arguing instead that the minstrel show began in Buffalo, New York, where E. P. Christy formed a band of three blackface musicians in June 1842—the same month that the 'Negro Oddities' act appeared at the Walnut Street Theatre in Philadelphia. Rather than debate the exact date and location of the 'first' minstrel show, I find it more instructive to note that multipart blackface performances by ensembles of three or more musicians and dancers emerged within months of each other in New York, Buffalo, Philadelphia and other northern US cities between the summer of 1842 and the winter of 1842/43.

5 With due respect to McConachie, I note that Lott—concerned as he is with the social *unconscious* of the minstrel show—makes no claims regarding the *conscious* intentions of either performers or spectators of the antebellum wench act.

6 According to Goldwyn, 'some guys will bring their young daughters along [with the wench brigades], but you don't see adolescent girls out there marching with their fathers' (2010). Ed Smith, Captain of the O'Malley Wench Brigade, explains the reasoning behind this prohibition: 'I can't watch everyone's kids, and the last thing I want is someone banging on my door saying, "someone grabbed my daughter in the parade, someone kissed my daughter in the parade"' (2010). Occasionally, an older adult woman will march as a wench, but the wench brigades remain overwhelming male.

7 Just before the 2011 Mummers Parade, the Oregon New Year's Association—a venerable fancy club—changed its affiliation to become a wench brigade, bringing the total number of wench brigades to eight. Only two fancy clubs and three comic clubs marched up Broad Street in 2011, and the fancy brigades 'are barely breaking even on their convention center show [on New Year's Day]' (Porco 2010).

8 In a notable exception to this pattern, William Brown—an African American theatre producer—staged *Tom and Jerry* in New York City in June 1823 with a primarily black cast, retaining the comic dance

by Dusty Bob and African Sal and appending a slave market scene to the end of Moncrieff's play.

9 In the early 1840s, the Walnut Street Theatre offered lower admission prices, more benefit nights for fire companies (a draw for working-class, male audiences) and a more popular repertoire than its main competitor, the Chestnut Street Theatre.

10 Following terminological conventions in minstrelsy scholarship, I use 'minstrelsy' and 'white minstrelsy' to refer to minstrel performances by white artists. 'Blackface minstrelsy' refers specifically to white minstrels performing in blackface, and 'black minstrel' describes African American artists like James Bland, who participated in the production of minstrel shows.

11 Following Krasner, I borrow the term 'mimetic vertigo' from Michael Taussig, who uses it to describe the entry of the self into the alterity 'against which the self is defined and sustained' (Taussig 1993: 237)

12 Kennedy identifies Spiroploulos as a 'freelance' mummer 'who went up the street without the sanction of any club on New Year's Day' (2007: 24), but Spiroploulos' Murray Club badge—clearly visible over his left breast—suggests that he is either a member of the Murray Club or the recipient of a pilfered badge from a sympathetic club member.

Works Cited

ABRAHAMS, Roger D. 1992. *Singing the Master: The Emergence of African-American Culture in the Plantation South.* New York: Pantheon Books.

BAKHTIN, Mikhail. 1965. *Rabelais and His World* (Hélène Iswolsky trans). Bloomington: Indiana University Press, 1984.

BLAND, James. 1879. *Oh Dem Golden Slippers: Song and Chorus.* Boston, MA: John F. Perry.

CHUDE-SOKEI, Louis. 2006. *The Last 'Darky': Bert Williams, Black-on-Black Minstrelsy, and the African Diaspora.* Durham, NC: Duke University Press.

COCKRELL, Dale. 1997. *Demons of Disorder: Early Blackface Minstrels and their World.* Cambridge: Cambridge University Press.

COOK, Will Marion. 1983[1947]. 'Clorindy, the Origin of the Cakewalk' in Eileen Southern (ed.), *Readings in Black American Music,* 2ND EDN. New York: W. W. Norton, pp. 217–32.

DAMON, S. Foster. 1936. *Series of Old American Songs, Reproduced in Facsimile from Original or Early Editions in the Harris Collection of American Poetry and Plays, Brown University*. Providence: Brown University Library.

DAVIS, Susan G. 1982. 'Making Night Hideous: Christmas Revelry and Public Order in Nineteenth-Century Philadelphia'. *American Quarterly*, 34: 185–99.

DOLAN, Jill. 2005. *Utopia in Performance: Finding Hope at the Theatre*. Ann Arbor: University of Michigan Press.

DOUGHERTY, Frank, and Ron Goldwyn. 1994. 'Anatomy of a Mummer: Yo, Wench'. *Philadelphia Daily News*, 30 December, p. M8.

DOUGLAS, George William. 1937. *The American Book of Days*. New York: H. W. Wilson.

DUBOIS, W. E. B. 1996[1899]. *The Philadelphia Negro: A Social Study* (Elijah Anderson ed.). Philadelphia: University of Pennsylvania Press.

DUMONT, Frank. 1914. 'The Golden Days of Minstrelsy: The Musings of an Old Timer'. *New York Clipper*, 19 December, pp. ii–iii.

DURANG, Charles. 1854. *Durang's History of the Philadelphia Stage Scrapbook*, VOL. 2. Library Company of Philadelphia.

EGAN, Pierce. 1821. *Life in London: Or, the Day and Night Scenes of Jerry Hawthorn, Esq. and His Elegant Friend Corinthian Tom, Accompanied by Bob Logic, the Oxonian, in Their Rambles and Sprees through the Metropolis*. London: Sherwood, Neely & Jones.

EMERY, Lynne Fauley. 1988. *Black Dance from 1619 to Today*. REVD EDN. Princeton: Princeton Book Co.

FISCHER, Gayle V. 2001. *Pantaloons and Power: A Nineteenth-Century Dress Reform in the United States*. Kent, OH: Kent State University Press.

FLETCHER, Tom. 1984[1954]. *100 Years of the Negro in Show Business*. New York: Da Capo Press.

GARBER, Marjorie. 1992. *Vested Interests: Cross-Dressing and Cultural Anxiety*. New York: Routledge.

GATES, Henry Louis. 1988. *The Signifying Monkey: A Theory of African-American Literary Criticism*. New York: Oxford University Press.

GOLDWYN, Ron. 1988. 'Fancy This: No More Secrets; 26 Parade Judges Strut out of Closet'. *Philadelphia Daily News*, 29 December, p. M2.

——. 2010. Personal interview. Philadelphia, Pennsylvania, 10 February.

Hill, Errol G., and James V. Hatch. 2003. *A History of African American Theatre*. Cambridge: Cambridge University Press.

Kennedy, E. A. 2007. *Life, Liberty and the Mummers*. Philadelphia, PA: Temple University Press.

Krasner, David. 1997. *Resistance, Parody and Double Consciousness in African-American Theatre, 1895–1910*. New York: St Martin's Press.

Lhamon, W.T. 1998. *Raising Cain: Blackface Performance from Jim Crow to Hip Hop*. Cambridge: Harvard University Press.

Logan, Olive. 1879. 'The Ancestry of Brudder Bones'. *Harper's New Monthly Magazine* 58: 687–98.

Lott, Eric. 1993. *Love and Theft: Blackface Minstrelsy and the American Working Class*. New York: Oxford University Press.

Masters, Patricia Anne. 2007. *The Philadelphia Mummers: Building Community through Play*. Philadelphia, PA: Temple University Press.

McConachie, Bruce. 2006. 'Cognitive Studies and Epistemic Competence in Cultural History: Moving Beyond Freud and Lacan' in Bruce McConachie and F. Elizabeth Hart (eds), *Performance and Cognition: Theatre Studies and the Cognitive Turn*. London: Routledge, pp. 52–75.

Moncrieff, W. T. n.d. *Tom and Jerry, or, Life in London in 1820: A Drama in Three Acts, from Pierce Egan's Celebrated Work*. London: Thomas Hailes Lacy.

Nash, Gary B. 1988. *Forging Freedom: The Formation of Philadelphia's Black Community, 1720–1840*. Cambridge, MA: Harvard University Press.

New Orleans Minstrel Show Program. n.d. Filed in 'Uncatalogued Minstrel Programs, Sa-Si'. Harvard Theatre Collection.

New York Dramatic Mirror. 1897. 'Vaudeville Correspondence: Philadelphia, PA'. 27 March, p. 20.

Perry, Chris. 1963. 'CORE, 400 Ministers, NAACP Gang Up on Mummers Parade Blackface'. *Philadelphia Tribune*, 31 December, pp. 1, 4.

Peters, Art. 1964. '5 Negro Bands Set to March despite Furor: Elks, Musicians from Local 274 Hired for Parade'. *Philadelphia Tribune*, 4 January, pp. 1, 3.

Porco, Rich. 2010. Personal interview. Philadelphia, Pennsylvania, 4 October.

Philadelphia Daily News. 2009. 'Bummer Parade', Editorial, 8 January. Available at: http://goo.gl/huQs7J (last accessed on 4 April 2016).

REED, Peter P. 2009. *Rogue Performances: Staging the Underclass in Early American Theatre Culture*. New York: Palgrave Macmillan.

ROACH, Joseph. 1996. *Cities of the Dead: Circum-Atlantic Performance*. New York: Columbia University Press.

SAMPSON, Henry T. 1980. *Blacks in Blackface: A Sourcebook on Early Black Musical Shows*. Metuchen, NJ: Scarecrow Press.

SMIRNOV, Natalia. 2010. Personal Communication, 4 January.

SMITH, Ed. 2010. Personal interview. Philadelphia, Pennsylvania, 10 November.

SOUTHERN, Eileen. 1983. *The Music of Black Americans: A History*, 2ND EDN. New York: W. W. Norton.

STANSELL, Christine. 1987. *City of Women: Sex and Class in New York, 1789–1860*. Urbana: University of Illinois Press.

STEARNS, Marshall, and Jean Stearns. 1968. *Jazz Dance: The Story of American Vernacular Dance*. New York: Macmillan.

SZWED, John F., and Morton Marks. 1988. 'The Afro-American Transformation of European Set Dances and Dance Suites'. *Dance Research Journal* 20: 29–36.

TAUSSIG, Michael. 1993. *Mimesis and Alterity: A Particular History of the Senses*. New York: Routledge.

TRAUSS, Sonja. 2010. Personal interview. Philadelphia, Pennsylvania, 7 January.

VIRGINIA SERENADERS. 1843. *The Virginia Serenaders Illustrated Songster: Containing all the Songs, as Sung by the Far Famed Band of Original Virginia Serenaders [. . .] throughout the Principal Cities of the United States*. New York and Philadelphia: Turner & Fisher.

WALN, Robert. 1819. *The Hermit in America on a Visit to Philadelphia: Containing Some Account of the Beaux and Belles, Dandies and Coquettes, Cotillion Parties, Supper Parties, Tea Parties, &c. &c. of that Famous City*. Philadelphia: M. Thomas.

WELCH, Charles E. 1991. *Oh Dem Golden Slippers: The Story of the Philadelphia Mummers*, REVD EDN. Philadelphia: Book Street Press.

WINANS, Robert B. 1984. 'Early Minstrel Show Music, 1843–1852' in Annemarie Bean, James V. Hatch and Brooks McNamara (eds), *Inside the Minstrel Mask: Readings in Nineteenth-Century Blackface Minstrelsy*. Hanover, NH: Wesleyan University Press, 1996.

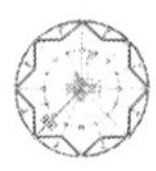

Chapter 6

REVEALED SPACES

The Burlesque Hall of Fame Weekend and Neo-burlesque Performance

Laura Dougherty

The Burlesque Hall of Fame Weekend (BHoF) takes place annually in Las Vegas, Nevada. With four days of performances, the BHoF Weekend in June is a reunion, a pageant, a living history and an international festival of classic burlesque and neo-burlesque produced by the Burlesque Hall of Fame. Since its founding in 1990, it has evolved into a spectacle that celebrates both the genre's history and its present incarnations. The event spreads out into the lobbies and hallways of Las Vegas' hotels, a tidal wave of sequined drag glamour. In keeping with the genre's tradition of parodic play, irreverence is queen at BHoF; it seems an untenable project to articulate the work done by this festival without employing, at least in part, the genre's quippy word-play and knowing, bawdy humour. It is, after all (and still): burlesque.

The event was first envisioned as a reunion weekend for former and current burlesque performers. As with a family reunion, the health of matriarchs, inevitable economic instability and the uncertainty regarding who will take the reins and organize the event all have, at times, sent doubt (or gossip, or both) through the neo-burlesque community each year. Will there be a reunion? For years the festival was a labour of love by and for the burlesque community. Though a marketable spectacle, now getting a mention in national and international news media,[1] often there were those in the neo-burlesque community who didn't believe the BHoF Weekend would materialize.[2] Yet it did, every year, creating a space in Las Vegas not only for this festival but for the burlesque genre.

I attended the 2006 (then) Miss Exotic World Pageant, the year it moved to Las Vegas, and the 2010 BHoF Weekend. The weekends' events are primarily attended by the burlesque community: retired burlesque dancers invited back as living legends, neo-burlesque performers from around USAmerica[3] and, increasingly, performers from other countries.[4] Aside from a few photo-bloggers and general fans, there are a few friends and partners of performers who attend the weekend's festivities. In this way, the festival is exclusive, produced by a community primarily for its own members. And because the audience is made up of so many performers and their friends, the audience always arrives dressed to impress. The festive state of this festival is embodied and displayed by the audience as well as the performers. Festival attendees plan ensembles and outfits for each night as if they were onstage themselves.[5] Because the main events all require tickets, most of the festival is private and the general public can neither see it nor join in spontaneously or accidentally.

I gained unusual access to the burlesque community because I accompanied a close personal friend who is a neo-burlesque performer. As such, I was able to move between the general audience space and the spaces created by more intimate conversations among small groups of performers, whether gathered at bars, at diners for post-performance 4 a.m. tuna melts, exchanges in hotel hallways and lifts, or in tech rehearsals. I was, in this way, both part of the majority of the audience—participants who know the performers, know their acts, have seen the same numbers before and know the living history (and, indeed, gossip)—yet atypical as I am not a performer myself but attended the performances and surrounding activities to witness and review the event.

For all who attend, there is a performed sense of homecoming to the BHoF Weekend, as if Las Vegas opens her loving countercultural arms to welcome the tawdry players. Pasties, tassels, heels and glitter abound in Las Vegas, after all. In *Strip Show: Performances of Gender and Desire*, Katherine Liepe-Levinson locates desire in urban centres: 'The geographies and topographies of the strip clubs in Montréal, Washington, DC, and Houston collectively represent dominant heterosexual male desire as "decadent," "opulent," "obscure," "fashionable," "slavish," "heroic," "show biz-like," and so on—but never as *natural*. Sexual desire in Western culture is, in fact, rarely represented through signifiers of the "normal"' (2002: 25). Illicit behaviour is a foregone conclusion in Sin City, if one believes the Las Vegas marketing campaign. Las Vegas, with all of its purposefully hyperbolic spectacle and decadence, necessarily informs the contours of the festival.

Neo-burlesque

BHoF creates a space for the overlap between the burlesque of the past and its remembered present. If neo-burlesque is a reversioning of burlesque tradition, in its present-day iteration, burlesque performance is predicated on quoting, nodding to, parodying and remembering its past. At BHoF, burlesque performers (the legends of the past) and the neo-burlesque performers (the leaders of the present) celebrate the performance tradition in a shared space, though there is a tension in how each remembers and understands that tradition. The burlesque performance tradition is often traced back to the 1860s, with the arrival of Lydia Thompson and the British Blondes in New York.[6] Burlesque in USAmerica in the early decades of the twentieth century ran parallel to the vaudeville circuit, entertainment that included variety acts, striptease and bawdy humour. By the 1940s, the trend of burlesque performance slowed while the pin-up girl aesthetic of girlie shows and photos in the 1940s and 50s gained popularity. Into the 1960s and 70s what was once referred to as burlesque performance became stripping and was relegated to strip clubs. The neo-burlesque movement began to build with staying power in the 1990s. From its beginnings in the late nineteenth and early twentieth centuries, burlesque has always incorporated parody in its tone (as the etymology of the genre's nomenclature suggests).

While striptease and parody have long been integral aspects of the performance form, it is striptease that most clearly exemplifies the form. 'Burlesque is glamour,' explains New York–based The World Famous *BOB*, one of the most well-known neo-burlesque performers (quoted in Baldwin 2004: 30). What can be confusing is that contemporary neo-burlesque performers generally refer to their performance form as 'burlesque' rather than 'neo-burlesque'. Colloquially, the moniker 'neo-burlesque' is trotted out to describe those performers and/or performances that incorporate complex and innovative aesthetics, in work that functions as performance art, or that is more steeped in parody, or that is purposefully uncomfortable or disquieting for its audience, rather than solely based in the aesthetic of classic striptease. 'Neo-burlesque' is more commonly used in critical scholarship than conversational description.[7] While the striptease of classic burlesque performance often features performers undressing out of elegant gowns, garters, stockings, opera-length gloves and boas, the striptease of neo-burlesque performance can involve a twist (a prop where a bra, pastie or G-string was expected), a narrative that fuels the undressing, spectacle, contortion, humour and disdain—some aspect of the style of movement or the style of costume specific to that performer or performance. In neo-burlesque, *how* the body is revealed is as integral to the performance as the revealed body itself.[8]

I enter the discussion of neo-burlesque through the New York City scene, where I began attending shows around 2000.[9] Performers choreograph their own numbers, and often work within an individual style or subject area. 'Striptease in this context is not solely about "taking off" but about "putting on" layers of meaning through the juxtaposition of what I call the four Cs: choice of music, choreography, costuming and concept' (Sally 2009: 7). As neo-burlesque has garnered more attention and popularity, it also has become more distinct in how it is organized. In the past 10 to 20 years, the norm for New York neo-burlesque has been single performers contributing one to three separate numbers to an evening's performance. The events are organized either by the venue, or, increasingly, by one of the artists who produces an evening's show at a venue. In the New York area, these performances take place in art/performance venues and/or bars,[10] on small stages either in small separate rooms or at the side or back of the bar. The house often collects a small to moderate admission cost, between $10 to $30, for an evening's line-up, with a mix of new and established talent. Performers often book each other for gigs. The grassroots style of the genre is part of the strength (if not charm) that builds the community but also necessitates that performers be organized, financially savvy and responsible producers. The performers acting as their own producers is part of the reason the genre has taken off, but it is one of its limitations as well.

Performers work under stage names, which may or may not be related to their aesthetics and styles. Within the burlesque community performers live in these names and personas, referring to one another only by the stage names: Sarah, Emily, Nicole and Rachel are better known as Dirty, Nasty, Tickle and Kitten. There are humourist performers who deal and reveal through parody and pastiche; classic striptease artists with gloves, boas and fans; vaudeville-esque entertainers who layer striptease with contortionist tricks and hula-hoops. There is a boylesque performer who performs in costume as a monkey, a performer who specializes in gore and fetish and performers who hone in on specific interests and subcultures.[11]

The personal aesthetics and content of each performer's shtick is a tradition carried over from the burlesque heyday. Whether classic, absurd or avant-garde in style, it is, of course, striptease that acts as the common ground of neo-burlesque. Ask a neo-burlesque performer the difference between burlesque and stripping and the quippy response is, 'About $500 a night,' while the more telling explanation might be that while strippers have customers, burlesque performers have an audience. 'Strippers, because their performance is a commodity and their ability to hustle the customers increases their pay, cut their acts down to the basics. No-frills, explicit moves are what the average customer desires, and the location of the dollars on the stage directs the movements of the dance. Burlesque acts don't change when tips are involved' (Baldwin 2004: 50). Despite the difference in the aesthetics, stripping in its current incarnation, and neo-burlesque, are descendant forms of burlesque performance.

The audience of a neo-burlesque show is generally made up of an artistic, sometimes-hipster crowd of 20- and 30-somethings. Crowds are a mix of gay and straight folk, though this is a slippery designator and nearly impossible to determine with any certainty given the omnisexual tone of neo-burlesque. Sexuality is performed for all to consume and celebrate, regardless of personal orientation. The audience is generally made up of both men and women, couples and mixed groups alike. While it is made up of all types, there is a specific unity to a burlesque crowd: all are there to be part of the show. Rather than the personal sexual gratification expected by customers at strip clubs, burlesque audiences are there to see the show *and* be part of it. After all, it just isn't burlesque without the hooting, hollering and festive nature of the audience and the anticipated exchange between audience and performer.

Burlesque as a form is based on parody. In its earliest forms burlesque subverted power structures of class and gender through ribald humour. Lynn Sally describes the 1860s British Blondes:

> The performers [. . .] talked in a way that often shocked Victorian-era sensibilities; dialogue was filled with double entendres and puns and the script could change daily to reflect current events. Nothing was safe from the Blondes' parodic grip. Not only did these little ladies sing bawdy songs and parody highbrow and popular culture alike, they did so while inverting gender roles (2009: 5).

Neo-burlesque plays on the traditions of the original form: a parody of a parody. Performers poke fun at (sometimes deconstruct) the form itself, and the expectations of the audience. The constructivity of gender is consistently addressed in the undressing of performed gender and sexuality. Even those performers who do not overtly use humour in their aesthetics are performing an exaggerated, extreme style of sexuality and of gender. In the constant and known presence of multiple layers of clothing—numerous layers that were always going to come off to reveal a body—suggest that any finished form is built by layers which, in their culmination, signify glamour or gender or both. The ubiquitous presence of bedazzled lingerie, false eyelashes, wigs, high-heeled shoes, glittered and/or touched-up bare skin point always, and necessarily, to the performance of gender. This hyper-performance of gender is parody that is expected and celebrated by audience and performers.

As a remembered performance form, neo-burlesque exhibits the necessary gap of performed memory; re-membering, not in terms of putting back together a whole, attaching limbs to a forgotten body, but the never-quite-like-the-original necessity of remembrance, a repetition with a necessary revision. Joseph Roach's often-rehearsed thoughts of memory resound here, 'the paradox of collective perpetuation: memory is a process that depends crucially on forgetting' (1996: 2). That which is rehearsed and remembered about burlesque performance in neo-burlesque can't, of course, be the exact thing once performed. Within the choreographed removal of clothes, more than flesh is exposed. At the BHoF Weekend a festive state, a palpable space is created because of the proximity of the bodies that are revealing a remembered past (the neo-burlesque performers) and the objects of remembrance (the original burlesque performers). More than mere juxtaposition of a performance tradition and its reinvented descendant, there is an active space, which affects how the form continues to evolve.

The Weekend's History

The BHoF relocated from Helendale, California, to Las Vegas, Nevada, in 2006. The Hall of Fame itself began on a goat ranch in the Mojave Desert, 30 kilometres off Route 66. Jennie Lee, a 1950s burlesque performer, founded the Exotic World Ranch, which she hoped would be a museum for curated collections and a gathering place for retired performers. She also founded the Exotic Dancers League, an intended union of striptease performers. With the help of Dixie Evans, another iconic burlesque performer, she started the Miss Exotic World Pageant at the ranch. The gathering was a celebratory reunion for retired performers and neo-burlesque artists, rich with the juxtaposition of generations, and their unique contributions to the genre, as well as a mash-up of glamour, glitter, boas and pasties in the hot, dusty and desolate desert. At that time it was a pilgrimage for performers. In order to rub up against those artists quoted in the necessarily nostalgic neo-burlesque performances, performers had to find their way there. Via planes, rental cars and caravans the pilgrims carved out a place in the histories of USAmerican[12] performance as they traversed the desert to get to a festive place that would mark the map.

In 2005, the event (and the Hall) moved to Las Vegas, and in 2010 was renamed the Burlesque Hall of Fame Weekend.[13] In its current conception, the BHoF Weekend is now marketed as a reunion, a competition and a tourist attraction. What happens to and for the genre of neo-burlesque performance at this yearly festival? How is the work done under the rubric 'neo-burlesque' advanced or undermined at the festive, fleshy BHoF Weekend? Who gathers, who performs and for whom? The BHoF Weekend—a festival, a competition and an ecdysiast convention—has contributed to the establishment of the performance form as a genre. The festival works to open up an exchange between the genre's past and present, marking the space between burlesque and neo-burlesque.

The Schedule

The Reigning Queen of Burlesque pageant and competition, the featured event, is held on Saturday evening of the four-day event held each June. Performers apply to participate. They submit a written description and a video of a specific act; the choice of act is usually determined by the availability of a viable video.[14] Approximately 15 performers are chosen for Saturday evening's main event. There are special subcategories for newcomers, group acts, variety acts, and boylesque performers. There are far fewer entrants for the subcategories than the main competition, from three to six in a given category, depending on the year. Select performers who are not chosen to perform in the Saturday evening competition are invited to perform on Thursday and Sunday evenings. Usually the Thursday-evening performance is a warm-up event of sorts, though it is held in the same theatre venue as the subsequent evenings' performances. The Friday-evening show comprises legends from the 1950s on who are retired from stripping, but don their pasties and doff their dresses once again. Interspersed with the legends are past

Reigning Queens and other neo-burlesque all-stars, who often perform numbers in tribute to well-known performers from the past. Those invited to perform on Sunday do so either poolside at the end-of-the-weekend pool party, or during the weekend's final performance held Sunday evening. Though the poolside performance is usually well attended, playful and celebratory, there is limited technical support and the attention of those gathered is not focused on the performers.

Admission to the three evening performances can be purchased separately or at the weekend rate of $250. Performers are given complimentary tickets to one evening performance but are not paid for performing. Surrounding these structured evenings of performance are after-parties both planned and unplanned. There is a bowling excursion; a poker tournament; an expo of costumes, memorabilia and artwork; a formal question-and-answer event with assembled legends; organized after-parties at select bars; and the pool party. Much like any convention, there is usually some event at any given time throughout the BHoF Weekend.

The Space between Neo-burlesque and Burlesque

Honouring the history of burlesque performance is certainly a primary component of the BHoF Weekend. For the Friday-evening performance, organizers bring in some different retired performers each year, but there are those who seem to be festival mainstays. Dixie Evans is a BHoF figurehead, and Tempest Storm performed each year up until 2011 when she turned 83. There is a clear purposeful nod to those who have gone before. The celebration of the genre's past has become more integral to the weekend's structure, although this may not be realized by all attendees. Dr Lucky calls the entire festival a 'living history': 'past is the present, it is about them [the legends], they are generous in including *us*' (2011).

The retired performers—'the Ladies,' as Nasty Canasta calls them—remount signature numbers and occasionally create new ones, in some instances stripping again for the first time in decades. During both BHoF weekends that I attended, Tempest Storm was the final performer of the evening. Tempest performed to the accompaniment of her personal drummer (she was the sole performer to use live accompaniment), and in the style that she originally performed some 50 years ago: she sauntered to one side of the stage, posed, shimmied a bit, then sauntered across the stage to the other corner to repeat the process. After a journey or two across the stage, she'd strip out of part of her ensemble. I could imagine her performances happening in a supper club while folks chatted over dinner, looking up only occasionally. The tone of her performance, the ease and simplicity of the seemingly unchoreographed movement, supported by the high-hat cymbal, was evocative of a past generation's style. When I first saw Tempest in 2006, my impression was that the performance read like a live artefact. The moxie and confidence of a 78-year-old woman performing striptease in high heels (she stripped down to a bra and underwear), charmed me, as did the crowd's reaction: celebratory catcalls, hoots and hollers were a verbal gesture of respect for a classic performer. Tempest's performances tend to drag on a bit. With all reverence to her 60-plus years of guts and guile in performing burlesque, she does not work to cultivate the constant connection with her audience that is so central to the neo-burlesque tradition. There is a tension in the audience: an appreciation for her contributions to the form but a waning interest in her current efforts.[15]

At the 2010 BHoF Friday show, Dr Lucky interviewed three of the invited legends onstage between acts as part of the evening's performance. The stories these performers shared were primarily about the working conditions of their early days in the business, how they were treated by venue managers, and how they interacted with clientele and with each other. Palpable space was created in the evening's rhythm with these interviews, which were a teaser for the formal question-and-answer session that was held on Sunday morning. The Q&A event was another platform for the past performers to share stories of their careers—how they got started, their signature numbers or events, notable memories in general. While there seemed to be a general appreciation for the stories and the performers who told them, I noticed little engaged dialogue between the generations. Several of the legends expressed gratitude and surprise that anyone would want to hear these stories, unclear, or previously unaware of how they functioned as historic markers for the neo-burlesque movement. Furthermore, many of the legendary performers didn't seem to grasp the parodic essence of neo-burlesque performance, or perhaps they just didn't appreciate or approve of it. But they moved in the spaces created for interaction by the festival organizers. Young performers singled out older performers, expressed gratitude, shared compliments, but when discussing contemporary performance the generation gap became apparent.

During the Q&A, someone from the assembled audience asked the entire panel for advice for young performers. One legend, Tiffany Carter (Miss Nude Universe 1975), answered:

> I know this is my personal opinion and I don't know if you will all agree with me, that you are cutting yourself off right here [points below her hip-bone] with G-strings and T-straps. [. . .] It makes you a lot longer, leaner and we always wore them up. Tight pull, all on the sides. If you have a little bit of a belly it cuts that off. That is what I noticed (BurlesqueBeat.com 2010).

A small moment. Perhaps it was lost on everyone else in the room, but I was particularly taken by how this bit of advice misses the mark for a few reasons. First of all, in contemporary styles, garments are ubiquitously low-rise and low-waisted, for everything from lingerie to pants. The sides of the G-strings worn by neo-burlesque performers couldn't reach up over their hip bones because they aren't designed or constructed to be worn that way. The more telling misfire of this kernel of wisdom is that it shows a lack of awareness that it is generally not the aim of the neo-burlesque performer to maintain any one envisioned or encouraged figure or size. Neo-burlesque is, rather, known for the inclusion of a wide range of bodies. The artistry of the form is in how the figure and its flesh are revealed, not in the shape or size of the revealed body; in the contours of the choreography, in what is hidden, and in the gestures to the audience that create the push and pull of the tease in the stripping. This is where the work of neo-burlesque resides. Neo-burlesque bodies are often more real or 'average' than a stereotypical stripper's physique (large—often surgically enhanced—breasts, tiny waist, round tush). The neo-burlesque landscape includes AA-cupped waifs and DDD-cupped, plus-sized curves. Through the years, I have often heard many different burlesque performers and audience members laud the community for such inclusion. The inclusive aesthetic is a badge of honour, with shout-outs to burlesque's roots in the freak shows of vaudeville and sideshow circuits.

The nostalgia that is so much a part of the BHoF works to create a generative space in the gap between burlesque and neo-burlesque; that little hyphen marks a charged space. The festival provides ample opportunity for chronicling and celebrating, a process that creates and allows room for growing the genre and expanding its inclusive reach. The hyphen between the present and its cited past in the term 'neo-burlesque' marks that space. That little line can separate and simultaneously join the root (past) with its prefix (present). The line is active and reaches towards the two components of the genre to loosely hold them together. The BHoF festival facilitates that reaching, confirming both the connection and the dividing line.

Contradictions are a vital and productive component of neo-burlesque. Along with the aesthetic of glamour are its antitheses: monstrosity, strangeness and the carnivalesque. The reveal in neo-burlesque, the climactic moment of a number, can be charged with a twist. There are performances where the final reveal is an undressed body—pastied breasts released from a bra, bejewelled underwear or G-strings revealing the contours of butt and pubis—but there are also numbers where a twist surprises and supplants the supposed and imagined revealed flesh. Pasties are not only bejewelled or tasseled but perhaps created from an unexpected (yet thematically derived) material, such as playing cards, flowers, googly eyes, fur, crosses, toy animals, photographs or tiny Groucho Marx nose-glasses. In those cases, the tease in the choreography that leads to the reveal results in a misfire of sorts. The final reveal is not about the sensual or suggested unveiled flesh, but it is a citation, an idea, a joke—it is parody. The form plays on itself and the expectations, traditions and promises of its understood relationship between performer and audience. The genre consistently works to destabilize heteronormative expectations of gender through the hyperrealized performance of gender, then by stripping that drag off of a body. And that all happens through striptease. It is parody, but not without contradiction, nor even without the danger of re-inscribing the norms that it works to unseat: 'Neo-burlesque is a decidedly queer art form wrapping itself up in a genre built on misogyny; it is post-post feminism that has turned around and found delight in showgirl glamour and has appropriated the icon of the pin-up as a possible site of transgression' (Sally 2009: 22).

The BHoF, with its misfires and unrealized juxtapositions of past to present, along with its successes, clears a space for such transgression. Tiffany Carter's G-string advice struck me as a surprising misfire, and that moment cleaved a gap between my expectations of the event and the reality. I attended the BHoF expecting more of the neo-burlesque experience: more elite performers with their best numbers, more performers in general, more performances and more of the sideshow influence. I was expecting a pageant, rather than a play on a pageant, forgetting, somehow, that parody is the name of the game.

Reigning Queen of Burlesque Pageant, 2010

Among the spaces created through this festival are those that mark the regional affiliations of performers. A strong showing at the BHoF can put a city on the map as a neo-burlesque hotspot. The BHoF Weekend is, ultimately, centred on the pageant competition, with the BHoF choosing a face (and body) to stand in for and otherwise market the genre as well as the BHoF's business. Any selection process considers a variety of factors around merit, loyalty, character, style and politics. In the years leading up to the 2010 pageant, a key element the Reigning Queens of Burlesque brought to the table—in addition to talent and skill—might have been their geographic affiliation. In 2009 the winner was Kalani Kokonuts, a Las Vegas performer who was not a regular in the neo-burlesque scene. The former stripper and showgirl performed in neo-burlesque venues occasionally, where she retained her high production values (read: Las Vegas showgirl aesthetic). The assumption held by many in the neo-burlesque community was that in a year when the BHoF had plans to open its new museum space[16] on Freemont Street, having one of Las Vegas' own as its Reigning Queen would serve the BHoF well.

The 2010 BHoF marked what could be called the Canadian Inclusion. Several of the show's hosts threw good-natured jabs at the great many Canucks present.[17] There were a few performers from Canada (mostly from Vancouver, Toronto and Montreal), but more noticeable was the presence of the Canadian crowd. Canada was there to represent and fans of the Canadian performers made themselves known. The hoots and hollers for Canadian performers such as Roxi Dlite, Lola Frost and the group Sweet Soul Burlesque were the most consistent throughout the festival. Roxi Dlite was more of a fixture in the neo-burlesque scene prior to her win. She placed as the first runner up in 2009. Talk among the performers (at least among those whose conversations I was privy to) was that Roxi was an odds-on favourite to win. As neo-burlesque gains steam in urban areas throughout Canada, notably in Vancouver, Toronto and Montreal, inviting those audiences into the fold by crowning their own Roxi Dlite the winner surely helps spread the bawdy word of neo-burlesque performance. While performers I spoke with seemed sure of Roxi's victory, they didn't show any animosity towards her or her success; only that how the winners helped the festival, the Burlesque Hall of Fame, and its reach seemed to be criteria for, if not a benefit from the Reigning Queen. To be clear, conversations I heard never smacked of jealousy, or of criticizing other performers; the more frequent topic was how the BHoF functioned, and to what end. As an outsider with insider access, I was struck by this topic—not about the skill or artistry of who might win, but more so what winning meant to and at the festival.

Size and Scope of the Pageant

So, how does what plays in Peoria (or the neo-burlesque equivalent) size up on the BHoF stage? Performers apply with their most show-stopping numbers and in 2010 *planned* show-stopping numbers they could use to apply to the BHoF. Numbers that are typically received well in small bars and performing arts venues don't work the same on a proscenium stage in front of several hundred audience members. What seems to be happening is that performers are pushing the limits of their own styles to include numbers that will play in Las Vegas, which in turn could push the genre as a whole towards bigger shows. As more performers work to perfect bigger numbers, audiences are coming to expect such showmanship and large-scale productions. This isn't solely a matter of aesthetics, but it has a material effect on the performers. The go-to aesthetic for the 2010 BHoF was striptease with some hugely oversized props. These included a 5-foot-high magician's top hat, a four-foot-tall apple, a 6- to 7-foot three-tiered cake topped with a mounted stag's head, a larger-than-life bull and a 12-foot-long smoking cigar complete with an ash tray. All of these scenic props were also load-bearing: the stripping happened atop the giant props.

Costs to have such props built, shipped or otherwise transported to Las Vegas, and then stored once back at each performer's home base are significant especially in relation to how much neo-burlesque performers earn.[18] Even if performers are able to store such a prop piece somewhere in their urban landscapes, transporting the prop to local venues for gigs would be an additional expense, that is, assuming the venue could accommodate the size of the prop. Many have to drop their Vegas numbers from their hometown repertoires. With performers earning between $50 and $200 in guaranteed pay (before tips or any other arranged for split of the door) for regularly scheduled gigs at bars in New York City, it is hardly cost effective to rent a car or van, or even take a taxi (depending on the city, and if the props could fit in a standard-sized car) to and from the performance. To accommodate and include numbers of such physical scope, venues are changed and the frequency of performances is decreased. The trend is increasingly towards holding a few large-scale shows a year rather than weekly performances, which is what is happening in the Denver neo-burlesque scene. Producers have to book larger venues and charge ticket prices that are considerably higher than the cover charge required for bars and smaller performance venues. Performers can't afford to create many large-scale numbers, nor is the burlesque audience likely willing to pay for admission to many large-scale shows. This is all to say that bigger numbers breed bigger numbers.

The performances at the 2010 BHoF were for the most part well performed, exquisitely costumed and visually striking. The spectacle was exhilarating, as spectacle is wont to be. Roxi Dlite's first-prize 'Smoking Cigar' number epitomized the 'Go Big or Go Home' modus operandi of the 2010 BHoF. During the act, she stripped out of a satin smoking jacket to the slimmest of slim-fit dresses. The lavender satin frock was laced up the entire back of the dress, its red laces against her pale skin across the several-inch gap between the edges of the dress, revealing her bare bottom. Once out of the dress, Roxi's striptease centred on what she would reveal from behind a lusciously full red feather boa. The decadence of the number peaked when an undressed Roxi, in pasties and a jewelled merkin,[19] straddled the 12-foot smoking cigar—the tip of which was, appropriately, lit. Roxi's classic choreography borrows heavily from a recognizable striptease vocabulary; there was no surprise in her movement. She was not working for parody. Roxi's aesthetic was pin-up-girl glamour and she worked beautifully within that framework: a delicious, decadent and smokin' number.

For me, watching from the banquet chairs, the space—both literal and theoretical—eked out by the outsized props highlighted the tension between innovation and exquisite showmanship that mark the current landscape of neo-burlesque performance. There were two performers at the 2010 BHoF weekend whose work was anchored by innovation, and thus stood apart from the rest. The performances of New York–based Ms Tickle and Nasty Canasta unfolded in unique and unexpected ways. Both performers placed in the pageant: Ms Tickle was named Most Dazzling and Most Innovative and won in the Best Debut category; and Nasty was named Second Runner Up in the Reigning Queen of Burlesque event.

Tickle's number began with her removing the long, white feathery plumes that formed a skirt. Throughout the number, she picked up the discarded plumes to use them for a fan dance, exposing jewelled fringe only barely covering her breasts and similarly fringed G-string with dual straps across the hips. She was dressed (and then undressed) all in white and neutral silvery jewelled tones. The number had an ethereal quality, which increased tenfold when Tickle, seamlessly and during the choreographed fan-dance moves, somehow connected the plumes in each hand and opened her arms, arching them out, up and back. The plumes had mysteriously come together to form wings on each arm—elongated and ethereal, these reaching wings each extended well past the fingertips of her out-stretched arms. We gasped audibly. The normal rhythm of the linear progression of the number nearly complete, the audience could only assume we had already seen the final reveal. Usually it is the removal of one final article of clothing, offering a glimpse of exposed flesh, but the unexpected twist in this number was the revealed costume piece—the illusion of the fans turned into wings.

Nasty Canasta's number, 'Dorian Gray', was as trimmed down as the big prop numbers were spectacular. Dressed like a flapper in a short, black, bobbed wig, a small hat, a simple, sleek, grey shift dress, gloves and a long strand of pearls, Nasty's music and choreography were consistent with the 1920s theme. At the opening, Nasty noticed a large portrait of herself, projected to her left. In the portrait, she was naked except for the same long strand of pearls. As soon as Nasty began her strip by taking off her hat, she realized that the hat then appeared in the portrait. A well-timed triple take and game of hat-on/hat-off with the picture was a lovely nod to vaudeville-esque physical humour. Nasty continued to strip—

FIGURE 6.1 (ABOVE). **Nasty Canasta 'Strippermom'.** Photograph by Jess Desluniers-Lee.

FIGURE 6.2 (RIGHT). **Nasty Canasta backstage at the Burlesque Hall of Fame Reigning Queen of Burlesque Pageant, 2010.** Photograph by Dr. Tang.

though her costume pieces were few—until she was naked (save for pasties and a thong), and her portrait-self was fully dressed. The number was quite brief in comparison to other performances, which served the nature of the number quite well. The twist in the 'Dorian Gray' piece, the reveal, wasn't Nasty's body but, rather, how we, as audience, saw it. The strip was timed perfectly to the portrait-self video and revealed to the audience how we watch, where we look and how the body is mediated in our consumption of it. The number was smart, tight and stood out smartly from the rest of the evening's performances.

Both Tickle and Nasty altered where we in the audience looked and how we read their revealed bodies. In so doing, they called attention to the consumption of gendered, sexualized bodies through a kind of bait-and-switch with the gaze. Striptease performance is necessarily about an audience's gaze; the choreography, especially in the push/pull of the tease, is planned to hold that gaze. The performer starts and stops to take off a given article, building anticipation in her audience for its promised and inevitable removal. These two numbers specifically, and neo-burlesque in general, create a space between the expected and the revealed, in a wholly self-referential way, a parody of striptease to destabilize the normative structures on the object—the body—stripped. These citational, charged bawdy moments gesture towards the utopian performative that Jill Dolan describes as 'small but profound moments in which performance calls the attention of the audience in a way that lifts everyone slightly above the present' (2005: 5). The work of neo-burlesque has the potential to offer such transgressive hoverings. Dolan charts a concept that is akin to the making strange or distancing of Bertolt Brecht's *Verfremdungseffekt*. Through exaggerated glamour, moments of surprising innovation and at times grotesque nakedness, neo-burlesque reveals brief moments that can illuminate the constructivity of gender. It is a performance based on gestural nods—nods to its past, nods to its audience. These moments can work as choreographed moves sidling near to the utopian potential of performance. Neo-burlesque performance, in its contradictions and parody, creates space between its present iterations and the originary burlesque it re-presents.

This is the richness I have always found in neo-burlesque: amassed together with an audience who necessarily knows the drill, called upon by the performer's gestures, tantalized and teased into wondering what will come off next and, finally, offered the reveal. The choreography, the concept, the costumes, the carnival atmosphere all engage my senses and my thinking about gender, sexuality and how we come together through this art form to undress and address social codes. Neo-burlesque performances can be crude, rough, loud and uncomfortable, and all of that, too, plays into the deconstruction of concepts of desire and sexuality. 'For, as participants well know, festivals, for all their joy and color, are also battlegrounds where identities are fought over and communities made' (Guss 2000: 172). The festivities that surround neo-burlesque performances unite performer and audience, and tease out of all of us an alternative understanding of the production of gender and sexuality. Dolan uses the rubric 'utopian performative' 'to indicate a performative that "does" utopia in its utterance' (2005: 173). Neo-burlesque can function as a performative that *does* utopia in the undoing of laces, the unfastening of hooks and the undressing of bodies. I do not suggest that the performances themselves are necessarily staged utopias, great no-places of deconstructed gendered norms, but that the scope of the BHoF gathering, with all of its misfires, its showmanship, its parade, its spectacle and its lived past is the doing of a kind of no-place. The space created is a place that offers perches to hover above present moments, a revealed kind of utopia. Whether the perch on which we hover is Roxi's smoking cigar or on the words of Carter's misplaced advice, the Burlesque Hall of Fame might offer a new perspective from the elevated space between—connecting past and present.

Notes

1 Most mass-market coverage of BHoF focuses on the performances by the living legends or on the quippy stage names of the performers, or on the sheer volume of glitter, crystals, tassels and boas:

> The performers have names such as Mimi LeMeaux, Delirium Tremens, Flame Cynders, Nasty Canasta or Trixie Little & the Evil Hate Monkey. The crowd howls and claps and whoops. It's very hard to turn into prose, convincingly, why this is worthwhile. But, I hope at least, it's enough to say that here's an authentic American popular artform [*sic*] that disappeared—and whose pioneering stars went unacknowledged—for the best part of 40 years. And now here it is, rediscovered and reinvented by a new, more elaborately tattooed generation: innocent, sexy, silly as hell (Leith 2006).

> The pageant was a tidal wave of movers and shakers. It is four hours of non-stop shimmying and tassle-twirling [*sic*] action of every shape and size. Looking on was the world press and a standing-room only crowd of kids, dogs and grandmothers. Why not? Women older than they are stripping in the pageant (Neal 2003).

2 In 2011, there was a greater disruption for the Burlesque Hall of Fame Weekend. A splinter group, first calling themselves the Sassy Lassy Burlesque Show, planned performances in Las Vegas during the BHoF weekend (2–5 June 2011), stealing legendary headliners Dixie Evans and Tempest Storm, mainstays of the BHoF. Sued for trademark infringement by the BHoF (the Sassy Lassy Nightclub was owned by BHoF Jennie Lee, and the BHoF owns all Sassy Lassy trademarks), the competing event changed the name of their event to the Dixie Evans Burlesque Show. Evans has been the caretaker and face of the BHoF since the death of founder Jennie Lee. The suit brought against the breakaway group alleged 'numerous burlesque pageant performers and attendees of the Burlesque Hall of Fame Weekend are boycotting Burlesque Hall of Fame's 2011 event because of the confusion as to which is the "real show" and "to wait and see who is still standing in 2012"' (Green 2011). The lawsuit accuses those responsible for the break-away group of 'intentionally creating confusion among the burlesque industry and family' (Scheck 2011). I think it is particularly relevant to how the BHoF

functions within the community that the attorneys representing the BHoF used the term 'family' in their suit.

3 It is a purposeful practice of mine to use 'USAmerica' when referring to the United States. As Gretchen Murphy notes in *Hemispheric Imaginings: The Monroe Doctrine and Narratives of U.S. Empire*, a project which explicitly exposes the active, if not colonial, implications of 'America': 'Even the name "America" bespeaks the crisis; conventionally used to designate the cultural identity of the United States, its implicit erasure of Latin America and Canada is now painfully apparent, leading Buell and others to suggest that one response to this global trend might be the "refashioning of American studies as a hemispheric project"' (2005: 1).

4 In recent years, there have been neo-burlesque performers from Canada, UK, Australia, Japan and Finland.

5 Nasty Canasta described the make-up of the BHoF audience:

> A huge percentage of the audience is performers; people in the audience have performed on a different night at the festival. I'm sure that there are random people there, but I have met very few of them, honestly, partly because it is in Las Vegas. For the New York Burlesque Festival there are a lot of people who live in New York and go to see it. But Vegas is a destination. As much as it's billed, people [who live there] don't go to there to see this. It's interesting because you are performing for people who *do this*, and are really well versed in it. It affects the choice of number and wanting to be there at all (2011).

Dr Lucky, a New York–based neo-burlesque performer who moonlights as a performance studies scholar and teaches an undergraduate course on burlesque at New York University, noted the importance of the audience as part of the spectacle:

> The audience [are] entertainers and as over the top theatrically as what's going on onstage. [It's about] seeing and being seen and being the most outrageous as you possibly can. It's a Technicolor musical acid trip Vegas crazy amusement park where it's sensory overload the entire time. Vegas is a transitory place. They don't give a shit about the BHoF. It's a transitory tourist crowd, and it's difficult to build momentum from a tourist industry, so it might not be the ideal location (2011).

6 See, for instance, Robert Allen (1991); Lynn Sally (2009); Rachel Shteir (2005).

7 Dr Lucky, in a phone interview, noted that a student of hers was interviewing another New York–based performer, Miss Saturn, and asked Saturn for her definition of neo-burlesque. 'Oh, is that what Lucky is calling it now?' Saturn quipped (2011). Much as neo-burlesque defies a bounded definition, when the label is used and by whom is similarly slippery. (For the use of neo-burlesque in critical scholarship see, for instance, Sally [2009]; Shteir [2005].) Neo-burlesque performers simply refer to themselves as burlesque performers, although I haven't heard or read of any opposition to the 'neo' prefix. However, when referring to current performers and the genre in its contemporary iteration, I will use 'neo-burlesque', and will use 'burlesque' to refer to performers from the genre's golden age, those who are the referred to as the 'legends' at the BHoF Weekend.

8 To clarify, there is fluidity between burlesque, stripping and neo-burlesque. Striptease is the common denominator. Some current neo-burlesque performers were previously strippers. It is my understanding that while it is not common for performers to consistently move between neo-burlesque performance and stripping, the distinction between the two genres seems less of interest to performers than to those writing or reporting on the performance. Some neo-burlesque performers refer to themselves as 'art-strippers'. There is overlap in choreography, in vocabulary, with the performers. My aim is not to make sure distinctions between the genres as much as to explore the genre of neo-burlesque performance.

9 I am careful to mention the specific geographic region and time as neo-burlesque has had different iterations, at times delineated by place or region. In the early 2000s, the Los Angeles neo-burlesque scene featured elaborate, professionally made costumes, while the New York scene was known for a DIY aesthetic, with performers building costumes for their numbers on their own. Currently, the Los Angeles scene includes a greater number of group performances and burlesque troupes than does the New York scene. While such categorization is by no mean definitive, as the genre continues to evolve, time and place are contributing factors to the aesthetic of a given performance.

10 A few venues that have held burlesque shows in recent years are: (In Manhattan) the Slipper Room on the Lower East Side, Rififi (now long-closed) and the Bowery Poetry Club in the East Village, City Winery in the South Village and Duane Park in Tribeca; (In Brooklyn) Galapagos Art Space in Dumbo and The Knitting Factory in Williamsburg.

11 'Boylesque' is a term used by the burlesque community to describe male performers.

12 Just as the then Miss Exotic World Pageant was garnering national and international recognition and attention in its new Vegas home, the name of the event was changed to the Burlesque Hall of Fame Weekend, with the winner of the main competition earning the title of the Reigning Queen of Burlesque (rather than Miss Exotic World). In personal conversations with performers I was told that there were legal issues with the name, specifically regarding trademark infringement claims made by the Miss World pageant. In all publicity and marketing, what was once referred to as Exotic World now became the Burlesque Hall of Fame, and the Miss Exotic World Pageant became the Burlesque Hall of Fame Weekend.

13 Nasty Canasta, in a phone interview, mentioned that when choosing a number to submit to the BHoF, choices were limited, at that time, by those numbers that performers 'happen to have video (and *decent* video) of. Because the spaces we work in in New York, especially, tend to be tiny and poorly lit, and because I personally have no access to decent video equipment, and even when we find someone to video a number it always looks like someone's uncle videotaped it from the back row, with people's heads in the way' (2011).

14 Sadly, early in her performance at the 2010 BHoF Weekend, Tempest lost her footing and fell on her right side. (Strangely, her drummer kept playing). The curtain eventually closed and the evening's performance ended while an ambulance was called. Tempest broke her hip, but had successful surgery.

15 The BHoF is an ongoing project. While there is a small storefront with a display of artefacts, it shares space with a coffee shop. There are archives still boxed and waiting for a more permanent and accessible home.

16 The following, posted on the blog BurlesqueBeat.com by J. D. Oxblood, captures the always cheeky tone of the neo-burlesque scene and notes the presence our northern neighbours:

> On Canada: Burgundy Brixx—who is running a cabal—told me why Vancouver was better than New York. Basically, you've got to have a corporate job in New York to support your burlesque habit. Because Vancouver is cheaper, and a more chill environment, you can work a little and play more. She made the move and regrets nothing. It's worth thinking about . . . Chatting with Norm, he relegated the Vancouvarinos' previous relative absence at BHOF to a kind of 'Canadian modesty.' You know—they're just not the gregarious motherfuckers that Americans are. But they came in force this year, and all I can say is I have GOT to get my white ass to some of those Canadian festivals (Oxblood 2010).

17 The World Famous *BOB*: 'Strippers make money and burlesque dancers put it into their next costume. I would love to see the bank account of anyone who says they're getting rich off of burlesque right now, because they would be a liar' (quoted in Baldwin 2004: 50).

18 A 'merkin' is a pubic wig or any constructed covering of the pubis.

Works Cited

ALLEN, Robert. 1991. *Horrible Prettiness: Burlesque and American Culture.* Chapel Hill: University of North Carolina Press.

BALDWIN, Michelle. 2004. *Burlesque and the New Bump-n-Grind.* Denver, CO: Speck Press.

CANASTA, Nasty. 2011. Telephone interview with author, 14 June.

DOLAN, Jill. 2005. *Utopia in Performance: Finding Hope at the Theatre.* Ann Arbor: University Of Michigan Press.

GREEN, Steve. 2011. 'Competing Las Vegas Burlesque Promoters In Legal Battle'. *Las Vegas Sun,* 25 April. Available at: http://goo.gl/OZXIp2 (last accessed on 23 July 2011).

GUSS, David M. 2000. *The Festive State: Race, Ethnicity, and Nationalism as Cultural Performance.* Berkeley: University of California Press.

BURLESQUEBEAT.COM. 2011. 'Legends Panel Transcript: Burlesque Hall of Fame 2010'. Burlesquebeat.Com, 2 June. Available at: http://goo.gl/-YEuKcd (last accessed on 23 July 2011).

LEITH, Sam. 2006. 'Why I Fell In Love With Miss Dirty Martini'. *Daily Telegraph*, 29 May. Available at: http://goo.gl/W7QyWa (last accessed on 3 August 2011).

LIEPE-LEVINSON, Katherine. 2002. *Strip Show: Performances Of Gender and Desire*. London: Routledge.

LUCKY, Dr. 2011. Telephone interview with author, 5 August.

MURPHY, Gretchen. 2005. *Hemispheric Imaginings: The Monroe Doctrine and Narratives of U.S. Empire*. Durham, NC: Duke University Press.

NEAL, Rome. 2003. 'The Crown Jewels of Burlesque'. *CBS News Sunday Morning*, 15 June. Available at: http://goo.gl/6Frpnt (last accessed on 23 July 2011).

OXBLOOD, J. D. 2010. 'On BHoF 2010—V. Denouement'. Burlesque-beat.Com, 2 July. Available at: http://goo.gl/7WrupQ (last accessed on 3 August 2011).

ROACH, Joseph. 1996. *Cities of the Dead: Circum-Atlantic Performances*. New York: Columbia University Press.

SALLY, Lynn. 2009. '"It Is the Ugly That Is So Beautiful": Performing the Monster/Beauty Continuum in American Neo-burlesque'. *Journal of American Drama and Theatre* 21(3): 1–23.

SCHECK, Justin. 2011. 'Wheels of Justice (Bump and) Grind for Vegas's Battling Burlesque Shows: Stripper Hall of Fame See Naked Aggression as Rivals Woo Its Octogenarian Ecdysiasts'. *Wall Street Journal*, 2 June. Available at: http://goo.gl/N4mocH (last accessed on 3 August 2011).

SHTEIR, Rachel. 2005. *Striptease: The Untold History of the Girlie Show*. New York: Oxford University Press.

Part Three

HETEROTOPIAS AND DYSTOPIAS AS CONTEMPORARY SPACES OF HEALING

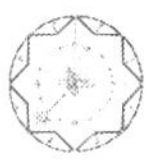

Chapter 7

HETEROTOPIAS OF POWER

Miners, Mapuche and Soldiers in the Production of the Utopian Chile

Néstor Bravo Goldsmith

Drawing from Michel Foucault's notion of heterotopias, I choose to identify and examine three distinct but related events that re-imagined Chile during 2010, the year of its bicentenary, namely: the rescue of the 33 miners trapped in the San José mine; the Chilean Military Parade performed in celebration of Chilean Independence; and the hunger strike by 32 Indigenous Mapuche people accused of terrorism by the Chilean State. A point of intersection in these three case studies is the decisive role the Chilean government played in eliciting, enacting and instrumentalizing the heterotopic sites to present and promote specific notions of national, ethnic and gender identities. Thus, the Chilean Military Parade is not an accurate reflection of reality, but a constructed, convenient representation of 'reality', staged according to the ideological agenda of the government in place. Subsequently, the parade produces and presents to its audience the Chile that could be as if it already were. The hunger strike, in turn, articulates a heterotopia of deviance that demonstrates the extremes of the situation of oppression the Mapuche are actually experiencing in their communities, and makes it visible for a national and international audience. Therefore, this enacted utopia reflects the nation as it is while fostering the nation that should be, at least according to the movement for Indigenous autonomy in Chile. Finally, the San José heterotopia enacts a utopian Chile through Camp Hope, which was an ideal and transitory 'city-state' conceived and produced by the Chilean government as a place where incompatible political, ideological and socio-economic systems and views are harmonized in a way that is not seen in everyday Chile.

The three events are of interest because in addition to following the six heterotopological principles formulated by Foucault, they also present two important characteristics. First, they have performance as the central constituent that defines their specificity and brings the heterotopias into existence. Here, performance seems to act as the interface, the point of interaction, and the suture between the conceived, the perceived and the representational social spaces each heterotopia articulates. Thus, these three cases represent a particular type of heterotopia that is enacted through performance.

Second, a relevant aspect that emerged from these case studies is that heterotopic places may not only mirror, contest and compensate for the flaws in their host society, but also refer to and intersect with other contemporaneous heterotopias enacted in it. If such interactions between performance heterotopias happen within a given society, then it is possible to extrapolate that they could also take place between contemporaneous heterotopias that emerge in different countries and cultures. If so, the mapping of utopias enacted, for example, in the macro-socio-geographies of Latin American countries could offer new perspectives to understand the sociopolitical processes that are underway in the region.

Camp Hope Heterotopia: Chronicle of a Disaster Foretold

On 12 October 2010, a temporary enacted utopia came to an end as a global audience witnessed the rescue of 33 Chilean miners[1] trapped in the San José mine. Since the tunnel had collapsed two and a half months earlier, the desert surroundings of the mine had become the scenario of a fascinating transformation, as the site began to be populated by the trapped miners' families, government authorities, rescuers, clerics from different religious denominations, politicians, soldiers, soothsayers, clowns, vendors and more than 1,600 journalists from all over the world. The pilgrimage to San José exponentially increased once it became known that the 33 miners were alive, an incident that turned dystopian tragedy into a moment of utopian hope.

The demographic explosion in San José challenged Chilean authorities to reconceive the raw perceived geographical place as a transitory village capable of hosting a projected population of more than 2,000 residents and a floating population of hundreds. In the mind of the planners, a peculiar city concept was formed, represented with the help of computer-aided design tools and finally materialized into 'Camp Hope', a small but perfect and functional city-state in the middle of the Atacama Desert.

Thus, the San José heterotopia was first discursively imagined by multiple protagonists and was carefully articulated by the government from the beginning. For almost three months, Camp Hope was produced as the place where an exemplary Chile was performed for a national and international audience, micro-managed right down to the smallest detail by controlling the timing of the event, orchestrating its *mise-en-scène* and broadcast, the entrance, actions and exit of the authorities involved, and filtering and concealing backstage key information about the episode that could have tarnished the perfect script and its dramatic arc.

From the government's point of view, the production of the Camp Hope heterotopia was never just about rescuing the 33 miners, which was the manifest, public purpose; it was also about demonstrating that the government 'can do things right',[2] and that it is capable of 'doing great things' (*Los Andes* 2010). Camp Hope provided and was articulated as the perfect setting to consolidate the instalment and the image of the new government by showing its efficiency, effectiveness, acumen and success in the face of difficult times.

Camp Hope offered the ideal place for rehearsing then-president Sebastián Piñera's technocratic approach to governance, which, until its politically poor handling of the Mapuche hunger strike, professed to be an effective and apolitical adaptation of technical expertise to the task of governance blended with high doses of presidential personalism (Fischer 1990: 18). Unlike the outside world where the government cannot control all the sociopolitical variables at play in current Chile, the setting of Camp Hope was such that the miners were passive victims waiting to be rescued, not deliberate or unpredictable individuals with agency to challenge the effort and decisions made on the surface by a team of technocrats. The miners could not act upon or change the developments; they could only be acted upon. And having the technical factor under control, the informational factor—a key element to tout Camp Hope to a massive audience—could also be controlled.

Thus, the government started catalysing a trialectic of space, knowledge and power (Soja 1996: 15) and enabling a site that soon would surpass the manifest purpose of rescuing the miners to become something else: a *temporal heterotopia* (Foucault 1986: 26) that would resignify, through performance, a utopian Chile. As San José was produced as a new location in the social space of Chilean society, it became the materialization of an ideal country, the Chile that could be, deceptively sold through the media as if it already existed.

Foucault defines temporal heterotopias as enacted utopias that are not oriented towards the eternal but 'linked to time in its most fleeting, transitory, precarious aspect, to time in the mode of the festival' (ibid.: 26). It is not only the transitory nature of Camp Hope that allows the enactment of the utopian Chile but also its isolation and location far from any city and town, the relatively small number of people involved and the clear definition of the operation.[3] The tragedy was not an event impossible to anticipate; it was not the *outlier* that Nassim Taleb referred to in his Black Swan theory (2007). On the contrary, it was a probable event, a 'White Swan' that owners of the mine, miners, engineers and authorities in charge of preventing accidents of this kind knew would occur. Between March 2004 and July 2010, the company had received 42 fines for breaching safety regulations, and three cave-ins provoked three fatal accidents in the mine. In the same period, it closed and reopened four times without complying with the safety regulations demanded by the inspectors. A report of the Labor Inspection of Copiapó, dated 9 July 2010, pointed out the lack of proper fortification of the roof, lack of permanent and visible signs posted in areas of danger, among other indications. The document also charges the company with a fine of $6,000 for its negligence (Mery 2010). Nevertheless, the mine reopened without meeting requirements and, just two weeks later, on 5 August, it collapsed again—this time trapping the 33 miners.[4]

The cave-in occurred around 2.30 p.m., and a few hours later the human geography of San José began to change drastically, as unexpected numbers of people arrived at the scene. Along with 26 rescuers from the Police Special Operations Group and firefighters, the miners' family members were the first to come, seeking reliable information about the fate of their loved ones.[5] Without a place to lodge, the families set up makeshift shelters close to the mine's entrance. The unlikely village grew to its peak in the days before the rescue took place.

The search for survivors reached its climactic moment when President Piñera answered the main dramatic question announcing that the 33 miners were all alive—Monday, 22 August, 17 days after the cave-in. This turning point morphed tragedy into *komos* (festivity) with a promising happy ending that would culminate two months later when the 33 were actually rescued. For a country that had been ravaged by a massive and devastating earthquake and tsunami a few months before, the news of the miners became a celebration of life, a sign of hope and national revival. With that typical heroic and poetic tone that Chileans use in times of triumph (and despair), many allegorized that the rescue of the 33 from the depths of the earth was but the very *padre-patria* that was about to be born again, thus reiterating the founding myth that portrays men as the central progenitors of the Chilean nation. Cristián Warnken, for instance, with his elegant prose, argued that the rescue was a re-genesis of the nation:

> It is the land that will give birth to 33 men. But in fact we are they who will be born, for we were sleeping and dead. An earthquake was not enough to wake us. We needed a Great Myth, to group around it: and this is not 'news' any more, but a myth born of the unconscious of the Chilean people. As if the republic would be born again, as if these 33 miners were its prodigal sons about to return. And until they return, Chile will not yet exist (2010).

According to Warnken, the dream from which Chile should awake is that of a country that 'has reneged on its own light to copy and dazzle itself with the spotlights, cameras, celebrities, the event and the "reality show"' (ibid.),[6] that is to say, from the Debordian dazzling light in which we are sunk, and where social relationships, the face-to-face, are mediated by images and the game of representation. Interestingly, Warnken's critical assessment of a Chile that had been spectacularized and seduced to perform for the camera was precisely what the current government was doing with the San José event to tout Piñera's technocratic model of governance, to engender new political figures and to throw a smokescreen over the national stage to camouflage the social conflicts that transpired in Chile at that time, such as the Mapuche hunger strike.

Yet, it seems that we, Chileans, prefer to believe in the cathartic trope created by Warnken, however illusory it might be, for the simple reason that, back on the surface of our imagined community, things are far from Edenic and we know (although almost never acknowledge) how urgently Chile needs a renewal, a purification, a kind of full-stop law that could end all the problems, conflicts and injustices that the country still carried on its back in the year of its bicentenary.

At dawn on 22 August, the rescue team learnt that the miners were alive after receiving a note tied to a probe that had reached their place of refuge. President Piñera, who was in the capital, was notified immediately. However, the news was kept secret even from family members for nine hours, until the president jumped onto the stage to give the news to the families and the world in person. The fact that the government delayed the release of such important news to the families shows the level at which it was micro-managing the event; by prioritizing the staging of this climactic moment, it hoped to maximize the effect.

From the point of view of its theatricality, the announcement made by the president was impressively constructed. At 3.15 p.m. he came out from the rescue zone surrounded by his uniformly dressed ministers with the characteristic red coats that only high officials of the government are authorized to wear. The entire camp gathered together in front of a raised platform where a deeply moved president proceeded to read the note received from the miners: 'Estamos bien en el refugio los 33' ('We are OK in the refuge the 33'). Grammatically incorrect,[7] the piece of paper profiled the low educational level of the miners that had at one point forced them to find jobs where, in general, technical literacy is not a requirement. Yet in the president's hand, the paper represented a government that worked on behalf of the working class, the most dispossessed, which is one of the tropes that Piñera's right-wing governmental rhetoric had been reiterating from the beginning to debunk the pervasive belief that conservative parties privilege the rich over the poor.

The celebratory speech that followed politically profited from the occasion by praising the efficiency of a government that 'keeps its promises', linking the incident to the bicentenary celebrations, recognizing the courage, patriotism and faith of the miners and their families and highlighting the exemplary union demonstrated by the Chilean people in a time of crisis.[8]

With the successful and happy outcome, the government gained political momentum as the managerial capabilities shown in Camp Hope favourably impacted the public perception.[9] With a global audience interested in following the event, the migration to the zone intensified, with hosts of journalists coming from around the world to cover the developments. The sudden demographic explosion obligated the government's planners to reconceive San José and make it sustainable for an expected population of 3,000, where no less than 60 per cent were reporters and journalists. The reconceived space materialized into the top cosmopolitan and exclusive Chilean city, the designated site where a utopian Chile would be enacted. With a possible successful rescue on the horizon, the government reengineered its communicational strategy and began to stage the rescue.

The final climactic moment happened sooner than expected. On 12 October 2010, when Chile celebrated El Día de la Raza (Columbus Day), and after 69 days underground, the 33 began to emerge from the mine. It was as if Warnken's masculine revival of the foundational myth of the nation had magically aligned with another foundational moment, 518 years ago. At any rate, it was the climax, the day Piñera said he had dreamt of: the setting, the lights, the music and the cameras readied to cover the moment when the land was to give birth.

The world watched as the government's live video feed opened with a panoramic view of the rescue zone: against a rocky background, a five-legged structure supported a large wheel above the shaft through which the rescue capsule, the red-white-and-blue Phoenix 2, would descend nearly 800 metres to retrieve the miners. Multiple fixed and mobile cameras were placed to cover the event from different angles. Stage left was the area reserved for the Chilean president, his wives and ministers who, along with the miners' wife and children, would greet the miners as each emerged from the capsule. A large Chilean flag flanked the authorities' sector. Stage right was the spectator area, with the miners' coworkers and family members. On the front left of the rescue area was a triage medical station ready to check the miners' health conditions. At 12.11 a.m., the first miner resurfaced, followed by the rest over the next 22 hours.

A miner exiting the capsule was first greeted by his wife and other family members of his choice, and was then welcomed by the president himself, who remained in the rescue zone for the whole operation. In that period of time, he received calls from several presidents and international celebrities,[10] while millions all over the world watched the event from their televisions, Internet and cell phones. In the United States, more than 10 million people watched CNN, Fox News and MSNBC as the first of the 33 was rescued (Mackey 2010). Mike Rowe, the host of the Discovery Channel's reality show *Dirty Jobs*, told CNN's Larry King, 'Whatever it is we call reality that passes for TV is nonsense compared to what really is happening right in front of us' (cited in Stelter 2010). The rescue in Camp Hope, however, was not pure reality but the assembling of the real, a *mise-en-scène*, an audiovisual device in action that put together a *version* of reality.[11] The Chilean government knew that it was an opportunity to project the image of the country to the world, and capitalize on it politically and economically. The government blurred news and entertainment into each other. Here the real was artificially produced as real to become 'hyperreal', pure simulacrum (Baudrillard 1981), where the protagonists, the victims, immersed in a real and dramatic situation, become performers of their own story, but according to the version of the owner of the event, the producer-director—the government. The anesthetization of the tragedy and the staging of everyday life in Camp Hope created and projected a heterotopic version of a perfect Chile into the videosphere.

According to Foucault, one of the roles of heterotopias is to create 'a space that is other, another real space, as perfect, as meticulous, as well arranged as ours is messy, ill constructed, and jumbled' (Foucault 1986: 27), and that is the case with San José. During the 69 days of its existence, Camp Hope remained in the margins of all spaces that commonly animate Chilean society and, although geographically situated on the periphery, this improbable city became the centre, the spotlight, the mirage in the middle of the desert where the gaze of millions of Chileans was focused. Thus, Chile was on tenterhooks for three months under the spell of the spectacle that the government and its strategic ally, the mass media, started to stage on day two.[12] At this point, Debord's third formulation, which sounds surprisingly similar to the heterotopian property of being in systemic relation with all the other sites of society (ibid.: 24), comes out pristine:

> The spectacle presents itself simultaneously as all of society, as part of society, and as instrument of unification. As a part of society it is specifically the sector which concentrates all

> gazing and all consciousness. Due to the very fact that this sector is separate, it is the common ground of the deceived gaze and of false consciousness, and the unification it achieves is nothing but an official language of generalized separation (Debord 1983: 7).

Its gaze on Camp Hope, the national audience witnessed not only how the Chilean president, one of his ministers and eventually the 33 themselves got onto the stage to become world celebrities, but also how this spot in the middle of the desert grew to become a kind of Tierra de Jauja (the Neverland of milk and honey), a place where the proverbial Chile was exemplarily enacted. Suddenly, Camp Hope became a model to which it was possible to juxtapose the other Chile, and so, to appreciate both its accomplishments and shortcomings.

In Camp Hope, a centralist government provided and satisfied all the necessities of its temporary citizens; but beyond its borders the income difference ratio between the richest 10 per cent and poorest 10 per cent of Chileans stands at 26.2 to 1 and persists as one of the most unequal wealth distributions in the hemisphere (UNDP 2009: 195). Camp Hope's health system was free, and the very minister of health tended to the trapped miners and their families; but in the other Chile, long waiting lists prevented people from receiving timely attention in public hospitals while the private clinics offered opportune but costly services. In Camp Hope, policemen were more often found playing football with children while smiling at the camera than violently repressing people and shutting down legitimate protests. The minister of education inaugurated a colourful classroom for elementary-school students in Camp Hope, giving free education to all children living there, in just one afternoon; while on the other side of the mirror, the educational system was still in crisis. And while in this Tierra de Jauja, the food, housing, education, public lighting, communications, TV transmissions, Internet and transportation were all free of charge, the economic neoliberal model continued to legitimize exploitation in the rest of the nation. Camp Hope was organized more like a socialist utopia than a capitalist one. Its economy was centralized and performed at its purest. The government acted as a paternalist and controlling entity, solving all the problems of this little country in a manner that would enrage economist Milton Friedman by just thinking about it. To be fair, I would say that Piñera used the best of these opposite economic concepts and, dialectically, he arrived at a synthesis that does nothing more than to prove that the enacted utopia of Camp Hope satisfies the third heterotopic principle: 'The heterotopia is capable of juxtaposing in a single real place several spaces, several sites that are in themselves *incompatible*' (Foucault 1986: 25). Here a market economy coexisted with a planned economy in a script that allowed such a hybridism to be staged by a neoliberal entrepreneur and right-wing politician, Sebastián Piñera.

Moreover, Camp Hope was eco-friendly while beyond its boundaries thermoelectric plants are authorized to operate in nature sanctuaries. Whereas there were no ethnic or class conflicts in Camp Hope, no crime, and the only jail remained empty all the time, the real dystopian Chile criminalizes Indigenous people, accuses them of terrorism and incarcerates them using laws cooked up during the Pinochet regime; and Chile's penitentiary system has the highest number of people behind bars in Latin America. Indeed, the plenipotentiary and efficient socialist/technocrat government that ruled in Camp Hope stands in stark contrast with the conservative and populist government privileging private companies that, in turn, privilege utilities over the well-being of their workers, as was the case in the San José mining tragedy.

Nevertheless, Camp Hope accomplished its double purpose of rescuing the 33 and revamping the government. During the camp's three-month existence, its central, bystander and cultural audiences[13] saw no deaths, and no homeless or beggars on its one and only street. Yet, the enactment of a temporal utopia has its double edge: by showing what a perfect Chile could look like, it reveals the lack-lustre Chile that remains. As with the feast of fools and carnival, transitory heterotopias vanish, leaving us with our everyday messy world. For Piñera, the time of celebration was also left behind as four months after the rescue his popularity was lower than ever before. Could he produce a new one? It was a tempting proposition.

Camp Hope was more than a narrative that addressed utopia; it was a materialization of a utopia. Though temporarily, Camp Hope perfected the social spaces and the institutions that operated and defined Chilean society at that moment. Without doubt, there is an enormous value in that accomplishment, and Piñera's government demonstrated that its team of technocrats can do things right, make wise decisions and meet the goals they set. The government in Camp Hope showed governance, and that is an objective, irrefutable datum. The problem is that once the production was done, and even during the performance stage of the heterotopia, the same characters that gave life to the story, answered the dramatic questions and solved the conflict—the president, the ministers, the policemen—played reversed characters in the everyday Chile. This questionable political cross-dressing becomes evident when juxtaposing Camp Hope to Chilean society. Yet perhaps the true scandal resided in presenting an official site as a place where the 'hierarchical rank, privileges, norms, and prohibitions' (Bakhtin 1984: 10) were all suspended or inverted for the participant, while outside, in the spectator's space, the 'existing hierarchy, the existing religions, political, and moral values' (ibid.) and norms remained unchanged. Camp Hope was, to some extent, the official feast presented as a carnival, a place where the authorities performed their official roles following a political script impossible to replicate on the main stage. In sum, it was a carnival for the temporal enjoyment of the ruling class, while the rest of us merely watched the feast, transfixed by our TV screens.

The Mapuche Hunger Strike: A Heterotopia of Deviance

Simultaneously, 1,100 kilometres from San José, in the southern region of La Araucanía, a 'heterotopia of deviance' (Foucault 1986: 25) was underway. While the 33 miners were rationing their food in order to survive, 32 other men—all incarcerated Indigenous Mapuche activists—were staging a hunger strike. At issue were millions of acres of ancestral lands, which had been expropriated by the Chilean government in the eighteenth century—an all-too-familiar tale in this hemisphere. Neither the national mass media nor the government paid attention to the strike, until massive street protests in support of the 32 exploded in different parts of the country, and the international community began to demand the intervention of the Chilean government.

The geopolitical conflict between the Mapuche people and the state stems from the two different spatial conceptions held by the counterparts: while the Mapuche's mental spatiality considers the usurped ancestral lands as still theirs, the state recognizes the current private Chilean settlements as the legitimate owners of the land. Without political representation in Congress, Mapuche groups organized protests and proceeded to occupy some farms and sabotage part of the infrastructure of mega-factories located in the region. The government answered by militarizing the zone in order to protect capitalist interests and to repress Mapuche mobilizations. Invoking an Antiterrorist Law created by Pinochet in the 1980s, the previous and current democratic governments incarcerated Mapuche leaders, accusing them of being terrorists. In doing so, the state reactivated a heterotopia of deviance, a space 'in which those whose behaviour is deviant from "required" norms are placed' (ibid.), a spatialization that has its roots in the marginalization and cornering of the Mapuche since the eighteenth century.

Unarmed against a body politics that criminalizes their demands as a people, the incarcerated activists gave urgent voice to their demands by refusing to eat solid food—pitting their bodies against the political body represented by the state. The hunger strike symbolized bearing the burden of political exclusion, and eating would jeopardize the protest in rejection of that exclusion. Although strictly speaking, political hunger strikes are not previously rehearsed but spontaneously written as they are synchronically experienced by the strikers, they also reenact past scenarios performed by other protesters. In that sense, the script is already written, but the setting, characters and aims are situationally and historically contingent (Taylor 2003: 28–30). The strikers' bodies become a signifier among other signifiers—the picture of the Cuban dissident Guillermo Fariñas, the Tamil militant Rasaiah Parthipan, Mahatma Gandhi and others—that build or add to an ongoing narrative, which could be called 'The exhibition of hunger strikers through the eras', as Roland Barthes puts it (2005: 82).

It is through a concerted hunger strike that the prison, the heterotopia of deviance par excellence, becomes a place where the confined 'indio prohibido' (Hale 2004: 16)—that one who rebels against the neoliberal multicultural politics sponsored by the state—gets the chance to contest the prejudices and be heard by the political body. On 15 July 2010, two weeks before the tunnel collapsed in San José, the 32 Mapuche confined in prisons scattered in the region[14] began a coordinated hunger strike demanding the suspension of the Antiterrorist Law, the demilitarization of the territory, the recognition of their status as political prisoners instead of terrorists, and the organization of a negotiation table to resolve the dispute over land and Mapuche autonomy. The Mapuche territory, which is already a place out of place within the country, was somehow relocated and spatialized in those small cells, and it is in this carceral space that the bodies of the 32 became the site of the insurrection and a means of pressure and negotiation. The body-territory of the 32 was secluded and restricted, as the land of their ancestors was likewise stolen and reduced. Unexpectedly, the hunger strike became a symbol of the Mapuche cause over their land and rights as a nation.[15] This heterotopia of deviation became a counter-space of Camp Hope with all its media paraphernalia and narratives of success and rebirth, because while the government was investing millions in rescuing the 33 miners, it left 32 Mapuche men to die.

Heterotopias of deviance, such as prisons, are to suspend the rights of individuals whose behaviour departs from the norms prescribed by a given society, but without inflicting physical pain, so that it is 'no longer the constituent element of the penalty' (Foucault 1998: 11). Therefore, the decision of the 32 to target their own bodies by fasting undermines the economy of Chilean prisons, which are obliged, at least theoretically, to monitor the health and welfare of individual inmates and ensure that proper procedures are pursued to preserve life.[16] With this political manoeuvre, the strikers subverted the system and made visible the injustice of a state that criminalizes their legitimate protest for ancestral lands.

Perhaps that is one of the reasons why the government first tried to render invisible the protest, and later, when it leaked out to the public, tried to delegitimize the act. President Piñera himself was in charge of discrediting the protest, saying that: 'In a democracy, a hunger strike is an illegitimate instrument of pressure' (Romero 2010). However, in a confrontation in which the body is more powerful than the disembodied logos, the strategy of verbal disqualification articulated by the government did not work. The hungering body is a place where words gradually cease, reducing the movement and the muting cry—and so, the governmental rhetoric aimed at delegitimizing the protest felt inappropriate, lost its meaning and was unable to compete against the body in pain. Consequently, on 15 September, seven days after Piñera's original declarations, and 66 days into the strike, the discourse of the government changed. Addressing the Congress in a plenary meeting to commemorate the bicentenary, Piñera said something unprecedented: '[W]e cannot ignore the fact that for decades, perhaps centuries, we have denied our communities of Indigenous peoples the necessary opportunities for material and spiritual progress for full integration into our republic' (cited in UPI Chile 2010).

The fact is that the discourse of the body changed the national conversation about Mapuche claims, and this shift was visible even in the republic's political masterminds.[17] Thus, it seemed that the body in pain began to rewrite the dominant narrative that has placed the Mapuche as a subaltern subject, and began to actualize the ancestral Mapuche struggle as a people.

Piñera's government was not prepared to face and solve a problem of such magnitude and historic transcendence. It was not Camp Hope, where technical decisions prevailed over any other consideration. The miners were passive victims waiting to be rescued, not agents with power to challenge the decision-making on the surface. The hunger strike offered a different scenario: it entailed a historical-political problem demanding complex political negotiations and legal solutions instead of calculated decisions supported by hard data. Here, the 'human factor' was not under government control as protesters acted upon a situation they viewed as one of oppression and injustice, and which the government had direct responsibility to solve.

The government's disengagement from the Mapuche cause during the first 50 days of the strike became untenable when one of the starving strikers was rushed to the hospital. As the news broke, a chain of events was put in motion. Street protests in support of the strikers stormed cities across the country. Four members of the House decided to join the strike and refused to leave the precinct, although they were soon forcibly removed from prison (visitors in transit do not belong to this heterotopia). The European Parliament sent an open letter asking the Government of Chile to intercede on behalf of the Mapuche. Chilean writers like Pedro Lemebel and poet Nicanor Parra, student associations, trade unionists, human rights defenders, *lonkos* (Mapuche leaders) and Catholic priests began fasting in solidarity. The body of the strikers in pain was mirrored in the body of others, surrogates, multiplied by hundreds.

Turning their punishment into a public spectacle exposed the injustice of their incarceration, and 30 of the 32 have since been declared innocent of the charges against them. Though the hunger strike prompted the modification of the Antiterrorist Law, better balanced the conversation between the Chilean nation and the Mapuche nation and established the ground for advancement towards the recognition of their and other Indigenous peoples, the paradigm shift from the *one nation, one cultural system* to a plural one will certainly take time. However, the celerity of social and political changes that new communication technologies elicit, plus the social awareness that popular movements such as those of the Arab Spring have raised, can shorten the process towards a culturally diverse Chile.

Through the hunger-strike heterotopia, the 'deviants' demonstrated that what was really crooked was the judicial system itself and the policies of assimilation sponsored by the state.[18] When the state offered an image of the Mapuche as terrorists, the 'terrorists' answered with nonviolent protest. When the system presented faceless accusers and witnesses, the 32 and those who joined them exhibited theirs openly. When the state staged the 'Mapuches permitidos' portraying them as desegregated and assimilated people, the Mapuche counter-performed a coordinated hunger strike in five different prisons, mobilized thousands of their *hermanas y hermanos* to go out in protest, marching together while waving their own national flag and chanting in *mapudungun*[19]. Finally, while the state cannot see outside the paradigm that conceives only one people for one nation, the Mapuche demand the right to be autonomous and proclaim a horizontal coexistence with the Chilean nation-state: two or more nations within one country.

The Chilean Military Parade: Enacting the Illusory Chile

If contingent one-time heterotopias like that of San José and the Mapuche have the potential to temporarily destabilize the culture in which they emerge, so do those temporal heterotopias that are already inserted and established in a given society as cyclical events, in the mode of festivals, fairs on the outskirts of the cities, parades and traditional national ceremonies (Foucault 1986: 26). These local heterotopias are not beyond the realm of normal expectations but are cyclic events established sometimes for centuries to respond to the demands and necessities of the society and, specifically, of those that organize or sponsor the events.

One prominent example of cyclical heterotopias in Chile is the Military Parade (MP), an official cultural performance sponsored and organized by the state since 1832 to commemorate Chilean Independence and glorify the role the Chilean Army played in that patriotic endeavour. The MP satisfies the principles of Foucault's heterotopologies (ibid.: 24–7): it is historically contingent as it functions according to what the acting government wishes to promote in terms of social discipline and social cohesion in a specific moment (Bristol 2001: 212); it has the capacity to juxtapose in a single space a plurality of other places found in Chilean society, as the performance enacts various ranks, institutions and functions (the military, the political and religious rulers, the cultural diversity, etc); it exists synchronically but also has the capacity to overlap past scenarios—battle scenarios, historical characters, key historical events —with enacted future convenient scenarios, such as the disappearance of the Mapuche conflict. The MP is also a segregated space where the repressive apparatus regulates access into the event. Finally, the MP enacts a convenient image of Chilean society, distorting aspects of the sociopolitical reality (Foucault 1986: 26–7).

Heterotopias such as military parades can be found in practically all Latin American countries. Besides being a palpable demonstration of the first heterotopic principle, which states that heterotopias can be found in any given society, this ubiquitousness offers a site to explore and compare how they respond to their own shared cultural system, and the extent of their similarities (ibid.: 26). According to Jorge Larraín, since the time of independence from European colonizing states, Latin American identity has been articulated alongside national identities. A shared history of colonial domination, a common language[20] and religion, independence wars fought in tandem by local and multinational *criollo* armies, and other socioeconomic, political and cultural factors have contributed to define a sense of belonging to a larger imagined South American community inextricably linked with national identifications (2001: 1).

The interplay between local and regional identities became apparent as most South American countries commemorated their respective bicentenaries during 2010 and 2011. In Chile, performances of essentialist military narratives emerged in the form of a military parade, battle reenactments and TV shows, to remind denizens that South American soil and soul were forged in the heat of heroic battles. This instrumentalization of foundational military stories to create a sense of regional unity and common destiny goes hand in hand with the iteration of abridged versions of national histories, which are presented in sanitized and amnesiac form, to erase from memory the trauma and the wrongdoings the militaries have perpetrated. Indeed, events such as military parades commemorating historical milestones become ideal vessels to retell a sterilized functional past in order to build community in the present and reinforce the existing pattern of social relationships (Bakhtin 1984: 686). For the same reason, a study of such cultural phenomena sheds light not only on the ideal or illusory image a particular nation touts to its citizens, and the concomitant erasures, but also explores the interconnectedness between the national and the regional in the Latin American context.

The MP offers a privileged site to enact a utopian Chile made in the likeness of the imagined nation by the current government. Also, it constitutes a paradigmatic site that materializes, articulates, promotes and sustains dominant ideas of cultural identities, a specific social order and versions of Chilean history; it does this by presenting a deceptive, illusory image of Chilean society. The Parade is a constructed and convenient representation of 'reality', staged according to the ideological agenda of the government in place, producing and presenting to its audience a curated version of the nation.

Heterotopias can change in function and meaning over time, according to the synchrony of the culture in which they are found (Foucault 1986: 25). The MP exemplifies such adaptation: although the score of the performance and its basic structure does not change much from one performance to the next, the verbal narrative that underscores the performance changes yearly. Uttered in a flamboyant prose style, the script reflects and conveys the government's political perspectives, conveying meanings and particular worldviews in support of their own idea of nation and their political struggle. The performance operates as type of canvas, ready to be painted on with the preferred ideological colours of the government in place.

During the Pinochet regime, for instance, the MP showed the military ideology at work as never before. The national representational space was literally taken by the armed forces: civilians were removed from the podium and the parade became an egotistic soliloquy where soldiers paid homage to soldiers and celebrated a new Chilean independence, gained on the battlefield.[21] According to Pinochet's words, on 11 September 1973, the Patria was liberated again, thus repeating the scenario of Chilean Independence, this time from the Marxist dictatorship (Pinochet 1977).

Cultural performances are snapshots of identity narratives that have been foregrounded at specific historical conjunctures, and the MP stages a threefold military version of national identities. The first is the insistence on the role that war and the warrior spirit of the Chilean ancestors played in forming a national identity (Larraín 2001: 145). Phrases such as 'a warriors' nation' and 'warrior race' are not only commonly repeated in the parade but also in official discourse. For example, when President Piñera spoke at the United Nations General Assembly in 2010, he defined the country as 'A nation of warriors and heroes that nevertheless has enjoyed unbroken peace during the last 130 years' (Gobierno de Chile 2010).[22] So internalized is this military version of identity that Chilean politicians from all parts of the spectrum frequently use words like 'battle', 'war' and 'surrender' to figuratively explain their public policies.[23]

The MP performance also marks identity (Schechner 2006: 38) by gendering the space in ways that reinforce patriarchal hegemony. The state assumes top-down stances in selecting, articulating and reifying certain identity narratives (while defusing or displacing others), utilizing it as an anti-entropic mechanism aimed at preventing the dissolution of the nation-state, maintaining the imaginary national boundaries. The MP carries on and displays a specific gender regime, which replicates the gender regime of the Chilean Army and reifies the essentialist discourse of hegemonic masculinities: a defining trait and a core value of the military.

The state uses the MP to convey, reproduce and reinforce the ideology of the ruling order in a specific historical moment, fulfilling its 'precise and determined function within a society' from year to year and from administration to administration (Foucault 1986: 25). In 1972, for example, the parade's central theme orbited around Salvador Allende's 'transition to socialism'. It was, of course, in a pre-dictatorship time when the army was still regarded as close to the people and as a non-deliberate institution subjected to civil authority. Yet in a perverse historical counterpoint, in the 1974 MP, Augusto Pinochet celebrated the purification of the nation from the 'intrinsically perverse' Marxist ideology. Presiding at the MP performance were the four commanders in chief of the four branches of the armed forces and order. Their uniformed presence occupied the same spot that President Allende, now dead, occupied two years before. In this context, the MP was a clear statement that the repressive state apparatus was obedient to the new political authorities and ready to fight against the internal enemy.

In 2006, Michelle Bachelet, the first woman president of Chile, presided over the MP along with her minister of defence, Vivianne Blanlot. The moment was politically significant as the military regime had killed Bachelet's father and tortured her and her mother. That year the stage of the MP, a space usually dominated by men, became a space where the traditional gender order of society was contested. Finally, in 2010, President Sebastián Piñera, in his inaugural speech, synchronized, in one rhetorical brushstroke, the San José and the MP heterotopias, capitalizing on the zeitgeist created by the first. The absence of women at the podium was again noticeable. Such examples show how the MP acts as a kind of weathervane, a revolving pointer that shows the ideological direction of the rulers. Highly controlled, it works according to the desires of those exercising political dominion.

The staging of the *indio permitido* (the allowed Indian) in the context of the MP is a notable illustration of how the political authorities use the MP to portray a convenient version of Chile. Aligned with the official military discourse which states the army 'has never practised any kind of discrimination against the Indigenous who have served in its ranks', and that they have 'the opportunity to progress in their positions as NCOs, and *even* officers' (Izurieta 2008), the MP portrays the Mapuche as fully assimilated in Chilean society.

During the Pinochet regime, the Mapuche had no physical presence in the MP, and any reference to them was through the typical tropes remembering the mythical Mapuche heroes, and the miscegenation between the Spanish conquerors and Mapuche warriors, which gave rise to the Chilean race, according to the national myths. In 2002, however, the MP included, for the first time, a delegation of Mapuche. Led by a *lonco* (tribal chief), the Mapuche entered the stage chanting and dancing traditional dances, then proceeded to pay tribute to the president. Such a gesture has been criticized by leaders of Mapuche groups who consider that they are honouring and legitimizing the Chilean state and the army—institutions that have historically persecuted and killed their people and stolen their land. Interestingly, during the 2010 MP, and as a reaction to the Mapuche hunger strike, the government reconfigured their performance in the MP, atomizing their presence by placing four of them scattered among a stock of 200 national characters. These 'assimilated' Mapuche were all carrying Chilean flags as a token of their integration.

Thus, the event works as a space of illusion (Foucault 1986: 26), which allows the government to invisibilize, harmonize and even idealize sociopolitical and geopolitical conflicts such as the Mapuche struggle. Even more, in this space, the always-complicated civil–military relationship is smoothly performed while the national-security doctrine learnt in the School of the Americas continues to haunt the military-school classrooms.

As long as massive public cultural performances sponsored by the state continue to be monolithic authoritarian spaces where a hypocritical Chile is enacted, Chilean democracy will never match the idealistic democratic rhetoric we proudly pronounce in the Senate Chamber. Events like the MP are not only thermometers of society but also its fever.

Conclusion

What do a prison located in Temuco City, a copper mine in the desert of San José and the O'Higgins Park esplanade have in common? Nothing obvious, at least until these three perceived spaces are transformed into particular representational locations where 'all the other real sites that can be found within the socio-cultural context, are simultaneously represented, contested, and inverted' (Ibid.: 24)—or heterotopias. In Camp Hope, the class structure, the economic system, hierarchical societal ranking and the historical *modus operandi* that prevail in current Chilean society were temporally suspended and idealistically performed by the government. In the MP, the ongoing geopolitical conflict between the state and the Mapuche was sanitized, while in the Araucanía Region, 32 Mapuche activists resignified those prisons as spaces of resistance and defiance against the Chilean state and its judicial system.

Performance Heterotopias

As much as the Chilean government was interested in invisibilizing the Mapuche protest, it was willing to make visible the search and rescue of the 33 miners in San José. Certainly, the process of rescuing the miners could have been a sober technical endeavour that could have taken place outside the media paraphernalia. Nevertheless, the government opted for producing, as a spectacle, a reality show that ensured the maximum number of spectators for its performance and built the perfect stage to captivate them: Camp Hope.

To say that the presence of spectators determined the behaviours of the all main protagonists involved in the three events allows me to formulate that in these case studies the production of heterotopias could not have been possible without the space-spectators-performers triad. This trialectic transforms the Newtonian absolute space (the empty stage) into a conceived Leibnizian relational space (actors will be placed in relation to spectators) to, finally, become a Lefebvreian lived space of representation where the performance takes place. Camp Hope, the hunger strike and the MP were consciously performed. Thus, the performative nature of these heterotopias is what I have come to call *performance heterotopias*, that is, heterotopias that are enacted through performance. Jill Dolan states that 'Theatre can move us toward understanding the possibility of something better [. . .] and fuel our desires in ways that might lead to incremental cultural change' (2006: 521), and uses the term 'utopian performative' to describe 'moments, which through their *doing*, allow audiences to experience, for a moment, a sense of what utopia would feel like were the claims of social justice movements realized' (ibid.). I use the term 'performative heterotopia' to refer to the set of behaviours that enact utopias, not in theatre but in the historical world, the representational space in which we live. In a sense, performative heterotopias blur the traditional distinctions between cultural performance, social drama and social performance as they cannot be reduced to one another, but they cannot be considered as separate either. It is in this matrix of relations that performance would act as the interface, the point of interaction and suture between discursive narratives and the real space.

Intersections

Heterotopias are real sites that have a general relation of direct or inverted analogy with the real space of society (Foucault 1986: 24). It is in the functional property of reflecting societal spaces that different heterotopias intersect. For example, while racial markers are erased in Camp Hope, and in the MP those markers are discursively and performatively homogenized, the Mapuche protest actually stresses racial differences. If an egalitarian society is enacted in Camp Hope, and in the MP a hierarchical and unequal society is performed as a cohesive one without social conflicts, the hunger-strike heterotopia denounces a repressive state, racism and a lack of egalitarian access to justice. These cross-references between heterotopias offer, then, alternative versions for the problems or conflicts of a given society has.

In this chapter, I have discussed how a single heterotopia is able to juxtapose, and even reconcile, a series of incompatible sites: in Camp Hope, a centralist economy working in tandem with a hypercapitalist one; in the MP, repressors and repressed are performed as harmoniously sharing the same space; and in the prison, a place which reifies the economy of suspended rights, and not the site to inflict physical pain (Foucault 1998: 8–9), the prisoners opt for self-flagellating their bodies through a prolonged fasting. Such internal juxtapositions show not only the subsisting contradictions and discontinuities that operate in society but also the ideological contradictions of those that conceived and produced a determined heterotopia. Thus, for instance, by juxtaposing Piñera's declaration about starting a new deal to the Mapuche people with the portrayal of assimilated and atomized Mapuche in the context of the MP, one cannot but question the true intentions of his government. Heterotopias, then, should be scrutinized inward as well as outward, and in relation not only to the society that they reflect, contest or invert, but also to other heterotopias.

A Last Reflection

As they change according to the synchrony of the culture in which they occur (Foucault 1986: 25), it is possible to say that heterotopias are always in process of becoming. This is an important realization because their dynamism assures that they are an actualized system whose informational thickness and meanings (conveyed through discourses and performances) are synchronically produced alongside the events unfolding on the stage of a given society. As it becomes clear that space is fundamental in any exercise of power, emerging and traditional heterotopias constitute an entry point to recognize, study and understand the ways hegemonic and subaltern groups instrumentalize them for their own political ends. Heterotopias may not only reflect, contest or improve what a society is in a given moment in history but can also act as transformative agents with material consequences. Therefore, heterotopias can be instrumental in rehearsing and presenting the spaces society needs to change.

Finally, I wonder what happens with heterotopias that are either already enacted or emerging in other societies, other Latin American countries, like the bordering nations of Argentina, Peru and Bolivia. Are those heterotopias talking to one another? Do they have points of intersection? How can a set of Latin American heterotopias, in their dynamic synchrony with their host societies, shed light on, for example, the slippery hemispheric imagined identity we talk so much about but cannot satisfactorily grasp in its perpetual becoming? Is it possible to map and juxtapose twin performance heterotopias such as the military parades performed in Peru and Chile? Could we analyse geopolitical conflicts between those countries and their war history through their military parades?

Heterotopology has been useful in studying local heterotopias and micro-geographies that were transformed into enacted utopias.

It would be fruitful to expand its application to analysing heterotopias located in the Americas macro-geography, and adopting hemispheric perspectives.

Notes

1 At least it was presented as such by the media, when in fact there was one Peruvian miner among those trapped.

2 On 9 February, the day he announced his first Cabinet, President Piñera declared the intention of establishing a 'new way of governing' characterized by 'doing things right . . . ' That purpose was reiterated innumerable times during his first year in office, and especially during the rescue of the 33 miners. After the successful rescue, the phrase morphed into the now popularized saying: 'Do it the Chilean way' (*La Nación* 2010).

3 In theatrical terms, Camp Hope satisfied three fundamental neoclassical rules: unity of time, unity of place and unity of action. First, the dramatic action evolved and was accomplished in the shortest time possible (sign of efficiency and effectiveness). Second, the action was restricted to one locale: Camp Hope. Third, the action used a relatively small group of protagonists performing one central story: the rescue, which actually is a subplot of the latent plot to establish the governance of the new government in terms of its effectiveness in decision-making and administration.

4 Mining accidents are common in Chile, especially in small and medium-size mines where, in the last decade, an average of 60 workers have died annually.

5 Although the company did not make public the news and inform the Emergency National Office authorities about the incident, five hours after the accident, personal phone calls spread the news like wildfire among the families, who rushed to the mine.

6 The media paraphernalia built up around the mine incident caught the attention of a national audience at a level comparable only to that obtained by the 2010 earthquake and by Chile's participation in the 2010 World Cup. If anything characterizes Chilean mass media, it is their selective search for news with the potential to be exploited—the more melodramatic or tragic, the better. Thus, the San José event

occupied the front pages of newspapers and the central section of informative radio and television during the rescue process and beyond. It was as if suddenly the searchlight was focused on San José, and the rest of the nation remained in the darkness.

7 The phrase 'Estamos bien en el refugio los 33' should have had a comma after 'refugio' to convey the idea properly.

8 President Piñera's speech can be viewed on YouTube: http://goo.gl/-trU48U (last accessed on 9 April 2016).

9 The benefits harvested by the government were many: the 'San José effect' helped to increase the popularity of the president in seven different categories of personal and political power in the months of the rescue. The Adimark poll of October 2010 showed that Piñera's approval rating went up:

> His 'ability to deal with crisis situations' has become his strongest attribute with an 81% approval rating, followed by 'active and energetic' at 80% and the 'ability to solve problems of the country' at 76%. The attributes of 'authority' and 'leadership' had ratings of 75% and 73% respectively, maintaining the positive trend shown since August 2010, and were closely followed by the attributes 'respected' (71%) and 'loved by the Chileans' (68%) (Adimark 2010).

10 British prime minister David Cameron and US president Barack Obama, among others, and salutations via Twitter from Ricky Martin, Sarah Palin and even from Commander Doug Wheelock, who sent his congratulations for the successful rescue from the Expedition 25, from the International Space Station, which orbited 350 kilometres from the earth.

11 In that sense, the event followed the structure of the reality-television genre. It is true that the miners were trapped, and that they were not actors, but once the cameras arrived into the mine and broadcast was made possible, the miners began to perform actions and activities for the camera, ergo for an audience. They knew that they were being monitored 24 hours a day, and soon after they were found alive they learnt that outside they were considered celebrities, and that their story was catching the attention of the world.

12 During that period, the attempt of finding those responsible for the tragedy, the time for accountability of entrepreneurial greed and

governmental negligence were surprisingly postponed, or perhaps irremediably forgotten behind the urgency of rescuing the victims. It was as if the whole mechanism of justice that society has designed to go after the culprits could not operate simultaneously with the rescue effort.

13 Following Kristin Valentine and Gordon Matsumoto's cultural performance analysis spheres, the audience at Camp Hope can be classified in three main categories:

(1) Central audience. '[. . .] those members of the culture who are physically present and who directly influence, and are influenced by' the performance [for example, family members and local journalists].

(2) Bystander audience. Those individuals who are 'present at the performance who are sympathetic but not part of the culture' [for example, foreign journalists].

(3) Implied or cultural audience. Those who, although not physically present at the event, are, 'in the minds of the participants, metaphorically looking over the shoulders of the participants and judging the appropriateness of their behavior'. In this case, Camp Hope's cultural audience included the millions of Chileans and international spectators who watched the developments on TV or followed the event on social media (2001: 74-80).

14 The 32 Mapuches were held in five different prisons located in the southern cities of Concepción, Lebu, Angol, Valdivia and Temuco. They communicated with one another through spokespersons chosen by Mapuche organizations to be the official representatives of the Mapuche in each prison. Also, family members that visited them served as liaisons to the external world.

15 Hector Llaitul, the leader of the protest, expressed well the Mapuche struggle:

> In the Mapuche territory there are laws that do not operate in the rest of the country. Where are the militarized lands? Where are they prosecuting political activists? [. . .] In what other place is the Antiterrorist Law invoked? To our knowledge, it happens only in the Mapuche land, which allows us to say that we live under a dictatorial state. Hence, for us the expressions

of resistance and self-defence are legitimate, especially if all political channels have been closed [. . .] in such circumstances our body is the only thing left to protest (*Clinic* 2010).

16 On 2 September 2010, the Supreme Court prosecutor Mónica Maldonado recognized that Mapuche political prisoners were being physically punished, by using methods and techniques prohibited by Chilean law and international treaties. According to her, the inmates were placed in solitary confinement and subjected to light deprivation to undermine their position. Maldonado also said that the torture procedures were applied with the consent of the authorities (Leiva 2010).

17 Shortly before the president spoke, Alejandra Sepúlveda, speaker of the House of Representatives, emphasized the debt to the Mapuche people and the rightfulness of their demands, saying, 'We owe it to our Mapuche brothers. They have known war and violence, and we believe it is time to seek progress and deeper reforms to resolve the just demands of indigenous people', and concluded her message with a surprising and unprecedented 'I apologize a thousand times if necessary, for the lack of dialogue and understanding in these 200 years of Chile' (UPI Chile 2010).

18 Echoing the claim, the president of the Supreme Court, Milton Juica, at the opening of the Judicial Year 2011, declared that '[i]n Chile the penitentiary system is in a state of complete collapse, and serious disregard for the rights and guarantees of those deprived of liberty, which requires an immediate solution for those who are obliged to do so' (Armaza 2011), and in the same ceremony the minister of justice Felipe Bulnes said that the 'human rights agenda begins in places of reclusion . . . ' (ibid.).

19 Mapuche language.

20 Certainly, in South American countries, there is a plethora of Indigenous languages spoken by their inhabitants; nevertheless here I am alluding to the 'common' languages imposed by the colonizers, in this case Portuguese and Spanish.

21 The Pinochet dictatorship claimed to have fought a literal battle against Allende's paramilitary forces. They call the clashes 'The Battle of Santiago'. Nevertheless, such a battle never existed as the political bases of Salvador Allende's government, and the few that resisted the coup, were killed, captured, neutralized or decimated

practically the same day as the seizure of power. The hyperbolic name 'Battle of Santiago' is used by Pinochet in Chapter 8 of his book *El Día Decisivo* (2009).

22 Contemporary Chilean historians such as Mario Góngora have helped to validate and reinforce this version of Chilean identity stating that Chilean identity was forged in the battlefield: 'It was through the Independence Wars, and a series of successive victorious wars that took place during the nineteenth century, that a nationalist awareness and a sentiment of "Chileanness" were created' (1992: 38).

23 Thus, for example, the minister of education, Joaquín Lavín, said, 'The President said that education is the mother of all battles, and the battle for development will be won or lost in the classroom' (*Educación* 2010). By the same token, the minister of health, Jaime Mañalich, after sacking the sub-secretary of health, declared, 'I firmly believe that the struggle, the battle for better health for our patients produces casualties, it is a battle that produces casualties' (*El Mostrador* 2011).

Works Cited

ADIMARK. 2010. 'Evaluación Del Gobierno. Octubre 2010'. Available at: http://goo.gl/RmQSWm (last accessed on 1 October 2010).

ARMAZA, Christiano. 2011. 'Críticas a la situación penitenciaria y pueblos originarios Marcan apertura del Año Judicial' (Criticism to the Prison System and Indigenous Peoples are the Main Subjects at the Opening of the Judicial Year). *El Ciudadano,* 3 March. Available at: http://goo.gl/1HBxE7 (last accessed on 3 March 2011).

BAKHTIN, Mikhail. 1984. *Rabelais and His World* (Hélène Iswolsky trans.). Bloomington: Indiana University Press.

BARTHES, Roland. 2005. 'Mythologies' in Julie Rivkin and Michael Ryan (eds), *Literary Theory: An Anthology*. Oxford: Blackwell, pp. 81–9.

BAUDRILLARD, Jean. 1981. *Simulacrum and Simulation* (Sheila Glaser trans.). Ann Arbor: University of Michigan Press.

BRISTOL, Michael. 2001. 'The Pageant' in Colin Counsell and Laurie Wolf (eds), *Performance Analysis: An Introductory Coursebook*. London: Routledge, pp. 210–15.

CLINIC. 2010. 'Héctor Llaitul, líder de la CAM desde la cárcel: "Nuestro cuerpo es lo único que nos queda para protestar"' (Héctor Llaitul, CAM Leader, from Prison: 'Our Body Is the Only Thing Left to Protest'). *Clinic*, 4 September. Available at: http://goo.gl/Yp5Jiw (last accessed on 4 September 2010).

DEBORD, Guy. 1983. *Society of the Spectacle* (Ken Knabb trans.). London: Rebel Press.

DOLAN, Jill. 2006. 'The Polemics and Potential of Theatre Studies and Performance' in D. Soyini Madison and Judith Hamera (eds), *The Sage Handbook of Performance Studies*. Thousand Oaks, CA: Sage, pp. 508–26.

EDUCACIÓN. 2010. 'Lavín sobre presupuesto: "La batalla por el desarrollo se va a ganar o perder en las salas de clases" (Lavín on Budget: 'The Battle for Development Will Win or Lose in the Classroom'). *Educación*, 1 October. Available at: http://goo.gl/cIIugJ (last accessed on 1 March 2011).

EL MOSTRADOR. 2011. 'Mañalich: "La Batalla Por Una Mejor Salud Tiene Bajas"' (Mañalich: 'The Battle for Better Health is Low'). *El Mostrador*, 25 January. Available at: http://goo.gl/Qt6s12 (last accessed on 25 February 2011).

FISCHER, Frank. 1990. *Technocracy and the Politics of Expertise*. Newbury Park: Sage.

FOUCAULT, Michel. 1986. 'Of Other Spaces' (Jay Miskowiec trans.). *Diacritics* 16(1) (Spring): 22–7 .

——. 1998. *Discipline and Punish: The Birth of the Prison* (Alan Sheridan trans.). New York: Vintage.

GOBIERNO DE CHILE. 2010. 'Presidente Piñera en su primera intervención ante la Asamblea General de la ONU' (President Piñera in His First Address to the UN General Assembly). Gobierno de Chile official website, 23 September. Available at: http://goo.gl/C9yuoZ (last accessed on 23 October 2010).

GÓNGORA, Mario. 1992. *Ensayo histórico sobre la noción del Estado de chile en los siglos XIX y XX* (Historical Essay on the Notion of the Chilean State in the Nineteenth and Twentieth Centuries). Santiago: Editorial Universitaria.

HALE, Charles R. 2004. 'Rethinking Indigenous Politics in the Era of the "Indio Permitido"'. *NACLA Report on the Americas* 38(2): 16–21.

IZURIETA, Oscar. 2008. 'Discurso de Clausura'. Available at: https://goo.gl/-AiFGSu (last accessed on 14 September 2008).

LA NACIÓN. 2010. 'Piñera promete "hacer las cosas bien" al estrenar gabinete' (Piñera Promises to Do Things Right by Announcing Cabinet). *La Nación*, 9 February. Available at: http://goo.gl/IEriOV (last accessed on 5 April 2016).

LARRAÍN, Jorge. 2001. *Identidad Chilena* (Chilean Identity). Santiago: Lom.

LEIVA, Ninoska. 2010. 'Mapuches en huelga de hambre son torturados como en Guantánamo' (Mapuches on Hunger Strike Are Tortured as in Guantánamo). *Radio U Chile*, 2 September. Available at: http://goo.gl/-Ms7CQd (last accessed on 2 September 2010).

LOS ANDES. 2010. 'Piñera: "Cuando Chile se une somos capaces de grandes cosas"' (Piñera: 'When Chile Is Together Capable of Great Things'). *Los Andes*, 13 October. Available at: http://goo.gl/QbAIhK (last accessed on 5 April 2016).

MACKEY, Robert. 2010. 'Latest Updates on the Rescue of the Chilean Miners'. NYTimes.com, 12 October. Available at: http://goo.gl/af609I (last accessed on 14 October 2010).

MERY, Herman P. 2010. 'Resolucion De Multas 6279'. Letter to IPT Copiapo, 9 July. Available at: https://goo.gl/aJm2kb (last accessed on 16 August 2010).

PINOCHET, Augusto. 1977. 'Discurso del general Augusto Pinochet en cerro chacarillas con ocasión del día de la juventud: el 9 de julio de 1977' (Address by General Augusto Pinochet in Chacarillas Hill on the Occasion of Youth Day, 9 July 1977). Available at: https://goo.gl/FGhuuA (last accessed on 21 October 2009).

——. 2009. *El Día Decisivo* (The Decisive Day). Available at: http://-goo.gl/cuQJbi (last accessed on 3 February 2009).

ROMERO, Martín. 2010. 'Piñera: "Huelga de hambre es un medio de presión ilegítimo"' (Piñera: 'Hunger Strike Is a Means of Illegitimate Pressure'). *La Nacíon*, 8 September. Available at: http://goo.gl/oDYiiL (last accessed on 8 September 2010).

SCHECHNER, Richard. 2006. *Performance Studies: An Introduction*. New York: Routledge.

SOJA, Edward W. 1996. *Thirdspace: Journeys to Los Angeles and Other Real-and-Imagined Places*. Cambridge: Blackwell.

STELTER, Brian. 'In Coverage of Mine Rescue, Watching, Waiting and Counting'. NYTimes.com, 13 October 2010. Available at: http://goo.gl/-rhhg33 (last accessed on 13 October 2010).

TALEB, Nassim Nicholas. 2007. *The Black Swan: The Impact of the Highly Improbable*. New York: Random House.

TAYLOR, Diana. 2003. *The Archive and the Repertoire: Performing Cultural Memory in the Americas*. Durham, NC: Duke University Press.

UNDP. 2009. *Human Development Report: Overcoming Barriers; Human Mobility and Development*. New York: Palgrave Macmillan.

UPI CHILE. 2010. 'Presidenta de la Cámara en Congreso Pleno: "Pido perdón mil veces" al pueblo Mapuche' (Speaker of the House at the Plenary Congress: 'I Apologize a Thousand Times' to the Mapuche People). *El Mostrador*, 15 September. Available at: http://goo.gl/Ck07ug (last accessed on 15 September 2010).

VALENTINE, Kristin, and Gordon Matsumoto. 2001. 'Cultural Performance Analysis Spheres: An Integrated Ethnographic Methodology'. *Field Methods* 13(1): 68–87.

WARNKEN, Cristián. 2010. 'Mineros Chilenos: El rescate de la Patria' (Chilean Miners: The Rescue of the Fatherland). *Surysur*, 26 August. Available at: http://goo.gl/kzSwwQ (last accessed on 30 August 2010).

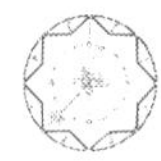

Chapter 8

MOURNING EN MASSE

Tucson's All Souls' Day Procession

Rachel Bowditch

FIGURE 8.1. **Tucson All Souls' Procession, 2013.**
Photograph courtesy of Nadia Hagen.

> *The moment you write about a festival, it is already obsolete because it is a living, breathing organism that is undergoing constant transformation and evolution. All we can hope to accomplish as scholars is to capture a glimpse, a moment in time—fleeting and ephemeral—of a lived, visceral experience.*

Around twilight on a crisp November Sunday, swarms of people clad in black-and-white face paint and creative home-made costumes emerge on the streets from every direction outside the Hotel Congress in Tucson, Arizona, carrying puppets, banners, effigies, floats and posters with photographs of the dead of all shapes and sizes. There is no clear distinction between pavement and street; between official performers and spectators—everyone is a participant. There is a sombre sense of excitement and anticipation. A large-scale sculptural urn assisted by guardians from the performance troupe Flam Chen weaves through the dense crowd collecting handwritten prayers and offerings from passers-by. Day of the Dead motifs of black-and-white skeletons, flowers and masks dominate the visual landscape mixed with a fusion of hybrid imagery that evokes death, memory and celebration.

Without warning, the mass of 100,000 festive bodies begins to move forming an over-three-kilometre-long procession through the streets of Tucson. Crowds of people line the streets; however, unlike the Macy's Day Thanksgiving Parade and other official processions, there are no street barriers separating those marching in the procession and those observing—the lines are porous and blurred. Participants move fluidly in and out of the procession between spectating and marching: dancing, drumming, walking and mourning. The procession culminates at a large open dirt lot where a stage awaits for the urn to arrive. Flam Chen, a pyrotechnic performance troupe from Tucson and organizers of the event, stage a fire aerial performance followed by the symbolic burning of the urn filled with the community's prayers and wishes.

This event, known as the All Souls' Procession, occurs each November, a celebration founded in 1990 by local artist Susan Johnson. The collective, community-invented ritual is loosely drawn from practices surrounding All Souls' Day and Día de Los Muertos, both celebrated widely across the Americas. The procession began as a personal gesture of grieving for Johnson's father—an impromptu gathering of 20 close friends and relatives walking through the streets adorned in handmade costumes. Over the more than 20 years that have followed, the procession has grown to a critical mass of bodies meandering en masse along a three-kilometre route through downtown Tucson. Several aspects of the event—the history and evolution of the procession, the evolving relationship with the city of Tucson, the personal and community altars, the ritual of burning of the urn and the finale—serve as powerful modes of community healing. They act as a vehicle for what procession organizer's Nadia Hagen and Paul Weir call 'festal culture', creating a necessary, hopeful utopian space to process trauma and create a sense of community identity.

Festival Palimpsest

The history of All Saints' Day and All Souls' Day can be traced back to the medieval Celtic ritual practice of Samhain, signifying the end of summer and the completion of the harvest, marking the transition of the seasons (Cosman 1981). As Jack Santino in *Halloween and Other Festivals of Death* points out, the ancient celebration of Samhain could be considered the prehistory of modern Halloween (1994: *xiv*). He notes how Samhain was widely practised in ancient Ireland, which converted to Christianity in 300–400 CE (ibid.: *xv*). The syncretic practice of grafting Christian festivals onto ancient festivals was a way to ease conversion. According to Santino, 'the early church adapted and accommodated the traditional religious beliefs and practices of those it sought to convert. Many of the festivals and holidays we enjoy have resulted from this policy and were derived in some part from already existing festivals and celebrations', creating what he calls a 'palimpsest of festival culture' (ibid.: *xvi*). Samhain, the Celtic New Year, was celebrated on 31 October and 1 November; the last day of the previous year, became identified with death (ibid.: *xv*). The Celts believed that the spirits of the dead returned to earth on that night to cause mischief and chaos. On this night, the boundaries between the living and the dead were blurred. During Samhain, bonfires were lit to guide the spirits and people wore costumes and masks dressing as spirits, witches and ghosts (ibid.).

Around the end of the first millennium, the Catholic Church fought to extinguish these pagan rites by appropriating the practices and renaming the celebration to honour the dead: All Saints' Day (1 November) and All Souls' Day (2 November). All Souls' Day was known as All-Hallowsmas, and 31 October was All Hallowed's Eve or Hallow'e'en (Hilker 2009).[1] Santino writes:

> Many traditional beliefs and customs associated with Samhain, most notably that night was the time of the wandering dead, the practice of leaving offerings of food and drink to masked and costumed revelers as the Eve of All Saints', the Eve of All Hallows, or Hallow Even. It is the glossing of the name Hallow Even that has given us the name Hallowe'en. [. . .] About A.D. 900, the church recognized that All Saints' had not supplanted the pre-Christian customs, so in an attempt to get closer to the original intent of the festival, it declared 2 November as All Souls' Day. This day is in recognition of the souls of all the faithful departed who had died during the previous year. It is obviously much closer in spirit to the Celtic Samhain than is All Saints' Day. [. . .] The spirits of Samhain, once thought to be wild and powerful, were now said to be something worse: evil. [. . .] Thus, the customs

> associated with Hallow Even included representations of ghosts and human skeletons—symbols of the dead—and of the devil and other malevolent, evil creatures, such as witches (1994: *xvi*).

When the Spanish conquistadors arrived in the New World in the sixteenth century, they brought the Christian All Souls' Day with them. As Valeria Menard notes, by the time the Spaniards arrived, the Aztecs already had in place a complex system of festivals dedicated to death (2000: 149). The ancient Indigenous peoples of Mexico (Purepecha, Nahua, Aztec, Totonac and Otomí) had their own elaborate festivals dedicated to the dead, with a month-long festival—in honour of the lord of death Mictlantecuhtli and his consort Mictlancíhuatl, the goddess of death (Carmichael 1992: 25). The Aztec believed in 13 layers of heaven and 9 levels of the underworld (ibid.: 26). Upon death, souls went to Mictlan, 'the place of the dead' (ibid.: 27). According to Stanley Brandes, on 3 November, 'the Nahua, descendants of the ancient Aztecs celebrate el *Día de los Accidentados* (the day of those who died an accidental death) and *el Día de los Matados* '"the day of those who were murdered"' (2006: 8). He notes how in pre-Columbian thought 'one's fate in the afterlife depended more on the manner of death than on one's deeds while alive' (ibid.).

The Spanish appropriated Indigenous practices and grafted them onto their Christian All Souls' festival, resulting in yet another syncretic fusion and hybrid festival known today as Día de los Muertos or Day of the Dead, which merges aspects of both European and Aztec beliefs and customs (Palfrey 1995). Brandes suggests that there has never been an 'authentic' Day of the Dead: 'through vast expanses of space and time, there have emerged many different Days of the Dead, each responding to the needs and aspirations of local celebrants' (2006: 15). Festivals such as Day of the Dead, All Souls' Day and Halloween are cultural palimpsests, products of continuously shifting worlds, resonating with what

Arjun Appadurai has termed 'diasporic public spheres'[2] (1996: 22). Through these diasporic public festive performances, the layers of encounter are rendered visible and brought to the surface. As Regina Marchi illuminates, there is a historical connection between the Day of the Dead celebrations and popular resistance in the Americas (1994: 268). These festivals create an alternative public sphere for communication making both tradition and the contemporary moment 'pervasive, vital, ongoing, and highly visible' (Turner and Jasper 1994: 149).

While Día de los Muertos is celebrated across the Americas, celebrations are not universal and vary from country to country, with further differences from one region to the next (Marchi 2009: 3). The Day of the Dead in Latin America is most elaborately celebrated in regions with large Indigenous populations in southern Mexico, Guatemala, Bolivia, Peru and Ecuador (Marchi 1994: 264). Mexico has become internationally famous for its Day of the Dead celebrations, particularly in the areas of Oaxaca, Michoacán, Puebla, Veracruz and Yucatan, where 'people create aesthetically intricate altars, and engage in a variety of Day of the Dead processions, vigils, popular theatre, arts and handicrafts' (ibid.).[3]

In Mexico, 1 November, Día de los Inocentes (Day of the Innocents), also known as Día de los Angelitos (Day of the Little Angels), honours deceased children and infants; and 2 November, Día de los Muertos, honours adults. Typically a three-day celebration, Día de los Muertos begins on the first day with a visit to the cemetery to clean and decorate the graves with flowers, votive candles and *ofrendas* (offerings); the cemetery becoming a portal between heaven and earth (Menard 2000: 149). Often these gatherings are social events that include eating tamales, *calaveras* (sugar skulls) and *pan de muerto* (bread in the shape of a person), singing and storytelling. A toy skeleton hidden in the *pan de muerto* is good luck for the person who bites into it—the person symbolically 'takes a bite of death and thereby inoculates themselves against the fear of death' (Turner 1999: 140). Home altars, a popular Día de los Muertos practice, are laid out on a table with votive candles, burning *copal* (incense), photographs of the deceased, *calaveras*, yellow or orange marigolds or chrysanthemums (*cempoalxochitl* in Nahuatl; a symbolic remnant of the Aztec festival), plus foods and beverages such as beer, tequila, coffee, corn, rice and beans (ibid.: 23). In predominantly Latino communities in the United States, some of the largest festivals can be found in Texas, Arizona and California.[4]

The Early Days: Forging the Procession

The Tucson All Souls' Procession could be seen as a unique hybrid festival that is suspended between All Souls' Day and Día de los Muertos celebrations as well as bearing a striking resemblance to Samhain. The procession began in 1990 as a personal healing ritual when founder Susan Johnson lost her father and needed to find a way to grieve his passing outside of the traditional methods of mourning a loved one. With a degree in art therapy, Johnson had studied the influence of ritual in the healing process and designed her own ritual to process her pain. In an interview with Erin White at the *Arizona Daily Star*, she stated, 'All Souls' Day is one of the oldest holidays celebrated in the world. [. . .] I wanted to create an artists' parade, not just a celebration of one culture. The merging of art forms with the heaviness of death became a very beautiful thing. It brought down a lot of barriers between the different cultures' (quoted in White 2006). After the first procession, Johnson says, she felt transformed: 'It opened up my heart and let me connect with things that were frightening to me. [. . .] The parade is a really powerful vehicle to express anger and rage constructively. To create and use your own creation—it is transforming' (ibid.).

Recruiting performers and friends from the downtown Tucson arts scene, she organized a three-day event to commemorate her father. When the event first started, it was by invitation only. Johnson made masks and costumes in her studio with friends and the evening culminated in an intimate procession of about 20 people processing through the streets of downtown Tucson. The response to the early processions was overwhelming and she received over 250 letters thanking her and asking how they could be involved the following year. For the first several years, the procession was relatively small, with at most a few hundred people mainly from the downtown art crowd. At the end, everyone would gather around a bonfire to tell stories of loved ones. Local artists started hosting mask-making workshops and spent weeks making puppets, costumes and floats, and inviting the community to participate free of charge. For the next eight years, Johnson organized the procession and workshops; in 1998 she passed the organizational reins over to Nadia Hagen, founder of the fire performance troupe Flam Chen.[5]

Hagen stumbled across the procession in its third year, quite by accident, when out riding her bicycle at 2.00 a.m.[6] She recalls that everyone was dressed up and pushing decorated shopping carts—what she refers to as 'insta-floats', complete with generators for lights and music (Hagen 2010). When asked how she inherited the procession, Hagen said that the process of changing of the guard was organic. She started as a participant, showing up in costume and walking the route. Then, she began to think about what she was going to do the following year and started building things weeks before the event. Prior to Hagen's involvement with the procession, she received a grant to produce a similar event on April Fools Day in 1996, with a parade component that went around downtown. Attended by approximately 300 people, the April Fools celebration was similar to the All Souls' Procession. Johnston and Hagen began discussing their two events and Hagen proposed ideas about a performance finale to end the procession. As Hagen recalls, Johnson was supportive of her ideas and enthusiasm and handed over control of the procession. Johnston wanted to keep the event small and intimate but Hagen envisioned the potential impact on the community. She advertised the procession with posters inviting the entire community to participate (ibid.).

In 1997, the crowds started spilling onto the streets which had to be closed for safety reasons. As the procession continued to expand, Hagen quickly realized she needed an infrastructure to manage the event and formed an umbrella non-profit, Many Mouths One Stomach, to fiscally manage and organize the event. Soon after Hagen became the artistic director of the procession, Paul Weir,[7] her husband and the technical director of Flam Chen, became a central organizer and technical director of the procession, taking the finale to new heights of innovation and spectacle. The line between Flam Chen and Many Mouths One Stomach is often blurred with Hagen and Weir serving on both boards and artistic steering committees. However, this fluidity has caused tension on the Many Mouths One Stomach board among those who feel the need to delineate between the two organizations (Hagen 2010). While a small group of organizers manages the event, it takes over 280 volunteers approximately 2,500 hours to run the procession. No one receives a full-time salary; however, a few organizers and artists receive a small stipend, between $100 and $500. As Hagen realizes, 'None of the stipends are remotely close to the amount of time that people put in' (2010).

The procession continued to grow exponentially each year through word of mouth, viral marketing and fliers posted around downtown Tucson, doubling in size each year—by 2001, more than 2,000 people were participating and by 2009 the procession had grown to 30,000.[8] Hagen describes the current All Souls' Day event as Johnson's child: 'You birth a child and you don't know how it is going to turn out. And that is what the parade is for her. It is like a 15-year-old. It's like a wild teenager, running down the street naked' (Weir 2010). Johnson started a counter-event, another smaller procession on the actual Día de los Muertos that retains the intimacy of the original procession.

As the procession has continued to expand, tension between participants and spectators has surfaced—those actively engaged in mourning and spectators who want to party. As procession organizer Matt Cotton of Tucson Puppet Works laments, 'I like that it's growing, but what matters to me is the sincerity of the small acts that happen at the workshops and during the parade' (quoted in White 2006). There are different factions of community ownership and investment in the event. On the one hand, some participants are so personally invested that they contribute greatly to the event with time, money and effort. However, this devotion puts them at odds with the 'snackers', as Hagen refers to non-participating spectators (2010). Many people just show up with their lawn chairs to observe the spectacle, much as they would passively watch TV. However, Weir sees attendance at the parade as a process of initiation: people show up with their lawn chairs but soon realize that they can participate by wearing a costume and walking in the procession. Next year, ideally, they are converted and fully participate (Weir 2010).

Staging National Trauma After 9/11

As it has evolved over two decades, the All Souls' Procession has become Tucson's unofficial signature cultural event. According to Weir, the event gained this iconic status in 2002 after the pivotal procession commemorating 9/11. While there have always been subtle political undercurrents, the procession in 2001 served as a public platform for processing national trauma. For Weir, the wars in Iraq and Afghanistan aided in solidifying and unifying the procession around a larger public purpose beyond individual mourning. According to Ann Kaplan, there are varying degrees of trauma and it is important to distinguish between personal trauma and collective trauma (2005: 1–2). For the majority of Americans, trauma is experienced on a regular basis through the media, with such traumatic images as the tsunami in Southeast Asia, the devastation of Hurricane Katrina and the harrowing earthquakes in Haiti and Japan. On 11 September 2001, US citizens in New York, Washington DC and Shanksville, Pennsylvania, experienced tragedy first hand, while the rest of the nation encountered mediated versions of the event, replayed over and over on every news channel. Kaplan identifies this phenomenon as 'secondary' or 'vicarious' trauma (ibid.: 20). She argues that viewers of the media, 'like therapists working with trauma victims, are often vicariously traumatized. [. . .] Vicarious traumatization may be an inevitable part of sharing what others have suffered, but it too can have socially productive aspects in specific contexts' (ibid.: 21–2). She coined the term 'empty empathy' in analysing the function of war photographs in relation to viewers and how the repetition of traumatic images produces a numbing effect (ibid.). She explores how people can 'move beyond sharing trauma and engage in witnessing, which is a new level of responsibility. "Witnessing" thus involves a stance that has public meaning or importance and transcends individual empathic or vicarious suffering to produce community' (ibid.: 22–3). As Kaplan notes, the trauma of 9/11 created a new collective subject and a civic cohesiveness that had not been experienced before (ibid.). Through mediated images of 9/11, temporary publics were formed around the national trauma to produce collective spaces of healing. The Tucson All Souls' Procession was one such space. Kaplan states, 'Complex interconnections between individual and cultural trauma—such that, indeed, where the "self" begins and cultural reactions end may seem impossible to determine. [. . .] Short-lived but real creation of new public-sphere communities as specific crises are "translated" from group to group' (ibid.: 2).

In the aftermath of 9/11, the need to transform personal trauma into collective trauma was seen in public gatherings such as the All Souls' Procession—the street transformed into a fertile space for spontaneous public offerings and collective healing (ibid.: 12). However, Kaplan points out, 'It gradually became clear that national ideology was hard at work shaping how the traumatic event was to be perceived' (ibid.: 13). The national tragedy was quickly co-opted by politicians and others who, overnight, translated the tears of trauma into a nationalist cry for war and revenge. This tragedy formed two publics, the one portrayed by the media and the other public that was silenced and manipulated (ibid.).

In 2001, the procession offered an alternative civic space for the public to express their dissent against the call for war. It was a safe haven for people to witness others who also felt alienated and frustrated with what they saw in the media; who wondered, as Hagen did, 'Why do I not agree with this cry for war? Why do I not feel this way? Why am I not seeing the situation this way?' (Hagen 2010). Just by virtue of going out on the street, donning a costume and mask, and being present with others was an affirmation of a different set of values than those being propagated by the media and by the government. Hagen remembers the solidarity felt by those gathered and a general feeling of unity—a counter-public against the 'rally to revenge' (2010). The gathering of bodies en masse in the streets forged a positive healing community space to remember those killed during the attacks and heal the personal and national wounds, building a powerful sense of collective and individual agency.

For Weir, the procession is the antithesis of the controversial right-wing conservative Cremation of Care gathering, first convened in 1878 and held annually at the Bohemian Grove, north of

San Francisco.[9] A Druid-like effigy is burnt beneath a giant statue of an owl, symbolizing the release from worldly concerns and responsibilities—in recent years, such burdens included the pre-emptive wars in Afghanistan and Iraq, the oil spill in the Gulf of Mexico, among other manmade catastrophes (Anderson and Binstein 1992). For 17 days, over 2,000 of the world's wealthiest and most powerful conservatives, including US presidents, foreign heads of state, politicians, industrial barons and CEOs gather to rid themselves of their worldly cares. President Herbert Hoover called it 'the greatest men's party on earth'; others have named it a 'summer camp for millionaires' (Moore 2004). Participants don red medieval robes and chant mysterious texts spurring conspiracy theories about simulated child sacrifice and devil worship. For Weir, the All Souls' Procession is the 'Restoration of Care', which energetically dispels the negativity put forth by the Cremation of Care (2010). Since 2001, the procession has been a public forum for political critique and expressive gestures of resistance—signs and floats protesting the genocide in Darfur, the wars in Iraq and Afghanistan, honouring New Orleans and its residents after Hurricane Katrina, and in 2010, protesting SB1070, Arizona's anti-immigration laws. The procession in 2011 became a public memorial for those those killed during the attempted assassination of Arizona Congresswoman Gabrielle Giffords, a potent site for community grieving and healing.

The Economies of Festival: Leveraging Space

Up until 2002, the procession finale occurred at the Mat Bevel Institute; then it was moved to the Franklin Street docks to accommodate the influx of people. In 2012, the finale site moved to the Mercado San Agustín on West Congress, an open dirt lot large enough to accommodate 30,000 people. In the early years, participants did not seek permission to parade in the streets; however, as the crowds grew, permits were needed for safety and crowd control. Weir notes how their relationship with the civic events board has changed over the years—the procession is an economic engine that wields a certain amount of leverage and respect (Weir 2010). However, surprisingly, despite their enthusiasm for the procession, the City of Tucson did not financially supported the event in any way for many years. As Weir and Hagen emphasize, the procession grew out of the subversive, anti-establishment punk aesthetic of the Tucson downtown arts scene. Hagen notes the long history of censoring festive behaviour, referring to the French Revolution, which grew out of a festival: 'If people gather in the streets and express how they really feel, then they will storm the Bastille' (2010). Hagen feels the city's position is hypocritical because, on the one hand, it wants to promote a vibrant culture and quality of life while, on the other, it fears the uncertainty and chaos of the procession. The city vacillates between these two positions and, at any moment, has the power to shut down the procession. Both Hagen and Weir were surprised that they weren't shut down during the George W. Bush era, when the Department of Homeland Security was founded and many civic rights were revoked. Hagen admits that not being bound by city funds is liberating and gives them artistic autonomy (ibid.). The police and fire department and one guy in traffic control, according to Hagen, are what make the whole thing possible.[10]

In 2010, the All Souls' Procession carried an estimated $65,000 price tag (Ward 2010). Over the years, various grants have funded workshops for the community, but when the procession grew too large to be contained on the pavements, the grant money went to the city to pay for police officers and security (Nichols 2000). The city grants no longer cover street closures as they do for other festivals sanctioned by the city. While the procession raises funds from a variety of sources, including grants, private and corporate donations, the All Souls' Film Festival and other event fundraisers, it is always a struggle to make ends meet.[11] The bulk of the procession gets funded by the fire performance troupe Flam Chen, which earns most of their money touring out of state as they are hired to perform all over the United States and Canada (Weir 2010). While the procession does not receive corporate sponsorship, they have received grants from Union Pacific railroad and other small, local businesses. The organizers have resisted corporate sponsorship, likening the event to a public funeral, as Weir remarks, 'At your funeral, you wouldn't want a Pepsi banner, would you?' (quoted in Ward 2010). For the first time in 2009, a big donation hat was passed around the crowd collecting between $4,000 and $5,000 (Weir 2010).

The organization consists of a cell-like pod infrastructure that is flexible and durable allowing volunteers to move fluidly into and out of the organization. Both Hagen and Weir hold institutional memory that allows the organization to exist from year to year. Recently, Many Mouths One Stomach commissioned an economic impact study of the 2013 All Souls' Procession to provide leverage needed to secure city funds (Ward 2010). The study made clear that the procession brings 17.5 million dollars into the City of Tucson and draws over 100,000 people to downtown Tucson. As of 2014, the city finally became a financial supporter of the procession, contributing $10,000 to the 2014 parade (Hagen 2010).

The Ancestor's Project: From Personal to Community Mourning

Several important parts of the All Souls' event take place the night before the main procession: the personal altars vigil, coordinated for many years by former Flam Chen performer Alysa Volpe;[12] the community altar, coordinated by Susan Johnson; and the Procession of Little Angels—their version of the Día de Los Angelitos. This parade to honour children who have died, called the Procession of Little Angels (taken from the Mexican Día de los Angelitos), comes

FIGURE 8.2. **The Ancestor's Project, projection on the side of a building in Downtown Tucson, 2012.**
Photograph courtesy of the author.

at the end of a full day of children's workshops and performances at the downtown Joel D. Valdez Main Library Plaza. Johnson's community altar is one large evolving memorial where the entire community can add a memento, photograph or candle, whereas the personal altars are created by individuals and dedicated to specific people. The personal altar vigil begins around noon and ends at midnight, and most people stay for the entire vigil, sharing stories and anecdotes of loved ones. Personal altars have been part of the Tucson All Souls' Day commemorations from the beginning, but in 2006, the organizers provided a space for people to set up personal altars in front of the downtown library. To create a personal altar, a participant needs to reserve space in advance by registering on the All Souls' website. Volpe would map out the space and designate specific areas for each altar (there are between 30 and 60, depending on the year). The altars are not curated in any way; the only time Volpe has asked an individual to change an altar is when it was centred on a petition to legalize marijuana. Sometimes altars are symbolic or thematic, but Volpe feels strongly that the altars should not be political spaces because they are meant for those who are sincerely grieving: 'I have people whose child was murdered' (2010).

Kay Turner notes that the word 'altar' usually brings to mind 'the great high altars in churches and temples dedicated to God and ceremonially tended by a priest, rabbi, or minister' (1999: 7).[13] An altar 'makes visible that which is invisible and brings near that which is far away; it marks the potential for communication and exchange between different but necessarily connected worlds, the human and the divine' (ibid.: 7). Personal altars as instruments of communication are creative, transformative spaces that serve as a portal between the sacred and the profane. Turner believes 'bringing private altars into a public setting reveals aspects of the deeply historical tradition of altar-making in startling new ways revealing family legacy, creativity, and social networks' (ibid.: 23).

Jack Santino indicates a relatively recent and growing international phenomenon of spontaneous shrines and public memorials of death often triggered by the untimely death of cultural icons such as Princess Diana and Michael Jackson or the tragedy of 9/11 (2006: 5):

> The marking of the place of a shocking death with a spontaneous shrine consisting of flowers and personal memorabilia has become part of the global expressive repertoire, seen most dramatically at the site of the Oklahoma City bombing, in London and Paris after the death of Princess Diana, and in New York after September 11, 2001, Madrid after March 11, 2004, and London after July 7, 2005 (ibid.: 8).

These spontaneous memorials offer potent sites for public rituals of mourning. He constitutes 'public' as being performed before an audience whose spectatorship is both fluid and unpredictable (ibid.).

These public performances of 'rites of separation' as defined by Arnold van Gennep are what Santino calls 'performative commemoratives' (ibid.: 9)—'the concept includes but is not restricted to spontaneous shrines—invite participation, unlike the funeral procession one happens to run across. They also invite interpretation. Once set out before an undifferentiated public, the polysemy inherent in these assemblages allow for a broad range of readings and associations by passersby, regardless of the initial intentions of the originators' (ibid.: 11). These spontaneous memorials are truly popular in the sense that they arise from the 'folk' or people of the community. 'They invite participation from strangers. They are "open" to the public' (ibid.: 12). As Santino notes, they 'reflect and comment on public and social issues' (ibid.: 12).

> These personal offerings represented by posters, shrines and altars make the private visible within the public sphere. [. . .] We who build shrines and construct public altars or parade with photographs of the deceased will not allow you to write off victims as mere regrettable statistics. We insist—the shrines insist—by their disruption of the mundane environment, their calling attention to themselves—they insist on us acknowledging the real people, the real lives lost, the devastation of the commonwealth that these politics hold. By translating social and political actions into personal terms, the shrines are themselves political statements. [. . .] The shrines insert and insist upon the presence of absent people (ibid.: 13).

These acts of public mourning construct a visible relationship between the deceased and those who leave notes and memorabilia (ibid.). Santino asserts that 'spontaneous shrines place deceased individuals back into the fabric of society, into the middle of areas of commerce and travel, into everyday life as it is being lived' (ibid.).

In the Tucson All Souls' Procession, altars and spontaneous shrines vary from person to person; many contain photographs of the deceased, votive candles, poems, sometimes fruit and food. Some are erected just once; others reappear each year. Volpe recalls, 'I have a husband and wife whose son died when he was 22 of a drug overdose. So every year, they come and create an altar' (2010). Volpe's belief in the significance of altars extends into her own home, where she maintains wall-to-wall altars. Every year she creates her own altar at the procession, which varies from one year to the next but usually contains pictures of her deceased father, grandfather and grandmother, carnations, trinkets and fabric. If someone she knows died recently, they are added (2010). It gives her the opportunity to be present with her grief and to remember those she has lost. Volpe points out that in our modern age, when someone dies their passing is processed with just a funeral and then those who have lost the loved one are expected to return to work and keep on going as if nothing happened—the grieving process is abbreviated. These personal altars allow people to extend that healing process and share it in a public, communal way. It provides a healing network where people grieving can be around others who are also suffering a loss. For Volpe, the personal altars capture the essence of what the procession is all about. She feels that most people come to the procession to check out the costumes and the finale rather than really meditate on the dead. As of 2014, Volpe no longer manages the altars as the community has spontaneously adopted the altar ritual without a single person coordinating and managing it.

Another altar of sorts is on display throughout the procession. Established in 2005, the Ancestors' Project is a visual public memorial that is often projected directly above the personal altars and on other civic buildings around Tucson along the procession route. By going to the All Souls' website, the public can upload images of their ancestors onto an online portal, which receives an average of 200 photos each year. Originally, these images were processed and colourized with sepia tones to give them an antiquated appearance by multimedia artist Adam Cooper-Terán,[14] director of the Ancestor's Project until 2009; but due to the volume, they are now projected as they are received in a slide-show format. For several years, the images were projected onto the City Court building at Sixth Avenue and Bennington, in storefronts along Congress Street, along Stone Avenue and at the finale site.

The Urn and Finale: Release and Transformation

Hagen and Weir's goal is to make the procession as participatory as possible, and in 2005 Weir designed a papier mâché urn to be carried throughout the procession route, into which people could place their prayers and mementos for the dead. As Hagen notes, they wanted to find a way for people to be involved and feel like they owned the procession. Since 2001, there have been burning sculptures at the finale but in 2005, upon receiving a grant from the Black Rock Arts Foundation (the Burning Man Organization's not-for-profit entity), the organizers introduced the urn—a giant sculptural steel sphere, 2.5 metres in diameter, full of prayers, which is set on fire. A 'Spirit Group', volunteers from the community, escort the urn through the procession to the finale and hand out paper and pencils for prayers. The first year, Hagen was surprised by how many people came prepared with prewritten messages, photographs and objects of significance to place in the urn. Hagen witnessed how difficult it is for some people to accept death: 'People can't always just let go. We watch people try. People put their arm in and then they pull it back. And they still have the thing in their hand because they can't quite let go. And they have to try a few

FIGURES 8.3a, b, c. **The Urn, 2013.**
Photograph courtesy of Nadia Hagen.

times' (2010). The first year, images of the deceased as well as Chinese Hell notes were glued to the outside of the urn, which they realized was a mistake when people started throwing money into a circular portal in the urn. Hagen muses over how much money that was meant as a donation has been accidentally burnt over the years.

The first year, when the urn arrived at the finale site, it was packed full of messages, which brought the backstage crew to tears, as Weir recalls (2010). Each year, Weir and Hagen climb into the urn's circular portal to sort through and make sure no one has put in anything dangerous—explosives, for example. Weir describes finding shoes, sweaters, socks, teeth and crystals inside. For Hagen, the urn is a potent symbol and physical manifestation of the cyclical nature of life and death—a portal to the afterlife and an invented community ritual for people to grieve outside of organized religion (2010). While small incidents have occurred over the years, there have been no major accidents. Weir redesigned the urn in 2010 so that it rests on a 7.5-metre steel tower hoisted up with a crane (Swindell 2010).

The procession ends in a spectacular finale performed by Flam Chen. The board of Many Mouths One Stomach meets in May to begin organizing the procession and the finale. Weir describes the 20-minute finale as a *pastorella*, which is basically the same from year to year with slight variations in theme and colour (2010). For Weir, the procession is a perfect fusion of rock and roll, shamanism and elemental awareness in one 20-minute performance. As Hagen remembers, in the early years, when the procession ended, there would be a big informal party and participants would burn puppets and sculptures (Hagen 2010). Hagen and Weir took that one step further and created an elemental fire spectacle.

Hagen is the primary choreographer and costume designer/constructer creating elaborate, imaginative, otherworldly designs. She also works with the Spirit Group that accompanies the urn, while Weir is the technical director and Head Rigger for the Procession and Finale performance. Hagen and Weir are the visionaries but they create an open structure that allows for individual input and creativity. Each Spirit Group is headed by its own volunteer director. Rehearsing for the procession is like band practice—performers meet several times a week to practise at various industrial artist warehouses around Tucson. Core members of Flam Chen fluctuate between 10 and 13 performers; however, an average of 75 performers are part of the finale. The procession is an opportunity for Hagen and Weir to bring local performing artists, community members and students from their Tucson Circus Arts School into one large performance.

In 2009, Hagen asked Randall Swindell[15] to take over as director of the fire performers. Swindell, who joined the procession in 2003, assembles around 12 fire performers and teaches them choreography for the finale. In order to perform with fire during the procession, anyone who handles fire must take a test on fire safety with the Tucson Fire Department and obtain a special licence (Swindell 2010). Weir designed the standard fire safety manual for fire performers and performance that is used by the fire department to this day. Safety is the primary concern when performing with fire, and Flam Chen has to adhere to strict standards, from the type of links on the chains of the poi[16] to the number of fire safety personnel needed per performer.

Some of the most innovative technological elements of the procession are the aerial helium balloon clusters and the Tetroons, 7-metre Mylar upside-down pyramids used by Weir in 2005. The balloons clusters cost anywhere from $3,000 to $8,000 in materials alone, according to Weir. The idea to use helium balloons came to Weir when he was brainstorming on how to do aerial work without using a crane. According to Weir, cluster ballooning has been around since the 1850s, although never to support an aerial rig.[17]

He noted that only three groups in the world use this technique. Their main balloon aerialist, Aurelia Cohen,[18] was fearless and was the first person who dared to perform over the massive crowd without a safety net. While there are many talented aerialists working with Flam Chen, Cohen took the leap that others couldn't. As Hagen notes, 'performing on the balloon rig is very different from static silks: being out in the elements the rig is in constant motion and the performer is literally clinging to the fabric for her life' (2010). Swindell recalls a frightening experience several years ago while Cohen was performing on the balloon rig during the finale—she was floating in a giant papier mâché egg when all of a sudden, she began convulsing uncontrollably. When she descended, she was shaking and in tears, unable to speak. When she finally came around, she described a sensation of spirits pouring out of the urn and through her body as she was suspended in the air over the crowd (Swindell 2010). Swindell admits that every one of the performers has had similar experiences.

Personal experiences and similar incidents have given the organizers a greater understanding of the kind of psychic energy they are working with. In 2010, the finale site was on an ancient Native American burial ground—a mass grave from a Civil War–era massacre. According to Swindell, the performers felt chills the entire time they were performing as the performance 'induces a meditative silence resembling a wake' (ibid.). Weir and Swindell see this ceremony as a community healing ritual to cleanse the space, releasing spirits that are trapped at that site. As Swindell describes it: 'It is exorcism in a massive public way. [. . .] It has a dark history that is hidden. I do feel like a lot of the procession has to do with healing that space. [. . .] They are dead but they are being thought of in a really intense way—or summoned. You can feel their presence' (2010). Swindell views Hagen and Weir as community shamans and the procession as a shamanic journey to the underworld. He believes that summoning this energy opens a portal to the afterlife: 'We are playing with something that is much bigger than any of us' (2010).

Forging 'Imaginary Communities' through Social Media

FIGURE 8.4. **Participant at the Procession, 2013.**
Photograph courtesy of Nadia Hagen.

In *Media and Ritual: Death, Community and Everyday Life* (2013), Johanna Sumiala asks how we might understand ritual in a constantly shifting transnational environment?[19] She observes how in contemporary society the line between 'producer' and 'consumer' is increasingly blurred; the traditional hierarchical role of the media is subverted transforming a passive consumer into an active agent through social media. In a public memorial of death, like the Tucson All Souls' Procession, social media is far more pervasive than mainstream media. A plethora of electronic devices flood the visual landscape capturing the event from multiple perspectives and vantage points, which instantly circulate via social media networks such as Facebook, Instagram, Twitter and YouTube. As grassroots reporters sprout up via social media networks, counter-narratives enter into the conversation vying for a piece of the 'attention economy'. The advent of social media transforms the passive consumer into an active agent in the visual economy of image and meaning making.

The media serves a ritual function in constructing what Sumiala calls a 'dramaturgy of grief' by disseminating symbolic images of mourning and memorialization that help the grieving process. Mediatized death rituals, according to her, manage public emotion and bring community together through symbolic communication such as lighting candles and placing flowers on community altars. Sumiala notes a significant paradigm shift occurring across the globe; the emergence of fragmented imaginary online communities whose boundaries are porous and constantly shifting. She argues that a close reading of these mediatized death rituals within this shifting landscape offers an important glimpse into our current moment and provides a deeper understanding of our selves and the diverse, imaginary communities we belong to—the Tucson All Souls' Procession is evidence of this. This temporary mourning community is reinforced via multiple social media networks bringing disparate communities together, forging a momentary communitas and utopian hope.

Why the Procession Matters

What does the All Souls' Day Procession mean for the community of Tucson—what function does it serve? Procession participant

Mickey Randleman prepared for the 20th anniversary of the procession by commemorating her late grandfather. She donned the dress she wore to his funeral and carried a letter and his photo. She notes, 'I have done the procession before but this year it will be more solemn for me because I'll be walking in my grandfather's memory' (quoted in Lewis 2009). For therapist Dr Karen McIntrye, the procession is healing: 'In our culture we are very afraid of pain, and we do this thing where we try to avoid it and pretend its not there. This is a great way to help deal with it. It helps people feel like they aren't alone in the depths of pain and loss. [. . .]' (in ibid.).

For Cooper-Terán the procession fulfils the public's need to mourn. As a part of the Ancestor's Project, he has observed how emotional people get when they see their relatives projected onto a public building: 'It totally transforms people and they are so grateful. The act is so powerful. [. . .] It stirs up dialogue. There are always stories that come out of these types of public gatherings when people start coming together with the intent to mourn or celebrate someone who passed' (2010). Another central organizer, Matt Cotten of Tucson Puppetworks, emphasizes that the procession is very different from Halloween: 'I think that's why this has gotten so big because people yearn for a ritualistic way to celebrate death and mourn people they've lost' (quoted in Bodfield 2003). Volpe feels the Tucson community is really disjointed, with a large confluence of people who have their origins elsewhere, and the procession provides an opportunity for it to temporarily coalesce (2010).

Hagen sees a significant shift in consciousness among a generation of artists who are channelling a shared energy and asking similar questions. Hagen's central questions are: 'What is it that our society lacks? What are we trying to respond to as artists? What is the call? What is needed?' (2010). For Weir, the most beautiful moments of the procession are like the one when the cop who has been working the procession all night approaches him and announces he is not working the procession the following year; he is going to attend and bring his family (Weir 2010). Or when the crane operator, who was sceptical at first, spoke after the actual performance about how moved he was by the event. Now Weir has trouble finding cops who are willing to work the procession because they all want to participate.

Weir believes that people gravitated towards the event because there are so few opportunities to mourn in the US: 'There's not a lot of room in Western culture for grieving in an exalted way—to express your emotions and your grief. It serves the role of festal culture. *Festal* is this very archaic word that references the core human need for celebration' (quoted in White 2006). Weir has a deep, personal attachment to the procession. The survivor of two suicide attempts, Weir believes he has died twice and has been to the other side. He understands what the urn looks like from the perspective of the dead:

> Being in that fourth, or fifth, or sixth dimension, not having a body, not having a mouth, or ears, or eyes—having vision 360 degrees, all directions at the same time. Knowing what it is—it is more important to me than the money or pain it causes in my physical body to work that hard—or any of those things. It transgresses all of that. [. . .] I feel I was put on this earth to do this ritual (2010).

As Hagen sees it, 'Artists like us are answering this call to what we need as a culture—to create a utopia. What do we need as a culture just to evolve? To not self-destruct' (2010). For Weir, fire triggers something profound in the reptilian brain that has been forgotten or buried. Festive events such as the All Souls' Procession are temporary, efficacious and transformative, evoking real-life changes in those who participate (Weir 2010). Events inspired by the Tucson All Souls' Procession are taking hold in other cities across the US, including Portland, Oregon, and St. Louis, Missouri, producing meaningful public forums to collectively mourn and celebrate the dead outside of official mainstream culture.

Notes

Sections of this chapter have been previously published in Rachel Bowditch, 'Commemorating the Ancestors: Performances of Death at the Tucson All Souls' Procession' in Chris Newbold and Jennie Jordan (eds), *Focus on World Festivals: Contemporary Case Studies and Perspectives* (Oxford: Goodfellow Publishers, 2016), 281–9.

1 The Romans celebrated a similar festival called Feralia in October to celebrate the passing of the dead (Hilker 2009).

2 Appadurai's concept further develops Benedict Anderson's 'imagined communities' to include the ways in which 'certain forms of mass mediation play a key role in imagining the nation and in facilitating the spread of this form to the colonial world in Asia and elsewhere' (Anderson 2006: 22). Here I extend Appadurai's theory to encompass festivals as 'diasporic public spheres' where multiple layers of convergence, diaspora and conversion can be glimpsed.

3 Two of the most commercialized Day of the Dead sites in Mexico are the 'now famous towns of Mixquic, a suburb of Mexico City, and Janitzio, in Michoacán—both relentlessly highlighted in glossy photo books and travel articles. Referred to by Mexicans and foreigners alike as the place to be to experience an 'authentic' Day of the Dead, these communities have become veritable pilgrimage destinations for tourists in search of 'tradition' (Marchi 2009: 128). Cultures around the world practise traditions for honouring the dead, which include grave visitation, building altars, making offerings and praying—for example, the Japanese Buddhist Bon Festival, the traditional Chinese Ching Ming Festival, Día de Finados in Brazil and Día de los Ñatitas (Day of the Skulls) in Bolivia (Palfrey 1995).

4 The Día de los Muertos celebration in San Francisco, which was initiated in its present form in the early 1970s, takes place in the Mission District, gathering over 15,000 participants and revellers. The event is celebrated with art, music, performances and a procession that begins between 24th and Bryant Streets and moves to Garfield Park. In Mesa, Arizona, according to artist Zarco Guerrero, Día de

los Muertos is an opportunity to 'pay homage to the Mexicans killed in auto accidents while being smuggled across the border' (quoted in Miller 2008).

5 Born in Manhattan, Hagen was raised by her grandmother. An autodidact without formal art or performance training, Hagen immersed herself in the punk underground scene and developed her aesthetic and performance skills touring with the industrial punk band Crash Worship, founded by Simon Cheffins. She would often travel through Tucson with the band and eventually settled there, over 20 years ago (Hagen 2010).

6 Hagen started Flam Chen in 1996 with her friend from France, fire performer Kesha Kramer. The name Flam Chen is based on the French word for fire chain (ibid.).

7 Weir, technical director of the All Souls' Procession and Flam Chen, has been living in Tucson since 1990 and has been participating in the greater art scene for over 20 years. His exposure to performance outside of music came from living in Yosemite National Park where he worked with a project called Project Bandaloop—a group of rock climber aerialists (see www.projectbandaloop.org). Working with Project Bandaloop was his first exposure to nontraditional performance and it opened his eyes to the power of performance in a public arena. In 1998 he joined the All Souls' Procession and elevated the level of spectacle with his technical savvy, using pyrotechnics on a grand scale to realize Hagen's vision.

8 The original procession route started at 516 N. Fifth Ave at 7 p.m. and proceeded down Fourth Avenue through downtown Tucson, culminating at the Mat Bevel Institute. The route in 2010 commenced at the Epic Café, 745 N. Fourth Avenue, and continued downtown, ending at the Franklyn Street Docks, near the North Stone Avenue underpass. The procession now begins at 6 p.m and the finale starts at 7.45 p.m. The specifics of location and duration vary from year to year.

9 Bohemian Grove, founded in 1872 by 'five San Francisco newspapermen, a Shakespearean actor, a winemaker and two successful merchants, with the goal of connecting "gentlemen" to the finer pursuits of literature, art, music and drama', has been holding annual gatherings at a 2,700-acre secluded redwood-forest sanctuary near the Russian River (Moore 2004). An hour north of San Francisco,

the private encampment includes 120 individual camps resembling an enclosed city with a library, a museum, an emergency health clinic and a fire station (Norberg 2010). Each year the event is met with protests by the activist group Bohemian Grove Action Network called the 'Resurrection of Care', and each year somebody tries to infiltrate the closed compound and fails (Benfell 2004). According to the *San Francisco Chronicle*, in 1991 four protesters hid in the trees on the fringes of the ceremony as they watched a model of an owl—the Grove's traditional symbol of 'Dull Care'—being destroyed by four explosions (Butler 1991). As *Gawker* pointed out, 'the Bohemian Grove is pretty much Burning Man for old dudes, the main difference being that the Grovers start their party by roasting a giant effigy, and the Burners end their party with one '(Thomas 2009).

10 In 2009 the All Souls' organizers paid $7,000 for street barricades and cops and that amount increases each year (Hagen 2010).

11 One creative fundraising solution was the creation of the All Souls' International Film Festival held a month after the event to allow participants to see documentaries and short films based on the All Souls' Day events. But since 2009 the film festival has been held before the procession as a way to raise funds and awareness.

12 Volpe started out as a fire performer and stilter in Flam Chen. Her first performance with Flam Chen was for the 1996 procession as a spirit dancer. In 1999, Volpe organized the finale while Hagen was on tour with her band. In 2007, Volpe shifted her focus from being a fire performer to organizing the altars (Volpe 2010).

13 Kay Turner notes, 'The first Western domestic altars were made in the Neolithic era around 5000–6000 BCE. In many pre-patriarchal cultures in Old Europe, the Near East, the Indus Valley, and the Mediterranean, altars were dedicated in households to insure the protection and advocacy of various life-giving and life-nourishing fecund goddesses' (ibid.: 12).

14 Involved in the arts his entire life Adam Cooper-Terán, at the age of 14, connected with the downtown art scene working on public murals with artist Pasco Azurelo. He first encountered Flam Chen and the All Souls' Procession when he wrote an article for the *Arizona Daily Star* about the downtown art scene. He began documenting Flam Chen's performances and was responsible for documenting and creating all media related to the procession.

Cooper-Terán has worked on and off with the procession for many years.

15 Swindell is a fire performer and stilt walker. As a teenager, Weir and Hagen taught him how to spin fire and walk on stilts. Up-and-coming Flam Chen performers are trained at Hagen and Weir's Tucson Circus Arts, a school dedicated to circus training. As Swindell notes, 'Flam Chen has single-handedly gotten hundreds of people to learn circus arts and theatre here in Tucson. Over time, they have taught many people, like me, who otherwise would not have been exposed to that stuff right out of high school' (2010).

16 Poi is derived from the Maori of New Zealand. While poi is a traditional part of Maori culture, lighting poi on fire is not and is a practice that developed outside New Zealand. Fire poi are made of Kevlar wicks attached to ropes or chains. The wicks are soaked in fuel, usually paraffin or white gas. 'Poi' is Maori for 'ball' and, originally, it was a flax bag used to carry small objects such as eggs. The Maori also use poi as a bag to crush food in, and it was adapted as a tool for warriors—to help develop strength, flexibility and coordination. Later, it was adapted for performance. The traditional performance poi (a light ball made of raupo—a swamp plant—attached to a flax rope) can be found in Maori action songs and dances, where it is swung around rhythmically to produce a percussive sound (Starzecka 1996: 46).

17 Weir recently connected with Don Piccard, the world's foremost balloon expert and a fifth-generation balloon master whose family holds the world record for the highest ascent and lowest descent. At the age of 87, Piccard agreed to meet with Weir and invited him out to his ranch in Minnesota to discuss ballooning technology (Weir 2010).

18 Cohen, who joined Flam Chen when she was 17, is responsible for training many new aerialists in Tucson at the Rhythm Industry, Flam Chen's studio space (Swindell 2010).

19 Sumiala's cites a number of contemporary death rituals as her focus—the death of Osama bin Laden, Steve Jobs, Michael Jackson and the Swedish foreign minister Anna Lindh among others—making her work vital and necessary to the present moment. In the case of Jobs, the high priest of technology who died in October 2011, his death instantly circulated around the globe transforming Apple

stores into pilgrimage sites and the Apple logo into a sacred transnational symbol. Increasingly, social media networks are becoming critical voices in the construction of the images that surround tragic events. An example Sumiala gives is after the tsunami in South East Asia, personal images from mobile phones were circulating on the Internet and on major news networks long before the official media teams were able to reach the disaster zone.

Works Cited

ANDERSON, Benedict. 2006. *Imagined Communities: Reflections on the Origin and Spread of Nationalism.* New York: Verso.

ANDERSON, Jack, and Michael Binstein. 1992. 'L.A. Smoke Clouds Bohemian Bash'. *Washington Post,* 1 June.

APPADURAI, Arjun. 1996. *Modernity at Large: Cultural Dimensions of Globalization.* Minneapolis: University of Minnesota Press.

BENFELL, Carol. 2004. '100 Call for "Resurrection of Care": Annual Protest of Movers and Shakers' Encampment Focuses on Love, Kindness'. *Press Democrat,* 19 July. Available at: http://goo.gl/uQbE6Q (last accessed on 11 April 2016).

BODFIELD, Rhonda. 2003. 'Revelers' Puppets Tell Personal Stories: Tucson's All Souls' Spectacle'. *Arizona Daily Star,* 2 October. Available at: https://goo.gl/2LJKZz (last accessed on 13 April 2016).

BRANDES, Stanley. 2006. *Skulls to the Living, Bread to the Dead.* New Jersey: Wiley-Blackwell.

BUTLER, Katy. 1991. 'Bohemian Club Ritual Disrupted by Protesters'. *San Francisco Chronicle,* 15 July.

CARMICHAEL, Elizabeth. 1992. *The Skeleton at the Feast: The Day of the Dead in Mexico.* Austin: University of Texas Press.

COOPER-TERÁN, Adam. 2010. Personal interview. Tucson, Arizona, 10 May.

COSMAN, Madeleine Pelner. 1981. *Medieval Holiday and Festivals: Calendar of Celebrations.* New York: Charles Scribner's Sons.

HAGEN, Nadia. 2010. Personal interview. Tucson, Arizona, 10 May.

HILKER, Carol. 2009. 'All Saints' Day and All Souls' Day—Celebrating Day of the Dead San Francisco'. *San Francisco Examiner,* 1 November. Available at: http://goo.gl/MqJYNT (last accessed on 13 October 2010).

KAPLAN, Ann. 2005. *Trauma Culture: The Politics of Terror and Loss in Media and Literature.* New Brunswick, NJ: Rutgers University Press.

LEWIS, Kelly. 2009. 'Healing Through Procession', *Zocalo Magazine* 30 September. Available at: http://goo.gl/rVlt7U (last accessed on 13 October 2010).

MARCHI, Regina. 1994. 'El Día de los Muertos in the USA: Cultural Ritual as Political Communication' in Jack Santino (ed), *Spontaneous Shrines and Public Commemoration of Death*. New York: Palgrave, pp. 261–83.

——. 2009. *Day of the Dead in the USA, The Migration and Transformation of a Cultural Phenomenon*. New Brunswick, NJ: Rutgers University Press.

MENARD, Valerie. 2000. *The Latino Holiday Book: From Cinco de Mayo to Día de los Muertos; The Celebrations and Traditions of Hispanic Americas*. New York: Marlowe and Company.

MILLER, Carlos. 2008. 'Indigenous People Wouldn't Let "Day of the Dead" Die'. *The Arizona Republic*. September 5. Available at: http://goo.gl/-bISUTz (last accessed on 13 October 2010).

MOORE, Derek J. 2004. '"Roughing It" Boho-Style: While Cabins Range from Rustic to Posh, Amenities All First-Class at Grove'. *Press Democrat*, 24 July. Available at: http://goo.gl/39iKRe (last accessed on 11 April 2016).

NORBERG, Bob. 2010. 'Weighty Guests Arrive for Annual Bohemian Grove'. *Press Democrat*, 15 July. Available at: http://goo.gl/m52tCt (last accessed on 11 April 2016).

PALFREY, Dale Hoyt. 1995. 'Day of the Dead'. *Mexconnect*. Available at: http://goo.gl/RR1ZJa (last accessed on 13 October 2010).

SANTINO, Jack. 1994. 'Introduction: Festivals of Death and Life' in Jack Santino (ed.), *Halloween and Other Festivals of Death and Life*. Knoxville: University of Tennessee Press, pp. xi–xxvii.

——. 2006. *Spontaneous Shrines and the Public Memorialization of Death*. New York: Palgrave.

STARZECKA, D. C. (ed.). 1996. *Maori Art and Culture*. London: British Museum Press.

SUMIALA, Johanna. 2013. *Media and Ritual: Death, Community and Everyday Life*. London: Routledge.

SWINDELL, Randall. 2010. Personal interview. Tucson, Arizona, 11 May.

THOMAS, Owen. 2009. 'The Piss-Poor Secrets of the Bohemian Grove'. *Gawker*, 2 April. Available at: http://goo.gl/aARdaz (last accessed on 11 April 2016).

TURNER, Kay, and Pat Jasper. 1994. 'Day of the Dead: The Tex-Mex Tradition' in Jack Santino (ed), *Halloween and Other Festivals of Death and Life*. Knoxville: University of Tennessee Press, pp. 133–51.

TURNER, Kay. 1999. *Beautiful Necessity: The Art and Meaning of Women's Altars*. London: Thames and Hudson.

VOLPE, Alysa. 2010. Personal interview. Tucson, Arizona, 11 May.

WARD, Coley. 2010. 'All Souls' Procession in Money Bind'. *Arizona Daily Star*, 26 September. Available at: http://goo.gl/glPYMr (last accessed on 11 April 2016).

WEIR, Paul. 2010. Personal interview. Tucson, Arizona, 10 May.

WHITE, Erin. 2006. 'All Souls' Procession'. *Arizona Tucson Daily Star*, 5 November. Available at: https://goo.gl/KrBYc2 (last accessed on 11 April 2016).

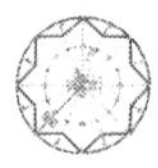

Chapter 9

PERFORMING DYSTOPIA

Hurricane Katrina and the 2006 Mardi Gras Parade

Katherine Nigh

> But to my country I want to say this: During this crisis you failed us. You looked down on us; you dismissed our victims; you dismissed us. You want our Jazz Fest, you want our Mardi Gras, you want our cooking and our music. Then when you saw us in real trouble, when you saw a tiny minority preying on the weak among us, you called us 'Sin City', and turned your backs.
>
> Anne Rice (2005)

The website for the New Orleans Convention and Visitors Bureau describes New Orleans as a 'European City on a Po-Boy Budget' (2008). New Orleans, Louisiana, is often advertised to visitors as the city in the United States 'least' like the US. The combination of the city's culinary, musical, architectural and linguistic traditions, among others, understandably could lead a visitor to believe at one minute they were visiting Paris and the next that they were on the island of Haiti. In addition to its distinct food and architecture, that the population of New Orleans is predominantly black and poor[1] probably plays a role in this attitude for those who identify US American identity as being white and middle class. It is also possible that the very thing that draws many of the city's visitors—its festivals and rituals—is one of the things that estranges New Orleans from those who consider performance and ritual separate from 'everyday life'. While people are drawn to visit New Orleans because of these festivals, the customs themselves can be perceived as bizarre and even sacrilegious. However, as scholars including Joseph R. Roach (1996) and Mikhail Bakhtin (1984) have illustrated, carnival and festive ceremonies such as Mardi Gras are much more socially rich and complex events than many who do not participate in such ceremonies perceive. These events are foundational elements in the formation of communities and, for many individuals, provide a sense of self-esteem and purpose. Ceremony and ritual reflect shared meaning to shape and strengthen group and personal identity, which is context specific. While the city was still physically devastated by the aftermath of Hurricane Katrina (23–31 August 2005) and its inhabitants were just beginning to process the emotional and psychological damage they and their loved ones endured, it may be difficult for those who do not come from New Orleans to understand how people could put on costumes, decorate floats and parade down the streets that, just a few months earlier, had been submerged in water. In other words, one might have asked what place festival, performance and joy had at a time when more perceivably 'serious' issues were at hand. To examine the 2006 Mardi Gras and the history of Mardi Gras in New Orleans is to understand that festival and performance is such an integral part of the individual and community identity that as part of the rebuilding process, there was no option *but* to go forward and have the parade that year.

While Mardi Gras can be seen as a utopic occasion where the most delightful and joyful world can be imagined and performed, the tensions between utopia and dystopia have always pervaded this event. During the 2006 Mardi Gras, these tensions took on a particular resonance, as participants displayed and performed both their frustrations with what had occurred after Hurricane Katrina and their hopes for an improved future in New Orleans after the storm. In her book *Utopia in Performance: Finding Hope at the Theater,* Jill Dolan writes: 'My investigation into utopia in performance, then, resists the effort to find representations of a better world; the word *utopia* means, literally, "no place", and this book respects the letter of its sense by refusing to pin it down to prescription' (2005: 7). Like Dolan, I choose not to use the word utopia in the context of a post-Katrina New Orleans and the 2006 Mardi Gras Festival as a place of hope but, rather, as she borrows the term from Thomas More, as a 'no place'—no longer the place it was, unclear as to the place it would become and certainly vulnerable to the visions of real-estate moguls and government officials eager to change the 'landscape' (and demographics) of the city. Local traditions and performances including Mardi Gras served as a site for the public declaration of anger, pain, frustration, grief and a love for a city that had seen and undergone a literal and metaphorical drowning just six months before. These performances were not utopic in the sense that they provided a hopeful vision of New Orleans. These performances are perhaps a perfect example of Dolan's sense of utopia in which, aligning herself with philosophers Ernst Bloch and Herbert Marcuse, she sees 'art as an arena in which an alternative world can be expressed—not in a didactic, descriptive way as in traditional "utopian" literature, but through the communication of an alternative experience' (ibid.). The 2006 Mardi Gras provided an opportunity for an 'alternative world' outside the one that could not easily be escaped, a world surrounding the inhabitants of New Orleans that was a constant reminder of what had taken place six months before and for the presentation of an alternative Katrina narrative to those dominating the mainstream media.

An event such as Hurricane Katrina is experienced both from the inside, by those who are located in the geographical and cultural nexus of the event, and from the outside, by those who experience the event from afar. Outsiders generally turn to the media to understand what they cannot see for themselves in person. Even those 'on the ground' will turn to the media to understand the 'larger picture' of what is happening in their community and to receive practical information of what damage had taken place in various neighbourhoods, where to go for shelter or to evacuate. Media coverage also served to frame the events taking place in the Gulf Coast area. 'Katrina was the first hurricane to hit the United States to the accompaniment of continuous (24/7) television coverage [. . .]. In social science terms, television constructed the frame of meaning to which the audiences and decision makers came to understand Katrina' (Dynes and Rodríguez 2007: 24). These frames are not neutral and they often uphold hegemonic structures, particularly of power and race; furthermore, they often omit information, causing gaps of knowledge that do not acknowledge the perspectives and narratives of often subjugated communities (see Conquergood 2002). The dominant narratives created by the media after Hurricane Katrina portrayed a 'black' city that was looting and out of control. It is important to examine the 2006 Mardi Gras because it offered a space to resist these dominant narratives and served as a stage for these counternarratives to be transmitted to the national audience who turned yet again to the media to be told just how far along New Orleans was in its recovery.

The 2006 Mardi Gras became a site for both utopic and dystopic visions of a post-Katrina New Orleans. Taking advantage of increased media attention, some Mardi Gras participants performed images of citizens who were not happy with the local and federal government and felt abandoned by the nation to which they belonged. Additionally, the differences in performances along racial and class lines only highlighted the social divisions that contributed to the events surrounding Katrina.

New Orleans and Hurricane Katrina

New Orleans is located on the southeastern tip of Louisiana, on the southern end of Lake Pontchetrain. The city is surrounded by water—both by the large lake and the Gulf of Mexico. In the late 1600s and early 1700s, when Louisiana was a French territory extending from the Mississippi River to the Rocky Mountains, the swamplands where New Orleans would come to be founded appeared to be uninhabitable. After a number of settlers passed through the area, Jean Baptiste Le Moyne de Bienville decided to found the city of New Orleans in 1718 and name it after the duke for whom he served—the Duke of Orleans. The city's origins were heavily influenced by French customs, architecture, language and laws. Though strategic because of its location near the Mississippi River and the gulf, it was otherwise considered a city to send the 'undesirables' of France (including prostitutes and criminals). In the 1760s, Louisiana was sold to Spain and the city's architecture and customs were then influenced by its new ruling country. Louisiana was given back to France by Spain and, in 1803, Napoleon sold Louisiana to the United States.

One of the factors that sets New Orleans apart among cities in the United States is its unique slave history. While there were slaves in New Orleans, as there were in many other parts of the United States, the French and Spanish laws and attitudes regarding slavery meant that, unlike in other parts of the country, slaves were allowed to buy their freedom; New Orleans therefore became one of the first cities where former slaves owned property and businesses, which aided the integration of African-derived ceremonies, music and food into the cultural landscape of the city. From this blending of traditions and heritages, jazz music evolved in New Orleans. While New Orleans may be advertised as a city that 'does not belong' in the United States, in many ways this city tells the history of the country in a way few others can. Within the food, architecture, music and people of the city exists a history of slavery as well as a history of the influence of French, Spanish and British settlers in the territory that is now the United States of America.

While the location made it ideal for trade and access, New Orleans, like many cities along the Gulf Coast, has always been vulnerable to flooding and hurricane-related natural disasters. The city is located below sea level and keeps its surrounding waters from flooding the city through a system of levees. In 1947, a hurricane flooded Jefferson Parish (a section of New Orleans) and killed 51 people (McCarragher 2008). Hurricane Betsy, which made landfall in September 1965, caused extensive damage and deaths in New Orleans and initiated the habit of many residents keeping axes in their attic in case they needed to cut through their roofs to escape a flooding home (as many did have to do 40 years later during Hurricane Katrina). Hurricane Katrina appeared on the weather map on 23 August 2005 and was initially considered to be a relatively non-threatening category-one hurricane. However, within a few days, Katrina had strengthened significantly and, by the time it reached the Gulf Coast, on 29 August, it became 'one of the deadliest and most costly hurricanes in US history' (Levitt and Whitaker 2009: 1). Russell R. Dynes and Havidán Rodríguez write: 'Katrina impacted an extensive geographical area of the United States, approximately 90,000 square miles, or about the geographical area of Great Britain' (2007: 23). Many Gulf Coast cities including Biloxi, Folsom and Golfport were devastated by the hurricane. However, perhaps both because New Orleans was well known (and in many cases beloved) before the storm and because of the dramatic images of a city seemingly completely underwater, it began to gather the most media attention after the storm. The devastation that impacted New Orleans did not come from the hurricane itself (rainfall or wind damage) but, rather, by the breach of multiple levees built to keep the many rivers feeding into New

Orleans from flooding the city. While many of the city's inhabitants prepared to clean up from the wind-and-rain damage caused by the storm, water began to fill the streets and people's homes. For those who lived closest to the levees, escaping the rapidly rising water was nearly impossible. While some were able to climb onto their roofs, others were swept away by water so strong it lifted homes off their foundations, moved large boats miles from their original locations and stacked items as large as cars and trucks on top of one another as if an artist had purposefully created some type of post-apocalyptic sculpture. Those who survived the water surge and made their way to higher ground were soon to discover they were only at the beginning of their ordeal. Owing to miscommunication, incompetency and neglect, it took an inexplicable amount of time for people to be rescued. One of the more horrific examples of what people had to endure if they survived the initial flood waters took place in the Superdome, home to the football team the New Orleans Saints, where tens of thousands of people seeking shelter from the storm had no food, water or toilets. Both inside and immediately outside the Superdome, dead bodies were left in the hot and humid summer weather to rot. After the immediate crisis subsided, New Orleans residents had to deal with insurance companies, the rebuilding process and finding loved ones who had evacuated or been relocated to other states. For many of those who had either left for or been placed in other states, the decision of whether to return to New Orleans became agonizing and nearly impossible.

Mardi Gras, Agency and Social Change

With such devastation after Katrina, organizing and executing an event such as Mardi Gras did invoke practical and ethical dilemmas for the city's organizers and inhabitants. Yet, Mardi Gras has been synonymous with New Orleans for over a hundred years and the decision to not have a parade in 2006 would not be one made without great consideration. The history of Mardi Gras in New Orleans reflects the complex political and cultural trajectory of a place that has Native American, Spanish, French, Haitian, African, Italian, Irish, German, Portuguese and other influences. Under Spanish rule, the predecessor of Mardi Gras emerged in the form of masked public balls that quickly became 'an important component of the cultural life of New Orleans' (Fox Gotham 2007: 24). Later, Spanish rulers decided that the mixing of various classes and races during the balls would 'encourage revolt and lead to criminal behavior' (ibid.). When the United States assumed control of New Orleans in 1805, public masked balls were banned; this prohibition is an early indication of the tension between more puritanical US customs and a town that would exist within and yet always outside this culture.

In the 1820s, after the ban was lifted, masquerade balls began to develop and were more associated with the time period of Carnival. Carnival organizations and private clubs that had 'clearly defined leadership structure, committee system, and secret rites of passage' were known as 'krewes' (ibid.: 31). In 1857, the Mystick Krewe of Comus held the first themed parade and ball—beginning the tradition of planned parades. These krewes also gave a sense of organization and order to Mardi Gras: 'By restricting participation and developing planned tableaux and costumes, the old-line krewes aimed to eliminate the aura of spontaneity and promote order through a controlled procession' (ibid.: 32). At this time, the public masked balls were legally meant to be segregated (though those laws were not always enforced [ibid.: 27]); however, the emerging krewes which were associated with private men's clubs and the social elite of New Orleans were exclusively white. This ordered and controlled Mardi Gras was advertised as a safe and fun activity for all to participate in; it was then that Mardi Gras became a tourist attraction for visitors to New Orleans who associated Mardi Gras with the white upper-class krewe members. However, amid this organized and controlled environment, role reversals, transgressions and political commentary have and continue to take place within and outside the Mardi Gras krewes. Early in its development, the exclusivity of the marching krewes resulted in the development of 'counter-krewes' or 'backstreet krewes' that would include and celebrate those who were not allowed to participate in the larger krewes. The Jefferson City Buzzards, which formed in 1890, comprised working-class men (as opposed to the rich and elite of New Orleans) and, shortly after, women formed a group called Krewe of Les Mysterieuses (ibid.: 44). African Americans also quickly formed their own groups and krewes since they were excluded from participation in the white elite krewes. The Mardi Gras Indians, who have received relatively substantial attention from performance scholars and cultural anthropologists such as Joseph R. Roach, are groups comprising African Americans masking as Native Americans. These groups began to form in the 1880s and still proudly parade. George Lipsitz writes: 'During Mardi Gras, New Orleans "high society" celebrates its blood lines and mythologizes itself as the heir to a powerful tradition of mysticism and magic [. . .]. The Indians subvert this spectacle by declaring a powerful lineage of their own, one which challenges the legitimacy of Anglo-European domination' (2003: 231). The Zulu Social Aid and Pleasure Club (which started as the Tramps Social Aid and Pleasure Club) was founded in 1909 and today is one of the best-known African American krewes in New Orleans.

There has always been a large difference between the projected images of Mardi Gras and New Orleans and the realities of the festival and place beloved to its inhabitants. News reporter Ken Ringle writes: 'TV cameras are always drawn to the drag queens, vomiting drunks and bare breasts on display in the French Quarter, usually by tourists. But Mardi Gras in New Orleans has almost always been more about neighborhoods and families' (2006). Writing about Cajun Mardi Gras in Western Louisiana, Carolyn Ware notes: 'For many Cajun women and men, Mardi Gras is not simply a once-a-year diversion, it is a deeply meaningful part of their religious, ethnic, regional, and community identity' (2007: 3). This statement could be made for many who reside in areas and/or belong to Mardi Gras groups, including the Mardi Gras Indians whose 'extraordinary artistry and craftsmanship of the costumes, which may take a year to build, taken together with the many-layered protocols of Sunday rehearsals, parade-day tactics and strategy, and music-dance-drama performance, make the honor of "masking Indian" a New Orleanian way of life' (Roach 1996: 194). For the Indians and other groups, their celebrations of Mardi Gras do not come close, literally or figuratively, to the Bourbon Street mayhem that many of us imagine when we think of this annual celebration.

This attitude towards Mardi Gras might also be indicative of larger misperceptions about similar events. Festivals such as Mardi Gras can be understood as a 'break' from everyday life—something that disconnects us from our jobs, families, responsibilities and realities. But festivals also create communities, responsibilities, jobs and, as multiple scholars have pointed out in the case of Mardi Gras in New Orleans and the larger area of Louisiana, they are often a central part of people's 'everyday' lives and identities (in the sense that they identify themselves as being a part of a group with similar backgrounds and values). Cultural anthropologists and performance scholars have theorized that festivals such as Mardi Gras extend beyond the superficial reputation they hold as an excuse to get drunk, enact repressed sexual desires and let go of everyday decorum; rather, festivals hold the potential for social commentary and social change. Fu-Kiau Bunseki explains: 'Festivals are a way of bringing about change. People are allowed to say not only what they voice in ordinary life but what is going on in their minds, their inner grief, their inner resentments [. . .]. Parades see true meaning' (quoted in Roach 1996: 251). Putting on masks and costumes, actions that seem to figuratively and literally mask one's identity and emotion, in fact offer the potential to reveal emotions that are concealed during 'everyday' life. In his discussion of New Orleans Mardi Gras, Roach points out: 'Both carnival and the law have operated as agents of cultural transmission, especially in conserving the exclusionary hierarchies of the social elite, yet both have also served as instruments of contestation and change' (ibid.: 243). The ability of the Mardi Gras festival to both 'conserve exclusionary' and to 'serve as instruments of contestation and change' seemed especially poignant in 2006—on the one hand, the parade served as a site for parade participants to express their frustrations with the racism and classism that both effected the portrayal of New Orleans in the media during and after the storm and also impacted local and federal government response to those in need; yet, on the other, it was no exception to the Mardi Gras events before it that were riddled with ethnic tensions, racism, sexism and classism.

In 2006, a number of krewes used the forum of Mardi Gras to express frustration about what had taken place in their city before, during and after Katrina. Some directly criticized politicians including Mayor Ray Nagin, President George W. Bush and Secretary of State Condoleezza Rice and organizations such as the Federal Emergency Management Agency (FEMA) for failing to provide for the city. Two krewes that performed such critiques included Krewe du Vieux and Krewe of Mid-City. The Krewe du Vieux, which is known according to their website for keeping the 'original' purpose of Mardi Gras by utilizing satirical themes (Krewe du Vieux 2011), made their theme 'C'est Levee', playing on the French term *c'est la vie* or 'such is life'. The Krewe of Carrollton's theme was the 'Blue Roof Blues', which made reference to the blue tarps that

FEMA provided in order to 'protect' people's homes from further water damage. These tarps arrived after homes had already been destroyed, and thus they became an iconic image of the post-Katrina Gulf Coast region. The Krewe of Mid-City parade had themes of 'New Orleans Culture'—culture as in mold (MSNBC 2006) and 'I drove my Chevy to the levee but the levee was gone'. They also reused a float that had been used in a previous Mardi Gras parade, with an image of Willy Wonka, in reference to Mayor Nagin's post-Katrina comments that New Orleans was a 'chocolate city'. These themes demonstrate the groups' willingness to directly confront some of the more contentious topics surrounding Katrina.

FIGURE 9.1 (LEFT). **Katrina Blue Roof Hat.**
FIGURE 9.2 (RIGHT). **Katrina Witch Costume.**
Photograph courtesy of Mark J. Sindler, March 2006. Louisiana State Museum. Hurricane Digital Memory Bank, Object #2629 and Object #2629.

While making more pointed criticism, they maintained the sense of humour and irony that reflects the culture of New Orleans.

In the midst of this type of humour and celebration, the expression of grief was displayed when krewes took the opportunity to hold memorials for those they had lost. The Zulu Social Aid and Pleasure Club created a memorial by lighting 10 candles for the 10 members of the club who died during the storm and a candle for the many non-members who died as well (MSNBC 2006). Again, to those unfamiliar with the complex history and performance traditions of New Orleans and Mardi Gras, displays of grief and mourning may seem paradoxical amid the revelry of Mardi Gras. However, in a city that regularly and publicly displays its grief through traditions such as jazz funerals[2] and that literally keeps their dead above ground,[3] the memorialization of those lost during Katrina was a befitting part of the 2006 Mardi Gras. Individual participants not associated with specific krewes also created costumes that expressed their personal perspectives on the storm and its aftermath. Figure 1 is an example of the use of costume to address iconic images and issues surrounding Katrina. One woman made a hat to look like the blue tarps that were distributed by FEMA. Poking out of the top of the tarp-covered roof is a small figure representing someone who has managed to climb onto their roof. The figure's arms are outstretched in a gesture mimicking those who, in real life, were waving their arms in the air begging for rescue. On the top and front part of her hat is a red X with the number 1 next to it. This symbol references the markings that were painted on people's homes after they had been searched for survivors or bodies. The numbers represented the number of bodies (those of humans and animals) and the date the house was checked. The parade participant has also painted this X on her cheek, like a badge of honour representing what she endured. The miniaturization of a scene familiar to many performs multiple functions: it reminds people of the horrific events that had taken place in the city not that long before (a reminder those in New Orleans did not need but one that may have had an impact for those *outside* the city) and it also demonstrates the absurdity and spectacular nature of what took place in the aftermath of the storm. A second participant (see Figure 2) uses the identifiable character of a witch (a term often used to describe Katrina) to make a political statement about the correlation between Katrina and the destruction of Louisiana wetlands—a message that takes on new meaning and relevance after the 2010 oil disaster in the Gulf of Mexico.

Audience or non-parade-participants, who have long been an essential part of the Mardi Gras experience (Ware 2007: 118), became even more vital in 2006 when all eyes were on New Orleans. During the first Mardi Gras after Katrina, there was an audience of those who were there to see the event in person as well as an audience who watched the event on television with an eye towards the recovery process. An important element of this Mardi Gras was the message it sent to the nation about New Orleans' recovery. In an interview about the 2006 Mardi Gras, Julia Reed stated: 'I mean, you know, it would send—there's nothing associated with New Orleans as Mardi Gras the world over. So I think if you say, OK, we're just going to throw in the towel this year. I really think it would send a signal to the rest of the country, to Washington in particular, to the world, that we're giving up' (in CNN 2006). Douglas Brinkley made a similar statement: 'And so Mardi Gras is a sign to the world, we're back, we've picked ourselves up; we've got a long ways to go, but we're not quitters' (in ibid.). These quotes demonstrate the pressure on New Orleanians to use the 2006 festival as a statement to the nation and to the world about the progress they were making in their recovery. Public performances such as Mardi Gras have layers of intended audiences that range from the small and intimate to the most distant of viewers. After New Orleans had been placed on the 'national stage' during Hurricane Katrina, participants in the 2006 Mardi Gras—whether or not they cared to play to the larger audience—had to be aware of this national attention and the presence of the media.

Counternarratives as Dystopia

In addition to defending their city, participants of the first post-Katrina Mardi Gras were presented with the opportunity to counter dominant narratives that emerged about New Orleans immediately after the hurricane. It did not take long for the conversations surrounding Katrina to become racialized. While white people who were 'taking food' and other survival items from abandoned grocery and convenience stores were described as 'survivors', black people taking the same actions they were described as 'looters' in media photographs depicting such activity (Agid 2007: 67). Sociologists Dreama G. Moon and Anthony Hurst were 'taken aback by the manner in which Katrina victims were often criminalized, demonized, and demeaned in many media portrayals' (2007: 125). They go on to argue that these negative images 'condition(s) or frame(s) our social attributions towards those groups' (ibid.: 137). Stereotyping is used to maintain domination and control by the hegemonic structures of the subjugated groups. The media portrayal of these communities feeds into already negative cultural assumptions about black people and shows how racism permeates media coverage of events including but not limited to Hurricane Katrina. Patricia Leavy writes:

> The press ultimately aims to tell a story that resonates with cultural beliefs and assumptions. The mass media is a commercial enterprise that reinforces dominant ideology [. . .]. It also bears indirectly on how the press reports an event, in terms of the kinds of social norms, values and socially constituted morality that are reinforced through their reporting (such as ideas about race, gender or nationhood) (2007: 12).

Because of the large number of black people living in the areas that were flooded and because of the seemingly slow response of rescue organizations—leading to a number of deaths that could have been avoided—the response (or lack of response) to New Orleans by the federal government was widely perceived to be racist. This sentiment was clearly articulated when, during a telethon to benefit victims of the storm, hip hop artist Kanye West looked directly into the camera and stated, 'George Bush does not care about black people' (quoted in de Moraes 2005). The negative portrayal of New Orleans' black population not only had implications on race relations but also directly impacted rescue efforts; for example, fears of violence dissuaded FEMA from entering the Superdome (CITE). *Times-Picayune* editor Jed Horne and Alisa Bierra (associate director for the Center for Race and Gender at the University of California, Berkeley) contend that the public was more likely to sympathize with this lack of effort if the city was 'that out of control' (Horne 2006: 109; Bierria and Liebenthal 2007: 33). Owing to these dominant narratives, the first Mardi Gras after Katrina served, for many, as a perfect opportunity to perform for the US public audience their counter-narratives to these media-created scenarios.

Some participants in the 2006 Mardi Gras had little concern about the general US audience and the valuable tourist dollars that were brought in by holding the parade. Such participants wanted to send a message to those displaced by Katrina—those scattered throughout the country as nearby as Houston and as far away as Seattle. Ken Ringle notes: 'That's the real imperative for holding Mardi Gras this year. Far more than the tourist dollars it attracts will be the signal it sends to those there and those absent alike that New Orleans is still alive, partying defiantly amid the pain' (2006). Those displaced by Katrina may not have been able to join in the festivities directly but by tuning into CNN or MSNBC—networks on which, months earlier, audiences were barraged by images of devastation—New Orleanians saw an image of their city evoking joyful memories. For them, the Mardi Gras experience that had once united families, churches, communities and strangers could unite again, even if mediated from afar.

National media reports emphasized the unifying nature of the 2006 Mardi Gras. Ringle writes: 'What's remarkable about Mardi Gras in New Orleans is the extent to which the entire city has institutionalized this defiant laughter, so that every class, race and condition shares it' (ibid.). But while Mardi Gras might have been celebrated across class and racial divides, like Katrina, it was not experienced in the same way by all. Chelsey Louise Kivland (2008) uses the symbols of hero, eulogist, trickster and critic to better understand the individual performances of specific communities in New Orleans within the larger overall performance of Mardi Gras. She argues that the Rex parade—the white, upper-class krewe of Mardi Gras—performed the role of the hero, with the group serving as a symbol of renewal and rebuilding which was the dominant theme of their floats (ibid.: 109). However, as she points out, this assertion is highly racialized. As the white, more privileged class of New Orleans, this group felt inherently more qualified or entitled to re-establish New Orleans—a type of manifest destiny, expanding imperialism as necessary and benevolent. Fox Gotham notes 'The different meanings and pressures of "recovery" and "rebuilding" are not distributed equally but signify entrenched inequalities and power relations' (2007: 198). Kivland writes: 'The parade's enactment of a kinship between the thematic statement of civility and the honors it bestows expressed the performers' claim to a dignified social status. The cultural exaltation of royal culture concealed the parade's racially segregationist practices by eliding the language of race for that of civility' (2008: 109). The white carnival krewe that, since its inception, had represented civility and order within the Mardi Gras tradition now presented themselves as having the civility that it would take in order to rebuild the city. Being white was associated with being civil and having the ability and the right to negotiate the rebuilding of the city, which, whether intended or not, had a very particular implication given the racial tension surrounding the events of Katrina. This mirrored the racism prevalent in media reports that captioned black people as looters and white people as trying to survive and get food for their families.

The Zulu parade, which has long been a 'counter' parade to the Rex parade,[4] had a theme of 'Leading the Way Back Home'. According to Kivland, the 'message' of their parade, which included stops at the convention centre, was that, in order to rebuild the community of New Orleans (understood to be a black community, representative of the majority of the population), those that had been displaced would have to return (2008). She refers to the participants of the Zulu parade as representing the 'character' of the eulogist since their parade included memorials for those lost and they recognized that renewal and regeneration could not take place without remembering those who were absent. The differences between these two groups' themes are indicative of a much larger division in the rebuilding, revitalization and restoration of New Orleans. Many city leaders, politicians and real-estate developers openly declared their intentions to take advantage of the displacement of the poor black population of New Orleans, to keep them out and to develop expensive homes where affordable housing was once available, making it difficult, if not impossible, for many to return to the city. An example of the explicit intentions to gentrify the city can be found in the words of James Reiss, who worked in Mayor Nagin's office: 'Those who want to see this city rebuilt want to see it done in a completely different way: demographically, geographically and politically' (quoted in Cooper and Block 2006: 292). Many housing projects around the city have been demolished to be newly 'renovated'—which many residents of New Orleans interpret as meaning 'white-washed'. By emphasizing the importance of the return of their community, specifically the black community, the Zulu parade challenged not only the underlying message of the Rex parade but also those who dismissed the importance of the return of *all* New Orleans residents to the city and those who actively stood in the way of their return.

The trickster emerged in the form of an organized group of male parade participants who wore T-shirts with logos that explicitly stated their anger and frustrations.

> From the end of the main thoroughfare of the parades, an oncoming group of ten or more black men walking in uneven but discernable lines with a steady, measured beat approaches the crowds of the mainline parades. The coordinated 'black mob', as one beholder calls it, moves against the stationary, mostly white crowds of tourists and locals, drawing the attention of all those they pass over and around. Long after the disruption passes, the striking commentary of the T-shirts that each marcher wears remains. Their white T-shirts boldly display the words 'Willy Nagin and the Chocolate City, Semi-Sweet and a Little Nuts' surrounded by the mayor digitally rendered in the costume of 'Willy Wonka', complete with cane, top hat, and three-piece suit (Kivland 2008: 112).

Again, race and racial divides play into this 'performance'. The group of men stand out against the group of predominantly white spectators because they break the 'unofficial' official rules of segregation that dominate the Mardi Gras experience. This rupture of protocol is in and of itself a performance. Furthermore, the messages on their shirts, as Kivland points out, remain even after the performers have passed by. In addition to challenging racial divides, this performance questioned the reliance on tourism in order to rebuild New Orleans—since slogan T-shirts are a popular purchase item for tourists (ibid.: 113).

Kivland's observations illuminate the discord between the national perception of events and local realities. Although the national media portrayed Mardi Gras as an emotional break or release from recent events, unification of communities and people of all races and classes coming together to celebrate, racial and class divides greatly impacted both the events surrounding Katrina and the first Mardi Gras after it. Some groups, who made themselves into performers, such as the 'T-shirt brigade' as Kivland refers to them, directly confronted those racial tensions. The use of performance and local traditions confronted the ironies and tensions that percolated in communities, especially the ones most affected by government neglect and the failure of the levees.

Utopia, Hope and the Future

Hurricane Katrina was devastating on many levels, the least of which was the disbanding of neighbourhoods and the close-knit relationships that existed there. After Katrina, New Orleans saw a loss of over half of its population, with some neighbourhoods in the city experiencing as much as an 85 per cent loss of its members. Rebuilding after the storm has happened in many forms, including the construction of buildings and the reinforcement of the levees that had failed the city. As important as that type of rebuilding is, efforts to rebuild the spirit of the city are also necessary because they give a sense of identity that acknowledges all of the city's roots and heritages. For the city's inhabitants to return to their performance and ritual roots, in a city where those are central to its identity and its multiple communities, was (and continues to be) a vital part of this rebuilding process. It is important to view these activities at Mardi Gras as primary—rather than alternative—modes of communication that are part of a long tradition of performance through which knowledge is constructed and transmitted, as scholars including Joseph R. Roach (1996) and

Diana Taylor (2003) have so eloquently described in their writing about performance and memory.

While the post-Katrina Mardi Gras could be seen as evidence of a city beginning to recover both financially and emotionally, there should be no confusing such return to traditions as evidence that things are back to normal in the Big Easy. Fox Gotham described the Mardi Gras krewes as providing 'order through a controlled procession' (2007: 32). In some ways the order and routine of the Mardi Gras parade might have provided comfort to those who had experienced such shocking displays of disorder and the complete upheaval of routine during the immediate and proceeding days and weeks after Katrina. At the same time, within this order, performances of disorder emerged in both representations of the chaos experienced during the storm, such as the costumes previously described, and in the actions such as the T-shirt brigade that interrupted a 'controlled' performance within the parade. People's anger, frustrations and heartaches are evident in their costume choices and parade themes. Mardi Gras, like the city of New Orleans itself after Katrina, served as both a utopic vision of what *could* be and a confrontation with dystopic representations of what *was*, for many, unpleasant realities.

In his book *All on a Mardi Gras Day*, author and New Orleans resident Reid Mitchell explores violent outbreaks during Mardi Gras festivities throughout the centuries. He asserts, however, that in Mardi Gras he finds a great deal of hope and conceives of it as a utopic experience in the more traditional sense of the word:

> I see in Mardi Gras much what I hear in a really good jazz band: a model for the just society, the joyous community, the heavenly city. I see a recurring ritual devoted to spontaneity, a festival in which a collective display is impossible without individual creativity, a form in which innovation is grounded in tradition [. . .]. And, despite considerable

> evidence to the contrary I trust I will find in my hometown the creativity and good humor that will allow the best to endure, even if it must endure side by side with old troubles that should be long gone and human failings that will last till Gabriel's horn (1995: 9).

Mitchell's words, published a decade before Hurricane Katrina, takes on an eerie prescience. The troubles that the city would endure could not have been imagined by even the most creative and apocalyptic of minds. Mitchell's understanding of Mardi Gras could not have been more true when people put their costumes on, got on top of their floats, picked up their instruments, put on their dancing shoes and hit the streets for the 2006 Mardi Gras. While the messages conveyed by their performances were not hopeful, the very act of putting on Mardi Gras conveyed some sense of hope that the best of New Orleans did and will continue to endure.

Coda

As further testament to the power of performance and its potential to create change and serve as a site for protest, performers have taken an interesting 'hit' after Hurricane Katrina. In the years proceeding the hurricane, the city introduced new fees that penalize musicians for performing on the street without a permit. The Mardi Gras Indians have been fighting against increasing fees, which they have to pay in order to march on the streets during Mardi Gras, and places such as Congo Square—an iconic place where slaves once gathered to dance and sing and that has since become a cultural and community centre, primarily for New Orleans's black population—were inexplicably shut down and closed off to the public after Katrina. (It has since reopened.)[5] Some could argue that these are coincidental casualties of a devastated economy. However, one cannot help but feel that something else has been going on—that policymakers, like real-estate moguls pouncing on the opportunity to develop, have used Katrina as an excuse to implement restrictions and social crackdowns that they have been planning all along. As performance scholars, social critics and engaged citizens, it is vital to continue attesting to the importance of cultural preservation as part of historical preservation. If officials, policymakers and real-estate developers shut down these sites of tradition, increase fees for performers and make it difficult for mostly working- and middle-class performers to return to New Orleans, then, while buildings may be replaced, tourists may return and traditions such as Mardi Gras enacted every year, they will only be superficial markers of a city restored.

Notes

1 According to the 2000 Census, 67.25 per cent of the population was black or African American. And, according to an MSNBC article, 30 per cent of the population live below the poverty level (Faw 2005).

2 Jazz funerals are the public parade of the dead through the streets with musicians and mourners following the coffin and often singing out loud.

3 Graves are often built above ground because of the muddy earth that makes underground burial difficult.

4 For further discussion on this rivalry, see Joseph R. Roach (1996) and Reid Mitchell (1995).

5 These fees and laws have continued to change since 2005.

Works Cited

AGID, Shana. 2007. 'Locked and Loaded: The Prison Industrial Complex and the Response to Hurricane Katrina' in Kristin A. Bates and Richelle S. Swan (eds), *Through the Eye of Katrina: Social Justice in the United States.* Durham, NC: Carolina Academic Press, pp. 55–76.

BAKHTIN, Mikhail. 1984. *Rabelais and His World* (Hélène Iswolsky trans.). Bloomington: Indiana University Press.

BIERRIA, Alisa, and Mayaba Liebenthal. 2007. 'To Render Ourselves Visible: Women of Color Organizing and Hurricane Katrina' in South End Press Collective (ed.), *What Lies Beneath: Katrina, Race and the State of the Nation*. Cambridge, MA: South End Press, pp. 31–47.

CNN. 2006. 'First Mardi Gras Celebration after Hurricane Katrina'. *American Morning*, 28 February. Available at: http://goo.gl/6zhr1p (last accessed on 2 March 2010).

CONQUERGOOD, Dwight. 2002. 'Performance Studies Interventions and Radical Research'. *TDR: The Drama Review* 46(2) (Summer) : 145–56.

COOPER, Christopher, and Robert Block. 2006. *Disaster: Hurricane Katrina and the Failure of Homeland Security*. New York: Times Books.

DE MORAES, Lisa. 2005. 'Kanye West's Torrent of Criticism, Live on NBC'. *Washington Post*, 3 September. Available at: http://goo.gl/8hGNYD (last accessed on 19 April 2016).

DOLAN, Jill. 2005. *Utopia in Performance: Finding Hope at the Theater*. Ann Arbor: University of Michigan Press.

DYNES, Russell R., and Havidán Rodríguez. 2007. 'Finding and Framing Katrina: The Social Construction of Disaster' in David L. Brunsma, David Overfelt and J. Steven Picou (eds), *The Sociology of Katrina: Perspectives on a Modern Catastrophe*. Lanham, MD: Rowman and Littlefield, pp. 23–34.

FAW, Bob. 2005. 'Katrina Exposes New Orleans' Deep Poverty'. *MSNBC*, 1 September. Available at: http://goo.gl/wcTP01 (last accessed on 27 September 2011).

FOX GOTHAM, Kevin. 2007. *Authentic New Orleans: Tourism, Culture, and Race in The Big Easy*. New York: New York University Press.

HORNE, Jed. 2006. *Breach of Faith: Hurricane Katrina and the Near Death of a Great American City*. New York: Random House.

KIVLAND, Chelsey Louise. 2008. 'Hero, Eulogist, Trickster, and Critic: Ritual and Crisis in Post-Katrina Mardi Gras' in Manning Marable and Kristen Clarke (eds), *Seeking Higher Ground: The Hurricane Katrina Crisis, Race, and Publicity Reader*. New York: Palgrave Macmillan, pp. 107–28.

KREWE DU VIEUX. 2011. 'Brief History of Krewe du Vieux'. Official website. Available at: http://goo.gl/hwOuw8 (last accessed on 10 May 2011).

LEAVY, Patricia. 2007. *Iconic Events: Media, Politics, and Power in Retelling History*. Lanham, MD: Lexington Books.

LEVITT, Jeremy I., and Matthew C. Whitaker (eds). 2009. *Hurricane Katrina: America's Unnatural Disaster*. Lincoln: University of Nebraska Press.

LIPSITZ, George. 2003. 'Mardi Gras Indians: Carnival and Counternarrative in Black New Orleans' in Jonathan Brennan (ed.), *When Brer Rabbit Meets Coyote: African–Native American Literature*. Urbana: University of Illinoi Press, pp. 218–40.

MCCARRAGHER, Barbara. 2008. 'New Orleans Hurricane History'. Available at: http://goo.gl/CpBLM7 (last accessed on 20 February 2008).

MITCHELL, Reid. 1995. *All on a Mardi Gras Day: Episodes in the History of New Orleans Carnival*. Cambridge, MA: Harvard University Press.

MOON, Dreama G., and Anthony Hurst. 2007. '"Reasonable Racism": The "New" White Supremacy and Hurricane Katrina' in Kristin A. Bates and Richelle S. Swan (eds), *Through the Eye of Katrina: Social Justice in the United States*. Durham, NC: Carolina Academic Press, pp. 125–46.

MSNBC. 2006. 'C'est Levee: Mardi Gras Back in New Orleans'. *MSNBC*, 12 February. Available at: http://goo.gl/v5HJm9 (last accessed on 2 March 2010).

NEW ORLEANS CONVENTION AND VISITORS BUREAU. 2008. Official website. Available at: http://www.neworleanscvb.com/ (last accessed on 15 March 2008).

RICE, Anne. 2005. 'Do You Know What It Means to Lose New Orleans?' *New York Times*, 4 September. Available at: http://goo.gl/nx39zm (last accessed on 14 July 2011).

RINGLE, Ken. 2006. 'Mardi Gras after Katrina: Laughing in the Face of Fate'. *Washington Post*, 27 February. Available at: http://goo.gl/CcKMCu (last accessed on 2 March 2010).

ROACH, Joseph R. 1996. *Cities of the Dead: Circum-Atlantic Performance*. New York: Columbia University Press.

TAYLOR, Diana. 2003. *The Archive and the Repertoire: Performing Cultural Memory in the Americas*. Durham, NC: Duke University Press.

WARE, Carolyn E. 2007. *Cajun Women and Mardi Gras: Reading the Rules Backward*. Urbana: University of Illinois Press.

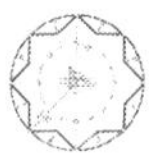

Notes on Contributors

Luis Alvarez is Associate Professor of History, Director of the Institute for Arts and Humanities, and Director of the Chicana/o Latina/o Arts and Humanities Program at UC San Diego. His interests include the history of race and ethnicity, popular culture and social movements in the US. He is the author of *The Power of the Zoot: Youth Culture and Resistance during World War II* (University of California Press, American Crossroads Series), co-editor of *Another University is Possible* (University Readers Press) and co-editor of *A History of Mexican America* (forthcoming, Routledge). His publications also include essays in *Latino Studies, Aztlan, Popular Music and Society, Perspectives, French Review of American Studies, Kalfou, Journal of the West,* and *OAH Magazine of History*. He has won numerous awards for his research, teaching, and service including fellowships from the Warren Center for Studies in American History at Harvard University, the Ford Foundation, the UC's Office of the President, the Institute for Humanities Research at Arizona State University, the Teaching Excellence Award from the University of Houston, the Center for Mexican American Studies at the University of Houston and the Equal Opportunity/Affirmative Action and Diversity Award from UCSD.

Rachel Bowditch is theatre director, Associate Professor and Head of the MFA in Performance in the School of Film, Dance and Theatre in the Herberger Institute for Design and the Arts at Arizona State University. Her book *On the Edge of Utopia: Performance and Ritual at Burning Man* (2010) was published by Seagull Books. She is currently working on two books under contract with Routledge about Richard Schechner's Performance Workshop and rasaboxes with Paula Murray Cole and Michele

Minnick (2018) and *Physical Dramaturgy* (2018) with Jeff Casazza and Annette Thornton. Bowditch's work has been published in *TDR: The Drama Review, Performance Research, the Journal of Media and Religion* and *Puppetry International* as well as book chapters in *Festive Devils in the Americas* (edited by Milla Riggio, Angela Marino, and Paolo Vignolo), *Playa Dust: Collected Stories from Burning Man* (edited by Samantha Krukowski) and *Focus on World Festivals* (edited by Chris Newbold). In 2009, she was an Institute for Humanities Research Fellow and is currently the president of the Association of Theatre Movement Educators (ATME). Her artistic work has been featured in *The Director's Vision* by Scott Shattuck, *American Theatre, New York Times, Rolling Stone, Theatre Journal, TDR: The Drama Review, Live Design, TYA Today, Newsweek, The Village Voice, the Wall Street Journal, Minneapolis Star Tribune, Minneapolis Daily Planet, Aisle Say Twin Cities, Channel 8/PBS, ABC 15 News, Channel 12 News, Univision* and the *Arizona Republic.* She presents her scholarship and theatre research at theatre conferences nationally and internationally. For more about her performance work, visit: www.rachelbowditch.com and www.vesselproject.org.

Néstor Bravo Goldsmith is Assistant Professor of Theatre Studies at the Department of Theatre and Dance at the State University of New York, Fredonia. A native Chilean, he is a performance studies scholar, performer, translator and theatre director. His service to the profession has been channelled through his work as founder and artistic director of the Festival de Teatro en la Frontera FETEF-Chile, as a member-at-large in the Performance Studies Focus Group at the Association of Theatre in Higher Education (ATHE), as president of the Asociación de Teatro de Temuco ARTES IX and as founder and director of Compañía de Teatro de la Universidad de la Frontera and of Compañía de Teatro Antumimik, Chile. His publications include essays in *GESTOS: Revista de Teoría y Práctica del Teatro Hispánico, Chasqui: Revista de Literatura Latinoamericana* and *Revista Apuntes de Teatro* (PUC). He has worked as a research assistant for Dr Tamara Underiner, and has collaborated translating essays and plays into *Spanish for the Youth Theatre Journal,* for the playwright Guillermo Reyes and for Compañía de Teatro Cuatro Elementos among others.

Lisa Doolittle is Professor in the Department of Theatre and Dramatic Arts at the University of Lethbridge (since 1989) and has served as the Board of Governor's Teaching Chair for 2015–17. She is a dance artist, educator and scholar for over 30 years in Canada and internationally, has developed innovative approaches for arts-based community-university collaborations around health promotion, issues in refugee, immigrant and indigenous communities, and inclusion of people with disabilities. Her scholarly publications, original productions and documentary films use the critical lens of Dance and Performance Studies to explore embodied performance as a catalyst for change. For a Social Sciences and Humanities Research Council funded national partnership investigating the arts in social change contexts, she coordinates the Teaching & Learning research, focusing on ways that pedagogy contributes to the effectiveness of the arts in community development and change agendas, in academic, professional and grassroots contexts. Her team is analysing data to contribute to a critical theory of pedagogy in the field, and is piloting a mobile arts and social change learning hub.

Laura Dougherty is Assistant Professor of Theatre at Winthrop University. She is a performance scholar, theatre director and voice and speech practitioner, teaches performance and theory as an artist/activist. Her research interests include using theatre—specifically Suzan-Lori Parks' *The America Play*—as a methodology for mapping linguistic and spatial borders of USAmerica, race, gender and sexuality in performance, and performance and/as citizenship, as well as investigations of gender, nostalgia and complicity in neo-burlesque performance. Her work has been published in *Theatre Journal*, *The Humanities Review* and *Playing with Theory in Theatre Practice* (Palgrave Macmillan).

Christian DuComb (PhD, Brown University) is Assistant Professor of Theatre at Colgate University. His research interests include street performance, practices of racial impersonation in the Atlantic world, and both US and South Asian theatre history. His first book, *Haunted City: Three Centuries of Racial Impersonation in Philadelphia*, is forthcoming from the University of Michigan Press, and his articles and reviews have appeared in *Performance Research*, *Theatre Journal*, *TDR: The Drama Review*,

Theater magazine, *The Encyclopedia of Greater Philadelphia* and *The Anatomy of Body Worlds: Critical Essays on the Plastinated Cadavers of Gunther von Hagens* (McFarland, 2009). His honours include the 2012 Cambridge University Press Prize from the American Society for Theatre Research and the winning entry in the 2006 *TDR* Student Essay Contest. His research has been supported by grants and fellowships from the Watson Foundation, the Winterthur Museum and Library, the Library Company of Philadelphia / Historical Society of Pennsylvania, the Central New York Humanities Corridor and both the Arts Council and the Research Council at Colgate University. DuComb is also an actor, dramaturg and stage director, and he performed with the Vaudevillains in the Philadelphia Mummers Parade from 2009 to 2013.

Ann Fletchall is Visiting Assistant Professor at Mississippi University for Women. She received her PhD in geography from Arizona State University in 2009. Ann is a cultural geographer whose research interests lie in media geographies, especially the televisual, cultural landscapes, and place-making. Her book (with co-authors Kevin McHugh and Chris Lukinbeal) *Place, Television, and the Real Orange County* was published by Franz Steiner Verlag in 2012. Ann's study of US influence in global trends in television appeared in *Mediated Geographies: Geographies of Media* (Springer Publishing, 2014). Her most recent essay on place-making through craft breweries with a case study in Montana is forthcoming in *Geographical Review*.)

Anne Flynn, Professor Emerita of Dance, University of Calgary, has been involved in the Calgary dance community as a performer, artistic director, teacher, writer, administrator and dance education advocate. Her research with Lisa Doolittle has received support from the Social Sciences and Humanities Research Council, and they are co-editors of Dancing Bodies, Living Histories. Flynn has written about multiculturalism and dance, Canadian women and dance, and applications of dance to health promotion, and presented her work widely. She has managed numerous community initiatives involving senior citizens and youth, and co-founded the Calgary Dancing Parkinson's programme in 2013 with the support of a national partnership grant on arts and social change. Flynn has served on the board of directors of local, provincial, national and international dance organizations, and is currently president of the US-based Congress on Research in Dance.

Kevin McHugh is Associate Professor in the School of Geographical Sciences and Urban Planning, Arizona State University. His interests centre in geographical thought and theory, accentuating explorations of space, place, landscape and movement. Kevin is co-author of *Place, Television, and the Real Orange County* (Franz Steiner Verlag) (with Ann Fletchall and Chris Lukinbeal), and co-editor of *Multiple Dwelling and Tourism: Negotiating Place, Home and Identity* (CABI Publishing). He has published journal articles across a range of topics in social and cultural geography, including essays in the *Annals of the Association of American Geographers, cultural geographies, Progress in Human Geography, Space and Culture, GeoJournal, ACME: International Journal for Critical Geographies, Urban Geography, Professional Geographer.* Currently, Kevin and collaborator Jennifer Kitson (Rowan University) are rethinking bodies, objects, things and atmospheres through a series of post-phenomenological experiments in proximal thermal and olfactory sensing.

Katherine Nigh is Assistant Professor at Temple University's School of Theater, Film and Media Arts and has also been an Instructor/Professor at Arizona State University, Whittier College and Florida State University. She is an artist/activist/scholar receiving her PhD from Arizona State University's Theatre and Performance of the Americas program (2011) and her MA in Performance Studies from NYU (2005). In 2013–14, she held a Postdoctoral Research Fellowship with the Hemispheric Institute in partnership with New York University and the University of Manitoba's Department of Native Studies under the direction of Dr Diana Taylor. This was a continuation of the work she has done with Hemi in the implementation of the Institute's Digital Video Library. She has had the honour and pleasure of working as researcher and sometime artistic collaborator with the likes of El Teatro Campesino, Grupo Cultural Yuyachkani (of Peru), and John O'Neal (of the Free Southern Theater/Junebug Productions). She is a performer, director, dramaturg, producer and performance artist. Her research and publications focus on theatre as a tool for social change/justice, performance of grief and mourning, national constructions of citizenship and belonging, and performance focused on race/ gender and sexuality.

Pegge Vissicaro, Professor Emerita of Dance at Arizona State University, is a dance culture scholar, socially engaged artist, and eco-somatic practitioner. She created the first online courses at Arizona State University and the first in dance worldwide with the intent to heighten awareness about how dance culture reflects the diversity of human experience. Using interactive media to promote constructivist-based learning communities, her innovative work investigated cross-cultural processes and led to the development of a textbook, *Studying Dance Cultures,* adopted by more than 20 universities worldwide. Vissicaro received a Fulbright to Portugal and two Fulbright Specialist Awards to teach dance education and technology. For almost three decades she has directed the performance company, TerraDance® and serves as Executive Director and President of Cross-Cultural Dance Resources. Key publications include book chapters and articles in *Age and Dancing, Ethnic Studies Review, Australia New Zealand Dance Research Society, Multimedia Tools and Applications, The Review of Human Factor Studies,* and the Foundation for Community Dance magazine, *Animated.* Vissicaro, also an accomplished West African dancer and drummer, produced the widely distributed dance music album *Terra Drums.* She actively presents papers and lectures, teaches master classes and conducts residencies nationally and internationally.

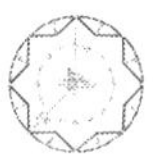

Index

Locators in italics indicate figures